CLASSICS OF CIVIL WAR FICTION

Classics of

Civil War Fiction

Edited by David Madden and Peggy Bach

University Press of Mississippi
Jackson & London

94   93   92   91   4   3   2   1

The paper in this book meets the guidelines for permanence and durability
of the Committee on Production Guidelines for Book Longevity of the
Council on Library Resources.

Library of Congress Cataloging-in-Publication Data

Classics of Civil War fiction / edited by David Madden and Peggy Bach.
         p.   cm.
    Includes bibliographical references.
    ISBN 0-87805-522-3 (cloth : alk. paper). — ISBN 0-87805-541-X (pbk. : alk.
paper)
    1. United States—History—Civil War, 1861–1865—Literature and the war.
2. Historical fiction, American—History and criticism.   3. War stories,
American—History and criticism.   I. Madden, David, 1933–
II. Bach, Peggy.
    PS374.C53C57   1991
    813'.08109—dc20   91-16947
                                                                                CIP

British Library Cataloging-in-Publication data available

For

Frank N. Magill

Supporter of Civil War Studies

CONTENTS

CONTENTS

CLASSICS OF CIVIL WAR FICTION

INTRODUCTION

I

This collection of original essays is a deliberate and, we think, a positive contribution to a debate that got under way only two years after the end of the Civil War. In 1867, the year in which one of the finest Civil War novels, *Miss Ravenel's Conversion from Secession to Loyalty,* written by a veteran of the war, John William De Forest, was published, William Dean Howells, editor of *The Atlantic Monthly* and father of realism in American fiction, lamented that "our war has laid upon our literature a charge under which it has hitherto staggered very lamely."

Almost fifty years later, in *The Spirit of American Literature* (1911), literary historian John Macy echoed Howells: "thousands of books were written by people who knew the war at first hand and who had literary ambition and some skill, and from all of these books, none rises to distinction" (12–13).

The debate is usually posed in the negative with this question: given the central importance of the Civil War in the history of the United States, why has no novel embodied, to the satisfaction of a majority of critics, the profound essence of that event? Most critics who touch on this debate agree that the great Civil War novel warranted by the magnitude and the central importance of the war remains unwritten. They give various reasons why it has not and describe what it should be when it comes to be written.

But claims, pro and con, are argued more incidentally than in sustained works of criticism. Given the tremendous interest in Civil War history, it is strange that very little literary criticism has been devoted to fiction about the war. *Classics of Civil War Fiction* is only the second book to be devoted exclusively to Civil War fiction.

The first, *Fiction Fights the Civil War* (1957), a title adopted from an article by Bernard DeVoto, is an indispensable descriptive and critical survey of over five hundred Civil War novels, with a subtitle that continues to be excruciatingly appropriate: "An Unfinished Chapter in the Literary History of the American People." It was written by Robert A. Lively, a historian with more than sufficient literary acumen who dared to venture his "Selection of the Best Civil War Novels."

We, too, have committed ourselves to quality choices. All but one (Lively represented Faulkner with *The Unvanquished*) of the novels discussed in *Classics of Civil War Fiction* (1950 being our limitation date), appear on Lively's list of fifteen. From the five hundred he studied, he chose thirty "Other Representative Civil War Novels." Plus or minus a few titles, the editors, not necessarily with the concurrence of our contributors, agree with Lively's list. Our own list at the end of this volume includes novels up to 1989. Lively includes a bibliography of all five hundred novels, along with a fairly complete list of critical articles and books.

Earlier, in 1950, Ernest E. Leisey provided a selective, annotated list in his more general study *The American Historical Novel.* Also useful is Arthur Taylor Dickinson's substantial, annotated list of novels in his even broader study *Historical Fiction* (1958). As late as 1969, only two and a half pages are devoted to criticism of Southern Civil War literature in Louis D. Rubin, Jr.'s, *A Bibliographical Guide to the Study of Southern Literature.*

Several notable articles joined the debate just before and after Lively's book appeared. In "Southern Novelists and the Civil War," published in 1953 and reprinted in *Death By Melancholy* (1972), southern critic Walter Sullivan did not declare a position on the question of quality; rather, having stated the importance of the war in the history of the South, he commented on *The Fathers, The Long Night, Absalom, Absalom!,* and several other southern novels on the implicit assumption that they were achievements of a very high order. "To the southern writer who would deal with the past, the Civil War is the most significant image of all. For it is the pregnant moment in southern history, that instant which contains within its limits a summation of all that has gone before, an adumbration of the future" (69).

One of the most famous books dealing with the literature of the Civil War is Edmund Wilson's *Patriotic Gore, Studies in the Literature of the American Civil War,* which appeared in 1962 during the period of what he called "this absurd centennial." (Interestingly, the only notable Civil War novel to appear within the four year celebration was Robert Penn Warren's *Wilderness,* 1961.) But Wilson limited himself to describing "some thirty men and women who lived through the Civil War, either playing some special role in connection with it or experiencing its impact in some interesting way, and who have left their personal records of some angle or aspect of it" (x). Of the works discussed in *Classics of Civil War Fiction,* he discusses only De Forest's novel and Ambrose Bierce's *Tales of Soldiers and Civilians* (1891). His excellent discussion of the nonfiction of the period provides a background for any study of the fiction published in the same period and later.

Another source of nonfiction recommendations is "A Confederate Book Shelf" in *South to Posterity* (1936) by Douglas Southall Freeman, a major biographer of Lee. A more recent, nonpartisan list, based on solicited recommendations, appeared in *Civil War Times Illustrated* (August 1981, pp. 46–47); *The Red Badge of Courage* is the only novel listed, a stark indication of its pride of place.

We pause in this brief survey of criticism on Civil War literature to observe that some of the finest Civil War novelists, several of whom are represented in this volume, also wrote some of the most intellectually vigorous nonfiction on the subject: De Forest's *A Volunteer's Adventures, A Union Captain's Record of the Civil War* (not published until 1946); Allen Tate's *Stonewall Jackson, The Good Soldier. A Narrative* (1928) and *Jefferson Davis* (1929); Robert Penn Warren's *John Brown, the Making of a Martyr* (1929); Andrew Lytle's *Bedford Forrest and His Critter Company* (1931); and Evelyn Scott's *Background in Tennessee* (1937). The Warren, Lytle, and Tate books, written in their Agrarian period, will surely be reissued by a university press; University of Tennessee Press reprinted Scott's in 1980. A major recent nonfiction achievement by a novelist is, of course, Shelby Foote's monumental *The Civil War, A Narrative* (1958–1974); his *Shiloh* (1952), unusually short for a Civil War novel, appeared during the Korean conflict era.

One of the most prolific and astute southern critics, Louis D. Rubin, Jr., has written almost exclusively on southern literature, but "The Image of An Army, Southern Novelists and the Civil War" (reprinted in his *The Curious Death of the Novel,* 1967) is one of the few pieces in which he has focused on Civil War fiction. Unlike Sullivan, he takes a clear position on the question of quality. Having observed that "more than a thousand novels have been written about the war by Southerners alone," he concludes that "most of the South's Civil War fiction . . . is wretched stuff. . . . No single Confederate war novel exists which we can read and then say with satisfaction and admiration *that* was the *Lost Cause; that* was Lee's army. . . . There is no *War and Peace* about the South and its army. . . . All we have is *Gone With the Wind*" (184, 185, 186). In light of those observations, Rubin discusses fifteen or so novels, including a few discussed in *Classics of Civil War Fiction,* that come close in various ways to achieving his definition of the great Confederate novel, a definition he makes clearest in the final paragraph: "What the Southern novelist who would create a great Civil War novel can do is not to forsake his sense of society and history, but add to it the ability of a Crane to see the lonely individual soul as well. . . . Through the perceptions of such a protagonist, the full tragedy of the Civil War might be captured in fiction" (206). One can imagine Rubin reading Lewis Simpson's essay on *Absalom, Absalom!* with particular interest.

In 1973, a midwesterner offered a critical survey of the contributions of both southern and northern writers to the literature. While it did not focus primarily on fiction, Daniel Aaron's *The Unwritten War, American Writers and the Civil War* encompassed far more fiction than Wilson's book, including examinations, however, of only six of the works of fiction discussed in *Classics of Civil War Fiction.* He quotes Howells, almost a century later, and, as his title declares, agrees with him: "as yet no novel or poem has disclosed the common soldier so vividly as the historian Bell Wily does in his collective portraits of Johnny Reb and Billy Yank." Aaron argues that most fiction failed to reveal "the meaning . . . of the War." "Some, like the majority of their fellow Americans (I paraphrase Oscar Handlin), draped the War in myth, transmuted its actuality into symbol, and interpreted the Republic's greatest failure as a sinful interlude in a grand evolutionary process" (xviii).

Aaron goes on to say that the lack of "'masterpieces' is no index of the impact of the War on American writers. . . . The War more than casually touched and engaged a number of writers, and its literary reverberations are felt to this day" (xviii-xix). At the end, Daniel Aaron quotes the judgment in 1916 of Sherwood Anderson, "No real sense of it has yet crept into the pages of a printed book" *(Windy McPherson's Son,* 21 – 22).

Daniel Aaron's own last line, "Our untidy and unkempt War still confounds interpreters," sounds the same negative note on which the debate began. Even so, almost twenty years later, he joins other critics and novelists in a continuation of the debate in the present volume. He focusses on Ross Lockridge, Jr.'s, *Raintree County,* a novel he did not mention in his book, about the quality of which there is much controversy; he praises it, but with reservations. In recent years, in conversation, he has said that he wished he had included Evelyn Scott's *The Wave* in his study.

At least several of the essays in this collection imply that the great Civil War novel just may not have gone unwritten, but our readers will have their own say about that.

II

Before we introduce the authors and their essays, some general questions and observations may provide a setting.

The question has often been posed: what criteria might one use to choose the best novels about the War Between the States by southerners? (Rubin ventured a few above.) What different criteria might apply in evaluating the work of northern novelists? If distinctions between northern and southern are relevant, how are we to determine what characteristics and qualities the great nonpartisan American Civil War novel should have?

While contributors to this volume do not explicitly pose any such criteria, implicit in some of the essays is an awareness that such questions have been raised. From the scant literary criticism on the subject one may derive a few general criteria; whether one feels that it is or is not relevant to apply them, they do constitute characteristics of the better novels that have been written. The Great American Civil War novel would perhaps:

dramatize an important or noble theme,
authentically depict family life on the plantation,
encompass the Antebellum Era, major battles, and the Reconstruction
   Era,
demonstrate exhaustive factual research,
reveal the war through the microcosm of a battle,
present the common soldier's view,
re-create events "as they really happened,"
"bring the war alive" for modern readers.

And, of course, it would exemplify the criteria usually applied to determine artistic excellence. It would be written out of a coherent philosophy of the Civil War, controlled by a complex artistic conception. The author should imagine new techniques for illuminating ways through which the war may become and stay part of the living essence of the character's and the reader's everyday consciousness.

In the ideal Civil War novel, the author's vision and purpose emerge out of the complexities of the war experience but transcend them. The novel succeeds in stimulating and engaging the emotions, the imagination, and the intellect to make the war agonizingly alive in the reader. Its point of view, style, and other techniques make the reader a collaborator with the author in creating a conception of the Civil War that will enable the reader, long after the fiction ends, to illuminate his or her experiences. It would be the novel Americans need to stimulate a revolution in our way of feeling, imagining, and meditating on an event that has determined the development of this nation and that continues to affect our behavior in ways we do well to see and understand.

Some would question whether the value of a particular Civil War novel need rely at all on all-encompassing criteria. It is, even so, a fact of American literary history that major differences between Civil War novels by southerners and those by northerners determine the criteria by which they have been evaluated over the years. For instance, it has been argued that it was industrialism that shaped the consciousness of northerners, and the Civil War was only a dramatic episode; but, it has often been argued, it was the War Between the States itself that shaped the consciousness of the southerner.

If the war is the central experience in the lives of southerners, in some sense every work of fiction by a southerner is an expression of the long-developing cause, the bloody agony, and the lingering effect of the war. The aim then of most southern novels about the war has been to defend, explain, or criticize, sometimes to extol or preserve the southern way of life.

The northern writer's aim is totally divorced from such an attitude. For the northerner, the North as a coherent region with a history and an identity, and his or her place in it as a northerner, has very little reality. The northern writer's perspective is: the Civil War was interesting as a human drama and it ended with an important moral victory. De Forest was moved to write out of the urgency of a participant who could imagine the southern young lady's point of view. *The Red Badge of Courage* (1895) is based on fact (and on Crane's reading of De Forest more than any other novelist) but imagined. By contrast, Joseph Pennell had actual divided loyalties, with grandparents on both sides, and like Faulkner's Quentin Compson, his autobiographical hero was obsessed generations after the war with that combined legacy. Given these contrasting visions, or attitudes, and purposes, it is not surprising that most Southern writers concentrate on the war's effect on the traditional southern aristocratic family on a plantation (Allen Tate's *The Fathers*, 1938, Ellen Glasgow's *The Battle-Ground*, 1902, and Stark Young's *So Red the Rose*, 1934). Relationships in the family unit are dramatized; that unity is disrupted by the intrusion of the war or by members of the family having to go to it; involvement in a major battle or in the eastern or western campaign is depicted; they return to the shattered family and all it signifies in the southern way of life. Ironically, one of the best with this plot structure was one of the first and finest of novels written by a northerner, De Forest's *Miss Ravenel's Conversion from Secession to Loyalty*. By sharp contrast, examination of the northern novels reveals a concentration on the common soldier in a specific battle, Crane's *The Red Badge of Courage* being the most famous example.

Whether the author is male or female, the focus, in serious as opposed to *Gone with the Wind* (1936) and other historical romances, is on male characters. A notable exception is Robert Penn Warren's *Band of Angels* (1955), narrated by a mulatto woman.

Southern novelists devote a great deal of space to the antebellum era

(Heyward's *Peter Ashley,* 1932, Tate's *The Fathers*), while northerners usually plunge into battle as quickly as possible, intent upon destroying the plantation family, with its slave economy, the cause of the conflict.

Although we have used the term Civil War fiction, we include the era of causes before and the era of effects afterward. The Civil War novel's time span is then from the events depicted in Harriet Beecher Stowe's prophetic *Uncle Tom's Cabin* (1852), published a decade before the war, to the World War II era of Pennell's *Rome Hanks* (1944).

In some of the novels, the war is mostly in the background, as in *Many Thousands Gone* (1931) and *Long Remember* (1934). In others, the war is an episode in a larger story, as in *Raintree County* (1948). Or, by contrast, it is not directly depicted, but memories of its causes and effects on into the present moment are dramatized, out of a rage to tell or explain, as in *Absalom, Absalom!* (1936), *The History of Rome Hanks* (1944), and *All the King's Men* (1946), (chapter 4).

This way of expanding the body of Civil War novels is anticipated by the fact that some novels we already think of as Civil War novels take up the war only at the end (*Peter Ashley* and *The Fathers*) to focus on causes or start with Reconstruction (Colonel William C. Falkner's *The White Rose of Memphis,* 1881, Josephine Herbst's *Pity Is Not Enough,* 1933, Richard Marius's *The Coming of Rain,* 1969) to focus on effects. Some of those novels are more effective conceptually, *The Fathers* from the South and Francis Grierson's *The Valley of Shadows* (1909) from the North, than many novels that are mostly about the war itself. Knowing what they know and still feel about the Civil War, the imaginations of southern readers especially are stimulated, within a provocative conception, by reading novels about the antebellum and Reconstruction eras.

In that perspective, *Huckleberry Finn* should be considered one of the great Civil War novels. In his essay on *Absalom, Absalom!* Lewis Simpson claims that *Huckleberry Finn* is "basically an exploration of the southern society that fought the Civil War." Some may consider it perverse to call Mark Twain's *Huckleberry Finn* a Civil War novel. But what if those who call it the Great American Novel are at least close to being right? They claim that it is the fullest expression of the American character and land, the American Dream and its nightmare obverse, not by the author's conscious intention, nor by any superabundance of diverse raw material, but by what it embodies and simultaneously implies about America then and America to come. What it most prophetically suggests, as Simpson declares, is the Civil War. If each American reads it with all she or he knows about the war conceptually and imaginatively in mind, it may shed a kind of light no conventional Civil War novel can. At the very least, reading this novel as a Civil War novel may alter the way one perceives all those novels more confidently called Civil War novels.

Another indirect illumination of the war is *Raintree County*, set in 1892 on 4 July, with flashbacks to the past, especially the war. And Joseph Stanley Pennell in *The History of Rome Hanks and Kindred Matters* features a protagonist like Quentin Compson who strives to make sense of his private present in terms of the historical past. In chapter 4 of Robert Penn Warren's *All the King's Men* Jack Burden tells us about his historical research into the tragic Civil War era story of his supposed distant relative Cass Mastern. Jack tried to escape from the present into his research only to discover that "the world is all of one piece," that to touch even the remotest strand of the web alerts the spider—and our past, present, and future merge in alarm.

The Civil War shattered the southern institutions and time has finished the process of destruction. Perhaps that is why fewer southern writers now write Civil War novels and those that have appeared recently are more likely to resemble northern novels with their concentration on battles—Shelby Foote's *Shiloh* (1952), Douglas C. Jones's *Elkhorn Tavern* (1980), Tom Wicker's *Unto This Hour* (1984)—rather than the traditional family-centered novel. Ironically, it is the popular historical romance novel that continues to focus on the plantation and the family, the vein most effectively worked by William Faulkner's great-grandfather Colonel W. C. Falkner in *The White Rose of Memphis,* Stark Young in *So Red the Rose,* and Margaret Mitchell in *Gone With the Wind.*

The central question of the Civil War novel raises other questions: Why is it that no major Civil War novel was written by a northern woman? Many would agree that of the better Civil War novels, several were written by southern women: Tennessee writers Mary Noailles Murfree, *Where the Battle Was Fought* (1884) and *The Storm Centre* (1905), Evelyn Scott's *The Wave* (1929), and Caroline Gordon's *None Shall Look Back* (1937); Virginia writers Mary Johnston's epic *The Long*

Roll (1911) and *Cease Firing* (1912), and Ellen Glasgow's *The Battle-Ground*. These southern women writers also wrote many non-Civil War novels.

For almost a century and-a-half, the Civil War genre of fiction has instilled certain expectations in readers as they pick up a new one. Many of those expectations are described in this introduction and in the essays to follow. It should be asserted on this occasion that a goodly company of readers want an end to, or a curtailment of, repackaging in both fiction and nonfiction about the Civil War.

With each repackaging of readily available facts, one gets the feeling that a time of acute critical reassessment is long overdue. The mania for the facts that the historian and too many novelists share has outlived its necessity. For the facts, we may consult *War of the Rebellion, A Compilation of the Official Records of the Union and Confederate Armies,* in one hundred twenty-eight volumes, with atlas, published in Washington from 1880 to 1901.

The obsession with authenticity produces some novels that are a kind of semidocumentary, a re-creation, like historical reenactments of famous battles on their actual sites, a parade of well-researched details in uniforms and armament, "brought back to life" by pretenders of our own day. Recent novels give us authenticity laced with imagination or imagination laced with authenticity—the effect is similar: an aura of artificiality. The reader may have the uneasy sense that the novelist, primarily committed either to the power of imagination or the force of fact, is straining to appease the neglected of the two masters.

A good many recent novelists and historians as well justify their notions for yet another Civil War book on the misconceived distinction between the military or political as opposed to the so-called "human" side of the story. Some reviewers of Civil War novels offer as criteria for excellence or distinction for a novel the fact that it "dares" to present "the human side." As opposed to what? The common soldier, it is presumed, is a creature somehow more authentic than the generals. It is a vapid distinction. The "human" eye-witness turns out to be someone who saw or remembered little more of the battle than the general who sat it out on the other side of a mountain or the civilian who cowered from it in a basement.

No eyewitness could ever produce a coherent view of any aspect of any major battle. Ironically, paradoxically, or just plain logically, the novelist or historian of the 1990s, possessed of millions of fragments and of his or her own sensibility, of a conceptual imagination, stylistic taste, and an intellect commensurate to the task, is far better equipped to give us a coherent view than a multitude of eye-witnesses.

It may be argued that the leaden blow of fact after fact blunts the writer's sensibility, inhibits the imagination. Once the formula takes effect, it is the formula itself one reexperiences page after page. Clearly, there are those who long to consume large doses of this formula. But those with a low tolerance for it may wonder, repeatedly, "Is this detail here because it is essential and illuminating to a conception derived from the author's vision of the war, or because the obeisance to fact dictates the use of it at this particular moment?"

From the beginning, fiction has offered a wide variety of fresh perspectives. De Forest gave us a northerner's perspective on the southern plantation owner and insight into a so-called minor battle, at Port Hudson, Louisiana. In his stories of soldiers and civilians, Bierce gave us a bitterly ironic vision of the universe. Crane gave us the perspective of the ordinary soldier. Kantor showed the battle of Gettysburg from the point of view of the townspeople. Scott's novel gave us a multi-faceted omniscient view of the entire war. Hers, along with Pennell's and Lockridge's, offered epic dimensions to the war. Faulkner showed how several oral perspectives affected the lives of survivors and descendants, both military and civilian.

Nonfiction has offered more than general histories and biographies and autobiographies; it has also taken up very special and specific subjects. It has dealt with some aspects that fiction has not approached, while fiction has done what nonfiction has not.

The success of the work of rediscovering and reassessing depends upon the simultaneous revitalization of Civil War fiction. Talk of the unwritten war might also include aspects that neither fiction nor nonfiction have explored sufficiently.

As they attempt to envision what might yet be done, future Civil War novelists would do well to survey the scope of the nonfiction that has already been written to determine what remains to be done. Fiction has not dealt sufficiently with: blacks, Indians, and other minorities, and with women in the war; with combat artists and photographers; with lesser-known historical figures such as Parson Brownlow, Edmund Ruffin, Oliver Wendell Holmes as a young officer and his famous father as a parent who searched for his son on the battlefield; with bridges, railroads, churches, and other structures as focus settings for key experiences.

There has been no comic Civil War novel remotely like *The Story of Don Miff, As Told by His Friend John Bouche Whacker, A Symphony of Life* (1886) "edited" by Virginius Dabney. Dabney was the Walker Percy of his day. His satirical vision, witty style, and comic innovative devices shift our perspectives as if we were riding in a square-wheeled carriage over a backwoods washboard road.

No book, fiction or nonfiction, has yet been written out of a coherent philosophy of the Civil War, controlled by a complex conception. Most Civil War books these days, nonfiction and fiction, are inspired less by conceptions than by mere notions: how about looking at the Civil War through a microcosm of the battle of the Crater? through Andersonville prison? from a science fiction angle?

Some of the most intriguing mysteries, paradoxes, questions, curiosities of American literature have to do with Civil War novels. For instance, it is strange that although most Civil War novels are by southerners, no southern writer of major importance, except Evelyn Scott and William Faulkner, has produced as his or her best work a Civil War novel. That is even more incomprehensible if you agree with the statement made earlier that many or most novels by southerners are in some sense expressions of the cause and effect of the Civil War.

The best southern novels do not generally compare well on artistic grounds with northern fiction about the war. Out of the North have come several classics, the best work of their authors: John William De Forest's *Miss Ravenel's Conversion from Secession to Loyalty,* Ambrose Bierce's *Tales of Soldiers and Civilians,* Stephen Crane's *The Red Badge of Courage,* MacKinlay Kantor's *Long Remember,* Joseph Stanley Pennell's *The History of Rome Hanks and Kindred Matters* (he wrote only one other, second in an unfinished trilogy), and Ross Lockridge, Jr.'s, *Raintree County* (his only novel), all discussed in this volume.

Most critics discuss Civil War novels or argue their relative excellence almost exclusively in terms of theme, while describing the raw material and the social and historical considerations, as if one theme more than another accounts for excellence. It is all the more curious then that the more intellectually conceived of the novels discussed in this volume, *The Wave, Absalom, Absalom!,* and *Rome Hanks* have not endeared themselves to critics of the past seventy years who lament the lack of a masterpiece—they usually don't even mention Scott or Pennell. Readers have been on their own then in their considerations of the aesthetic qualities of these and other novels. In the final analysis, of course, it is the aesthetic power of any work of fiction that enables it to continue generation after generation forcibly to have all its other effects on readers.

In their use of innovative techniques, *The Wave, Absalom, Absalom!, Rome Hanks,* and *Raintree County* are rare among Civil War novels.

The author's choice of point of view and the kind of style produced by point of view are of major importance in evaluating the achievement of Civil War novels and stories. The first-person, eye-witness account, usually in the spirit of the many collections of letters, journals, and memoirs kept by men and women, is employed mostly by southerners, as in *The Fathers, The Long Night, The Unvanquished.* The style of the first two is literary, the third vernacular.

Very seldom is the point of view third person, omniscient, but limited to the perceptions of a single character. *When the War Is Over* (1969), by Stephen Becker, a novelist who writes on De Forest's novel for this volume, stands almost alone. The prevalence of the omniscient point of view may explain to some extent the general impression that the Civil War novel is inevitably a very long novel. Artistic compression produced *The Red Badge of Courage* and *Shiloh,* but that most Civil War novels, including those in this volume, are over four hundred pages is inherent in the massiveness of raw material and in the intent of the author to capture the war and is encouraged by the omniscient point of view. Northern novels tend to run a little longer.

Whether the writer depicts the impact of battles on the members of a family or on soldiers in an army in a single major battle, the point of view that is most appropriate is, obviously, the godlike omniscient, and both southern and northern writers employ it most frequently. It promotes a chronological plot structure and a complex, rich, sometimes ornate, literary style.

Among the contributors to this volume are both southern and northern novelists and scholars, most of whom have published work on the Civil War. The works of fiction, chosen by the editors in consultation with the contributors, are by both northern and southern writers. All the essays were written for this volume, except those on Lytle and Scott (which has been considerably revised). The sequence of the essays is chronological. "Classic" extends to 1950. The year 2000 may be the limit of a follow-up volume.

A word about the wide variation in the length of the essays. We deliberately asked writers who would approach their choices quite differently, in the matter of length as much as any other consideration. Take, for instance, the first two essays. We very much wanted responses by Stephen Becker and Ishmael Reed to their choices of fiction from our list of fourteen works. A long essay by Stephen Becker on *Miss Ravenel's Conversion from Secession to Loyalty* (1867) is one kind of welcome response; a brief essay by Ishmael Reed on Ambrose Bierce's short stories is another.

George Garrett, along with a good many others, had long praised *When the War Is Over* (1969) as an unusual, neglected Civil War novel. We thought it would be interesting to invite the author of that novel, and a veteran of the Korean Conflict, Stephen Becker, to choose a title from our list. Becker is a native of Yonkers, New York, so in the first essay, a northern Civil War novelist looks at the work of an early northern novelist.

He provides a wide historical and literary context for the entire collection. Even when he hones in on De Forest's life (he "was a moderate Puritan, a New Englander descended from Huguenots") and his novel ("not merely realistic but wise, the creation of an artist coming to terms with the gap between the real and the ideal"), his generalizations help set the stage for the essays that follow. Like several other contributors, he comments readily from the point of view of a practicing novelist. De Forest's novel "has much to teach a modern novelist."

Because Bierce *had* to be included, we changed our original intention to confine ourselves to novels. Ishmael Reed, a Tennessean and author of several experimental and sometimes controversial novels, plays, and essays, became intrigued by our suggestion that Ambrose Bierce's vision of life in his stories might prove to be close to his own. In the midst of reading Bierce's work, Reed expressed his intense excitement on discovering a writer whose work he had known only in passing and became engrossed in reading *Tales of Soldiers and Civilians* (1891) and about Bierce's life and influence. Reed finds in Bierce insight into the slave-owning southern gentleman: "Throughout Bierce's work there is always a gentleman who is capable of the grisliest savagery. Bierce saw through the veneer of good breeding of the slaveowners who permitted their children to ride Negroes for fun. These characters, who always seem to be wary of offending their fellows . . . give little thought to shooting or hanging people." Laced like barbed-wire throughout his essay are references to later wars. "His pen is like the best state-of-the-art film camera, and one wonders whether that ghoulish carnival of death, World War I, would have been avoided if Bierce's sharp images of war could have been broadcast with the satellite technology of today."

Some years ago, James Cox delivered an extraordinarily dynamic and memorable lecture on *Huckleberry Finn*. We wanted the comments of such a man on a Civil War novel. Cox chose to write about *The Red Badge of Courage,* the novel generally considered to be the American masterpiece of the Civil War, a claim open to dispute. Like Reed, Cox was haunted by the war in the Persian Gulf during the time he was rereading and writing about Crane's novel, a novel as much about all war as it is about the Civil War.

George Garrett suggested that Virginian, R. H. W. Dillard, poet, novelist, and critic, might be happy to return to *The Battle-Ground* (1902). Dillard eagerly took on the task of arguing that it is one of the major novels—that, too, will be disputed—of Virginia novelist, Ellen Glasgow. "Her acute analysis of the position of women in a male-dominated culture . . . shaped her early fiction and set it apart from the romantic Southern fiction of the day. No wonder, then, that her Civil War novel is not just another mythic Valhalla of the Old Order, but is rather a complex study of the violent destruction of a deadly illusion of power and order, and especially of the effects of the illusion and its loss on a varied group of people who had always lived in its grip."

George Garrett, a native of Florida, poet, novelist, critic, renowned all-around man of letters, and author of historical novels of high quality set in the Elizabethan era, assigned to himself *The Long Roll* (1911), the work of yet another Virginian, Mary Johnston, whose historical novel *To Have and to Hold* (1900) was an enormous popular success. Having reiterated "several things that are usually said" about Mary Johnston's work, Garrett says a few that have not been said, including this; "I seriously doubt if Norman Mailer, for example, or, to be more recent, Tim O'Brien, have ever glanced at or even heard of Mary Johnston's Civil War books. [Garrett comments on *Cease Firing* as well.] But they owe her something whether they know it or not, as do we all. She prepared the way. And there are moments, passages and sequences in both . . . which are better writing about men at war than anything in *The Naked and the Dead* (or anything in James Jones for that matter [Garrett wrote a biography of Jones]) or the work of Tim O'Brien." He has more favorable comments for the World War II memoir *All the Brave Promises* (1966) by another of our contributors, Mary Lee Settle.

First choice, readers may want to know, went to the editors. After a decade devoted to rediscovering through many published essays and securing the reissuing of the works of Evelyn Scott, it was inevitable that Peggy Bach would choose *The Wave* (1929), until recently one of the most neglected of major Civil War novels. Bach argues that *The Wave* uniquely combines all the focal elements and techniques of southern and northern novels while going far beyond them, making all other novels seem spin-offs and expansions of materials in Scott's novel. The narration is stunningly omniscient overall but Scott renders all events—of every kind, on the homefront and in battle, in numerous settings North and South—from within the consciousness of over a hundred characters of every type. She modulates her style from impressionism to expressionism, from lyricism to a quality of severe intellectual scrutiny. She does not attempt to justify either side; and she is as objective as a foreign observer, de Tocqueville, would have been.

Told that Ishmael Reed had already chosen the stories of Ambrose Bierce, Mary Lee Settle, one of whose many novels, *Know Nothing* (1960) deals with the Civil War, asked rhetorically, "Well, you're certainly going to include John Peale Bishop's stories, *Many Thousands Gone*, aren't you?" Settle is a West Virginian writing somewhat impressionistically about stories set in that state by a writer who also was born and raised there. The book is "a connected series of stories . . . of no great matters, no battles, no heroes, or only one and a subtle one at that. Instead of the easier events, the battle cries, the burnings, the heroic deaths, there is the silent, grey dying fall of years of war."

That some of our contributors had never heard of some of the titles on our list of "classics" demonstrates no one's ignorance, rather the whole problem of the Civil War novel, a problem which is not alone explained by the paucity of literary criticism. The enormous fame of the popular success, *Gone With the Wind,* may suggest that another facet of the problem is misperception. Critics and serious novelists, like other serious readers, labor under the general impression that the so-called historical novel is an inferior genre. In his excellent *Fiction of the Forties,* Chester Eisinger mentions neither Joseph Pennell nor Ross Lockridge, Jr. Fine work, we have confessed, has also eluded the editors of this volume.

Rosellen Brown knew, of course, the most famous work of DuBose Heyward, *Porgy* (from which the Gershwin pop-opera, *Porgy and Bess,* was adapted), but she was not familiar with *Peter Ashley* (1932). Brown's essay suggests that there was some bliss in her ignorance, but we hoped for, and got, reservations about the quality of some of our choices. "What makes characters memorable . . . is their refusal or inability to simplify their choices and give us perfect models of behavior or belief. Why, then, is *Peter Ashley* at the same time so engaging a book and yet so irritating? And why does Heyward seem not so much the orchestrator of hard questions as the author slightly out of control?" "Is there a more familiar frailty of the Southerner than his allowing manners to overwhelm morals? *Peter Ashley* is a perfect exemplar of the conflict wrought in its author right before our eyes." Nevertheless, Heyward's novel is well-served by an essay written by this Southern writer, one of whose novels, *Civil Wars,* uses the metaphor of the Civil War for a modern story of the civil rights struggle of the 1960s.

A Michigan novelist and editor, Robie Macauley writes with personal feeling about the Civil War novel of Iowa novelist MacKinlay Kantor, *Long Remember* (1934). Kantor's is not an epic vision of the decisive battle of Gettysburg. "*Long Remember*'s realism is rooted in eyewitness accounts and recorded memories and it is less about a battle than about people—both soldiers and civilians—who found themselves swallowed up by a battle."

Generally considered one of the finest Civil War novels, Andrew Lytle's *The Long Night* (1936) was on our list from the start, and we were confident that a good many people would be eager to write about it, but we wanted to include in this book the insights of Robert Penn Warren, Kentucky-born poet, novelist, and critic, several of whose novels and nonfiction books are about or relate to the Civil War, *Band of Angels* and *Wilderness* (1961). Not in good health, he had to decline the invitation. Almost two decades earlier he had responded to David Madden's request for a brief, informal essay on his favorite neglected novel with a piece on *The Long Night* by his close friend. We reprint it here.

The Long Night is the tragic tale of private, family vengeance for the death of the patriarch that prefigures the public conflict of the Lost Cause. Lytle's technique is in itself a major expression of the clash of the two conflicts: he juxtaposes two first-person narrators, in the southern oral tradition, with his own omniscient narration out of the modern literary tradition; the reader must become a participant in the effort to experience and possess the two, related conflicts. Except for a technical defect, Warren praises "the conception of the story. . . . The work is full of realistic effects, the details of a real world and real people, but the whole is more like a ballad than a novel—a quintessential poetry of action, pathos, humor, and doom . . . . strangely like a dream."

Even when one knows a work very well, as Lewis Simpson clearly knows William Faulkner's *Absalom, Absalom!* (1936), the act of writing about it once more, for this new context, may stimulate, as it did for Simpson, a profound reappraisal which argues for the influence of Mark Twain upon his novel and that sheds new light on Quentin Compson, Faulkner's most autobiographical character. "Mark Twain was more than a distant forerunner of Faulkner. He created the model of the crucial role Faulkner enacted: that of the southern author as at once a participant in and ironic witness to the drama of memory and history that centered essentially in the never-ending remembrance of the great American civil conflict of 1861–1865." Reading his essay, one may well get the impression that his own choice for the Civil War masterwork is that novel.

Tom Wicker is a political writer for the New York *Times* and author of several novels, including *Unto This Hour* (1984), about the Civil War. When we suggested he write on *The Fathers,* he was, as he says in his essay, puzzled to know he had never heard of it. Once again, we welcomed a discovery essay and, as with Rosellen Brown, we offer here an essay that sees flaws in the achievement.

Introduction

Joseph Stanley Pennel's *The History of Rome Hanks and Kindred Matters* (1948) is another editor's choice. Although David Madden is, it must be owned here, on record as arguing for Evelyn Scott's *The Wave* as the greatest of all Civil War novels, he regards his discovery of Pennell's novel as a major event in his own development as a Civil War novelist whose "Sharpshooter" is still in revision.

Having reviewed the problems readers have had from the start in reading *Rome Hanks,* Madden offers suggestions for responding to the complex experience Pennell imagined; an understanding of the way he uses point of view is the major consideration. Young Lee Harrington, whose grandparents fought on both sides, sets out deliberately to recall and to meditate on the stories told to him by a friend of his northern great-grandfather and an uncle of his southern grandfather. As he remembers, talks to himself, and meditates, and even imagines what nobody could have told him, Lee weaves back and forth from past to present (around the time of World War II), mixing chronology. The ensuing confusion alienated reviewers and the many readers who expected a conventional Civil War novel.

The overall effect of this collection may be to convey a sense of our conviction that the war does not remain unwritten, but the essays by Wicker and Daniel Aaron, among several others, should allay any fears, that we have cast an uncritical eye over Civil War fiction.

Our survey of literary commentary on Civil War fiction created an interesting context for Aaron's essay on Ross Lockridge, Jr.'s, *Raintree County* (1948). Had Lockridge's novel succeeded—Professor Aaron argues that finally it doesn't—*The Unwritten War* may never have been written. "Of all the writers represented in *Classics of Civil War Fiction,* Lockridge probably comes closest to seeing the war from the perspective of a mystical midwesterner," says Aaron, himself a Chicagoan, "although to be sure from a marked northern bias." "*Raintree County* never got from impatient reviewers the thoughtful reading it needed and deserved." "Ross Lockridge, Jr.'s, novel, a mix of history and myth, encloses a single day, July 4, 1892, in legendary Raintree County, Indiana. As the hours tick on from dawn to midnight, flashbacks (some fifty in all) to distant decades gradually fill in the lives of the principal characters who have converged at Waycross Station . . . for the ceremonies. Thus the past is recaptured in the present and the future anticipated in the past."

Howells's question, taken up by others over the past century and longer, remains unanswered. We wonder whether Howells's question did not derive from a larger question in the popular imagination: why has the Great American Civil War failed to produce the Great American novel?

Americans seem to need to keep unanswered those two major, perhaps inseparable, questions about American fiction: why is there no great American novel? why is there no great Civil War novel? For Americans, the Civil War provides the single richest and most meaningful perspective on the entire American Experiment. Wouldn't the Great American novel then have to be simultaneously the Great Civil War novel?

Some readers are satisfied that *Huckleberry Finn* has been the answer to the first question since 1885, but for most readers, the first question remains unanswered. Most serious readers, North and South, agree that Stephen Crane's *The Red Badge of Courage* is the answer to the second question. But we are not alone in arguing that Crane's novel is more about war in general than it is about the American Civil War. In the consciousness of most of the public, North and South, Margaret Mitchell's *Gone With the Wind* is not only the greatest novel about the war by a southerner, but the greatest by anybody. *Gone With the Wind* is granted by most critics a kind of grudging admiration: strong narrative pace offset by shallow characterization, and so on. The phenomenal popular success of the novel and the movie make *Gone With the Wind* a monumental distraction from the serious debate, unless one sides in the current debate over the canon with those who argue that fiction should both reflect and affect society, in which case the general public would be right about Mitchell's novel.

We offer in these essays new substance for the debate—and, perhaps, some help in the individual reader's own attempts to achieve an answer.

David Madden   *Peggy Bach*

On John William De Forest's
Miss Ravenel's Conversion from Secession to Loyalty

STEPHEN BECKER

THE NOBLE SAVAGERY of the new world died in the bloody Civil War, and romanticism with it, a lingering double death, both to be reborn periodically as trivial sentimentality or wishful idealism. Romanticism was already dead in the old world, ground beneath railway cars, smothered by poisonous fogs, betrayed by child labor and bourgeois cynicism. When Victor Hugo's *Les Burgraves* was presented in 1843, a painter, asked to join the claque, answered, *"Jeunes gens, allez dire a votre maître que la jeunesse est morte."* The English generally date that death at 1832, with the great Reform Bill; some like Byron's death in 1824, Coleridge's in 1834 or Victoria's accession in 1837.

The agony was not brief; noble savages and romantics alike rallied often, and their ghosts still walk. And dates make no sense in these transitions, because the categories are never pure: romanticism (characterized by feeling and content rather than order and form, with emphasis on the sublime, emotional, supernatural and exotic) is feckless if it does not spring from an explicitly human setting, and realism (which prefers the familiar, typical and even banal, and recognizes that we are all frail vessels who will one day perish) is jejune if it does not implicitly contrast life and the ideal. Jane Austen was no romantic; the romantic Scott, with his "big bow-wow," admired her immensely, as did, later, the implacably Whiggish Macaulay. James Fenimore Cooper's extravagant plots and leafy prose (out of Chateaubriand by Samuel Johnson) contrasted with his strong sense of good and evil. His savages were often less than noble, his finely-chiseled whites often weak, his women often blurred cartoons, yet his gentlemanly political anguish—democracy or aristocracy—informs his novels. The gritty, cynical Balzac admired him; Hugo ranked him above Scott (later Conrad would call him "one of my masters," while Melville and D. H. Lawrence saw him as "the American novelist"). Balzac died in 1850 (the year of *The Scarlet Letter*), Cooper in 1851. *Moby-Dick* appeared in 1851, and may be the perfect fusion of dying romanticism and young realism, transcending both, surpassing American novels before and since. But a working novelist may admire all these efforts, all these men and women chained to the word, serving a life sentence in the name of an art, struggling to reconcile the conflicting demands of classical tradition, entertainment and livelihood. Good novelists are not competitive; they are a little band of brothers and sisters, and in the end it is us against them.

Eighty years of revolution and reaction, here and in Europe, came to temporary conclusions with the rebellions of 1848 there and the Civil War here, and serious writers, then as now, simmered when the world heated up. In Europe the quarrel was between reaction, moderating to conservatism, and radicalism, moderating to liberalism. Here the matter was at once more simple and more complicated. The Civil War was fought over slavery, despite the disguises of "states' rights" and "interposition." But slavery embodied many of mankind's most ancient struggles—between principle and practice, community and self-interest, truth and superstition; more specifically, between Christianity and barbarism. It is tempting to range Cavaliers, romantics and the Confederacy against Roundheads, realists and the Union—tempting but insufficient, though surely the latter had a sharper instinct for the human condition, for truth against illusion.

America's first literary realist wrote one enduring, flawed novel that stands as a milestone, has been largely neglected by critics and has much to teach a modern novelist; even its faults are instructive. John William De Forest was a moderate Puritan, a New Englander descended from Huguenots. He was born in 1826 and bred in Seymour, Connecticut (once Humphreysville), ten miles from New Haven. He was an intelligent, educated adult when the Mexican War broke out, and as a young man saw the Calhoun Resolutions in defense of slavery, the California gold rush, the Compromise of 1850 and Daniel Webster's decline; the Fugitive Slave Act, the publication of *Uncle Tom's Cabin,* the Kansas-Nebraska Act (repealing the Compromise and thus affirming Congressional neutrality on slavery in the territories and new states), the consequent birth of the Republican Party; "Bleeding Kansas," several noisy presidential elections, and the Dred Scott decision. He must have pondered Thoreau's long, passionate defense of John Brown and Hawthorne's shameless campaign biography of Franklin Pierce, an ugly bit of puffery by a great writer who even attempted to justify Pierce's supine deference to the slave states.

De Forest's education was irregular. He attended local academies and prepared for Yale—which meant, in those days, a familiarity with far more classics than even college graduates would be able to claim a century later. But his health was too dubious for the rigors of Yale, and he embarked instead on a gentleman's tour of the Middle East. This took him to Smyrna, Beirut, Jerusalem, the highlands of Syria, always in the company of, or wandering from the vicinity of, American missionaries in the area. (He remained nominally a Congregationalist all his life, but his work is not tendentious; it is even agnostic.) He learned something of the French and English. He met Arabs and African blacks, and observed the grand mix of Mediterranean peoples: Muslims and Christians and Jews, Greeks and Egyptians and Bedouin, Lebanese and Turks and Indians. "His first sight of a Turkish Negro was one of a man of dignity, independence, ease, intelligence and gravity" (Light, 21). His notes reveal a hope that all men would one day thrive in vague equality, but his natural attitude was the millennial attitude of white men: mankind's job was to raise itself to the level of the European and American white. To suggest otherwise would have puzzled these paragons. Yet it was not bigotry that moved them. They were swept along in the grand 19th-century flow of

politics and economics that bore humanity ever higher, ever better mannered, ever better educated, ever more sublime in philosophy and nobler
in action. The Great Chain of Being culminated in the British and
American upper classes.

De Forest was only twenty-three when he wrote his first book, *History of
the Indians of Connecticut from the Earliest Known Period to 1850.* It was
praised and reprinted. He deplored the white man's injustices, but also
the barbarism (in his view) of the Indians. He dwelt on the extermination
of the Pequots, the "largest and bravest" of the Connecticut tribes, and
concluded, "[T]he burning of the Pequot fort was . . . a piece of stern
policy, mingled with something of revenge, from which floods of argu-
ment could not wash out a stain of cruelty" (Light, 27). Already a cold
eye; scarcely frontier romanticism. (A nice footnote to literary history:
Hawthorne fretted about the Pequots, as his ancestors had labored vig-
orously to wipe them out; and of course Melville paid them homage with
his *Pequod.*) A modern biographer justly calls the book "the work of a
rational, though Christian, man whose angle of vision made him capable
of seeing that reality and human nature were exceedingly complex"
(Light, 27). (We may rejoice in that "rational, though Christian.") De
Forest's childhood, frailty and travels had distanced him sufficiently
from the ordinary to give him perspective. He was already withdrawn
somewhat from the cultural myths and slogans of his era.

He returned to Europe, this time on a more conventional grand
tour—England, France, Florence for a season; Trieste, Vienna and Ven-
ice briefly; then Graefenberg for the waters, which were rebarbative if
not roborative. He did the castles of the Rhineland, and spent the fall,
winter and spring of 1851–2 at Divonne near Lac Leman, immersing
himself not merely in the waters but in French language and literature
(though he would always write "esprit 'du' corps"), as well as the nervous
excitement raised by Louis Napoleon's coup d'état. Whether it was the
waters, or the sheer discomfort of the treatment, or maturity, or a natural
surge of strength to cope with foreign parts and ways, his health did improve. He gave over hydropathy and returned to civilization—Paris and
Florence, then Rome and Naples. In all he spent three years seeing the
world, wearing canvas sheets and shivering in pools, and reading omniv-

orously in French, German and Italian. When he returned to the United States at the turn of 1855 he was a "slim young man who liked an occasional cigar and glass of wine."

He also liked writing, or—at this stage—being an author. Any novelist will understand. In an early novel, *Seacliff* (1859), the hero asks, "What should a Christian preacher say of a man who would rather be Byron the young than 'such an one as Paul the aged'? And yet, I have been that man." Indeed: Europe, literature, an occasional cigar and a glass of wine—we are at some remove from either Calvin or Bunyan. He revised some of his letters from the Middle East, published them in magazines and collected them as *Oriental Acquaintance* (1856). He also met Miss Harriet Sillman Shepard, whose father, Dr. Charles Upham Shepard, was a professor of chemistry (in Charleston, S. C.) and natural history (at Amherst). He married the young woman in June of 1856. He and his wife belonged to New Haven, but spent much of their first two years, and many seasons thereafter, in Charleston, and De Forest developed attitudes toward "the Negro." His opinions were at worst condescending and at best moral and prophetic. Like many of his contemporaries, he considered "the Negro" a sort of advanced child with possibilities, but he was outraged by the institution of slavery, and reserved a special scorn for Northerners who moved south, became slaveholders, and abused abolitionists and free labor. History plays tricks. When De Forest wrote (undated, but surely in the 1850s), that better than bloody revolution would be "to have slavery melt into serfage, and serfage gradually rarify into freedom. This would take . . . six generations, a period not at all too long" (Light, 41), he was supercilious and callous; but it is our shame and not his that true freedom has taken even longer.

He wrote. *Putnam's Monthly Magazine* published *Witching Times,* a novel about the Salem witchcraft trials, in 1856–57. *European Acquaintance* appeared in 1859, as did *Seacliff,* a melodrama, almost a throwback to Monk Lewis and Ann Radcliffe, redeemed by its "accurate depiction of daily life and setting and . . . well-conceived and original minor characters" (Woodward, 131). His career was then interrupted; he left Charleston for New England shortly before the fall of Fort Sumter. He was thirty-five, and wanted to be a novelist; the stirrings of literary realism were exciting. But he was to serve his country for seven years, and to suffer the inevitable writer's agony: he saw life in the raw and had to prettify it for a bland and resisting public.

De Forest organized a company for the Twelfth Connecticut Volunteers and was commissioned a captain. He served in the Louisiana campaign in 1862, and in the Shenandoah Valley in 1864. Always, even when realism dominates overwhelmingly, good novelists distort, rather than report, real life, their own experience, to weave literal and accurate tapestries. De Forest was the first American to write realistically and grimly of war from first-hand experience. He was no Stendhal or Tolstoy because he was not master of the form—his episodes are less integrated, the flow meanders; because his characters (above all, his title character) betray somewhat their descent from literature's earlier "humors"; and because he was impelled by no powerful, overriding world-view. But his tapestry is stirring; the reader's attention does not flag, and the novelist will appreciate his methods. They are nowhere more interesting than in his finest novel, *Miss Ravenel's Conversion from Secession to Loyalty,* published in 1867. He had gone home in 1864 "with what then seemed a totally ruined constitution," but served for three more years in the Invalid Corps, first as historian and then as administrator of Reconstruction, with an office in Greenville, S. C. During those three years he wrote and published a novel that stands up—that is, to be blunt, better crafted and more absorbing than 99% of the American novels produced since, though these days that scarcely seems a compliment.

Where was the novel in 1867? *Madame Bovary* was ten years old. *War and Peace* was in the writing, and *Anna Karenina* was eight years off. We survivors, within sight of the twenty-first century, must not forget that the nineteenth is the grand century of the novel. (Fiction became an art in the eighteenth century, a craft in the nineteenth and an industry in the twentieth.) The literate audience grew constantly, undistracted by electric or electronic media, and when a new installment of Dickens arrived in New York, crowds thronged the dock; he and Thackeray were prime influences on De Forest. In 1867 Henry James was twenty-four, and while he would in the following year be called (by *The Nation*) "the best writer of short stories in America," his novels lay before him. Mark Twain was thirty-two and already famous, having just published *The Celebrated Jumping Frog of Calaveras County and Other Sketches*. Melville had accomplished his great work and ceased to write for the public—almost ceased to write prose at all. Hawthorne was three years dead, Thackeray four. All that remained to Dickens was the unfinished *Edwin Drood*. Conrad was ten years old, and Stephen Crane was not yet born.

Miss Ravenel's Conversion is not merely realistic but wise, the creation of an artist coming to terms (as Tolstoy struggled so agonizingly to do) with the gap between real and ideal, with the eternal rift between what he wished and what he saw. De Forest did not grieve or whine; he was, like many shrewd skeptics, sharp and decisive once he had formed a conclusion, and he writes a lively, confiding sort of prose, abounding in both cool observation and warm good humor. He appears occasionally but not as a character. The novel is not "narrated;" rather, its author interrupts from time to time, an occasional chorus, an Uncle Thackeray, an "I," addressing—almost buttonholing—the reader. His story begins in New Boston, the capital of Barataria, with a comment reminiscent of Hawthorne's Custom-house: "I ask pardon for this geographical impertinence of introducing a seventh State into New England, and solemnly affirm that I do not mean to disturb thereby the congressional balance of the republic. I make the arrangement with no political object, but solely for my private convenience, so that I may tell my story freely without being accused of misrepresenting this private individual, or insulting that public functionary, or burlesquing any self-satisfied community."

De Forest's Miss Lillie Ravenel is a daughter of the South, and when we meet her she is an ardent admirer of the brave and dashing rebels, but she is also the daughter of Dr. Ravenel, a "professor of theory and practice in the Medical College of New Orleans" (obviously a version—a most vigorous and engaging version—of Dr. Shepard), who will also profess firm opinions on almost any topic. He is a South Carolinian born, and a Northerner, if not a downright Abolitionist, by temperament. He meets our hero, Mr. Edward Colburne, on the third page, and on the fourth lectures him on Southerners:

29

"Nobody can tell me anything about those unlucky, misguided people. I am one of them by birth—I have lived among them nearly all my life—I know them. They are as ill-informed as Hottentots[!]. They have no more idea of their relative strength as compared to that of the United States than the Root-diggers of the Rocky Mountains. They are doomed to perish by their own ignorance and madness" (9–10).

Mr. Colburne is a young gentleman, rather *medium,* and is not accustomed to such Nestorian certitude. "It will probably be a short struggle," he says, inspiring Ravenel to higher flights:

"I don't know—I don't know about that; we mustn't be too sure of that. You must understand that they are barbarians, and that all barbarians are obstinate and reckless. They will hold out like the Florida Seminoles. They will resist like jackasses and heroes. They won't know any better. They will be an honor to the fortitude and a sarcasm on the intelligence of human nature. They will become an example in history of much that is great, and all that is foolish" (10).

And shortly he pays his respects to New Orleans:

"A man can't well live there the year round. He must be away occasionally, to clear his system of its malaria physical and moral. It is a Sodom. I consider it a proof of depravity in anyone to want to go there. . . . I staid until this stupid, barbarous Ashantee rebellion drove me out" (10).

But De Forest is nicely impartial:

New Boston is not a lively nor a sociable place. The principal reason for this is that it is inhabited chiefly by New Englanders. Puritanism, the prevailing faith of that land and race, is not only not favorable but is absolutely noxious to social gayeties, amenities and graces (21–22).

And a page or two along:

. . . remarked one of those conscientious but uncharitable ladies whom I have regarded since my childhood with a mixture of veneration and dislike. Thin-lipped, hollow-cheeked, narrow-chested, with only one lung and an intermittent digestion, without a single rounded outline or graceful movement, she was a sad example of what the New England east winds can do in enfeebling and distorting the human form divine. . . . Even her smile . . . was a kind of griping smile, like that of an infant with the colic (24).

De Forest is obviously a writer of dash and bite, who may be forgiven an occasional modern barbarism ("I suppose he would have courted her if she would have let him"). His plot is linear and chronological, and he uses five major characters, those we have met plus first a Lieutenant-Colonel Carter: "A little above the middle height he was, with a full chest, broad shoulders and muscular arms, brown curling hair, and a monstrous brown mustache, forehead not very high, nose straight and chin dimpled, brown eyes at once audacious and mirthful, and a dark rich complexion which made one think of pipes of sherry wine as well as of years of sunburnt adventure" (26). And later, in New Orleans, Mrs. La-rue, a woman of the world, secessionist, Roman Catholic, far too attractive. The minor characters are vivid but De Forest is economical, and his canvas is not Tolstoyan; he may remind us more of Meredith (who recommended four characters, two major and two minor, for the short novel, and was himself, while extravagant in style, economical in casting).

In New Boston Colburne falls for Lillie, who appreciates him but is more attracted by Carter's panache and manliness. Colburne is gentle, thoughtful and mannerly (a touch of Bezuhov and of De Forest himself); he is cousin to the classic virtuous younger son. Carter is more "manly," literally or figuratively redolent of cigars, whiskey, women, battle, courage (a touch of Kuragin and some unknown model); he is cousin to the classic swashbuckler, and he reminds secessionist Lillie of the cavaliers she has admired in New Orleans. Colburne is New Englander, Carter a native Virginian; the prim puritan shows to disadvantage. Carter has been stationed in Louisiana, and regrets never meeting Lillie before; Colburne sits silent. But Carter takes a shine to Colburne, and later asks him to command a company in Carter's regiment; of course Colburne agrees. The novelist again: Colburne agrees because he cannot show himself deficient in patriotism or courage, but also because he is enamored of Lillie, and must compete with this corsair; and also because he is, despite his gentle nature, excited by the prospect of combat.

The scene shifts to New Orleans, where the two officers are posted, and whither the Ravenels return (it is in Union hands, remember). Colburne is smitten, but Lillie's view of love (and war) is romantic still: the dashing Carter is more to her taste. Enter a complication: Mrs. Larue, the widow of the late Mrs. Ravenel's brother, "not more than thirty-three years of age and still decidedly pretty."

> Her complexion was dark, pale and a little too thick, but it was relieved by the jet black of her regular eyebrows and of her masses of wavy hair. Her face oval, her nose straight, her lips thin but nicely modeled, her chin little and dimpled; her expression was generally gay and coquettish, but amazingly variable and capable of running through a vast gamut of sentiments, including affection, melancholy and piety. Though short she was well built, with a deep, healthy chest, splendid arms and finely turned ankles (143).

Echoes of the romantic, surely; everything but "fine shoulders." She is the dark lady: tricky, fickle, sexy, and "in politics, if not in other things, Mrs. Larue was as double-faced as Janus." She has a mind of her own, and can be clever and devious and proud; she is human, warm and alive, where Lillie is a portrait on canvas; and De Forest seems far more comfortable writing of her than of the chaste young lady so like his own wife.

The scene is set, the cast assembled. Lillie's romanticism will lead her to marriage with Carter, who will sin (it is implicit) with Mrs. Larue but die gloriously; and Lillie's agonized discovery of his infidelity (and her aunt's treason) will convert her brutally from plumed officers, rebellion and romance to good sense, loyalty and reality. This takes most of the war, and afterward a grown-up Lillie will heed her affectionate father and love her faithful Colburne, and all will end happily.

But "happily" is too strong. After the "occupation" of New Orleans, the siege of Port Hudson and the defense of Fort Winthrop, after the first realistic, anguished combat writing in American fiction; after the Red River campaign and the battle at Cane River; after Colburne's courage and Dr. Ravenel's dogged attempts to revise the blacks' view of life and labor; after drunkenness, incompetence and corruption among the Union officers; after sickness, blood and betrayal on the large and small scale both, nothing can end happily. De Forest enjoys echoes of the old-fashioned; he writes of "segars" and uses "wofully;" but his dead soldiers are a new element in American fiction, and so are his iniquitous officers. He saw plenty of bitter murderous combat. A century and a quarter has passed, and we are now inured to catastrophe and massacre. Consider the impact upon a decent, well-mannered New Englander of battles in which men were shot, decapitated, blown to bits; or lay bleeding, screaming, later gangrenous; thieved and drank and whored where possible; died in dozens and hundreds and thousands, the flower of the Confederacy and the pride of the Union.

But the civilian world was American Victorian, and that age required façades, appearances. The respectable dodged the reality of good and evil long after the Civil War forced them into extremes of both; hypocrisy was essential to public order. So the novelist who rubbed his reader's face in reality was a radical, taking dangerous chances. We owe De Forest more than we have acknowledged.

Yet his title character is his least vigorous. Lillie Ravenel is almost a failure. De Forest was hedged about with taboos he could not conquer, or perhaps even identity.

One glimpse of reality was denied him, as it was denied all men, and indeed most women, until recently: the hazy glimpse of a woman's life and possibilities. Lillie is not insipid; she is no Clarissa, no Shamela. But De Forest was writing about a woman in a man's world, and he knew little of women. She was almost certainly based on his own wife, which would constrain him even further. The ancient tradition of great women in literature—Medea, Antigone, Lady Macbeth, Cleopatra—had little to do with reality: these were mythical figures or archetypes. De Forest could not leap the gap between them and real women. Women writers had already done so. Jane Austen's women were neither sacred nor profane, but human, ironic, emotional, often vying with men on equal terms; the Bronte sisters' women were more passionate; and perhaps it was thanks to these pioneers that De Forest even approached the portrait of a real woman. Surely Cooper and Scott, Melville and Hawthorne were little help.

De Forest was writing about armies, battle, horses, whiskey, swindles, slavery, adultery, death: what chance has a virtuous woman against such literary splendors? She may not vote, or ride alone, or claim rights over her husband's property; she may not, except in the most limited setting, smoke or drink. Her lessons have covered French, watercolor and pianoforte, rather than love and mortality. The seductively sluttish Mrs. Larue is far more attractive: Miss Ravenel is *good,* as much "humor" as person, so the modern reader longs for a human mistress like Mrs. Larue. Edmund Wilson identifies Miss Ravenel as "the girl"—"the ideal, the touchstone, the democratic princess . . . breathless suspense as to whom she will marry. . . . maidenly modesty combined with common sense and a will of her own, instinctive good taste and good manners . . . the cynosure" (Wilson, 708). To paraphrase Wilson, she alone among the major characters is a conception, not a creation.

De Forest assures us in the first chapter that Miss Ravenel

> was very fair, with lively blue eyes and exceedingly handsome hair, very luxuriant, very wavy and of a flossy blonde color lighted up by flashes of amber. . . . tall and rather slender . . . fine form . . . uncommon grace. Colburne [presented to her] was flattered by the quick blush and pretty momentary flutter of embarrassment. . . . (12–13).

When she marries the rake Carter, halfway along, and he leaves for the front two days later, De Forest writes a paragraph that may bemuse us:

> She was womanish about it, and not heroic. . . . Nevertheless she did not feel the separation as bitterly as she would have done, had they been married a few months or years, instead of only a few hours. Intimate relations with her husband had not yet become a habit, and consequently a necessity of her existence; the mere fact that they had exchanged the nuptial vows was to her a realization of all that she had ever anticipated in marriage; when they left the altar, and the ring was upon her finger, their wedded life was as complete as it would ever be. And thus, in her ignorance of what love might become, she was spared something of the anguish of separation (245).

High sentiment, and not low sensuality. The author speaks of "pure emotions," words "so sacred with woman's profoundest and purest emotions that they must not be written." Nothing here of the bridal night; and "intimate relations" implies no more sensuality than the old term "intercourse" for conversation. Early on De Forest gives her speeches like this: "Now, papa, you are too bad. Mr. Colburne, don't you think he is too bad?" We almost hear the lisp, see the dimple. Still, give the author his due: he wants to work a great change in Miss Ravenel, and is not illogical to begin so close to *tabula rasa*. Halfway through the story she is still saying, "What! Have you been fighting, too? You dear, darling, wicked papa!" But she is about to fetch linen from their trunks to bind up the wounded: she will know blood and bedpans.

And how unfair to demand of De Forest a modern outlook! He was scarcely more physical about the amoral Mrs. Larue, of whom William Dean Howells could not think "without shuddering." Even so, Harper's refused to run the novel in their magazine, and renegotiated the contract to provide for book publication only. De Forest wrote that he made "no objection to your reform of the story. If it goes into the Monthly of course it ought to be made proper for families. Only I think it ought to be understood that . . . the Colonel did frequently swear and that the Louisiana lady was not quite as good as she should be." Later critics suggest that the novelist's realism "made it inevitable that feminine novel-readers would avert their eyes," and that Lillie's marriage to Carter "might have sullied her" in those readers' eyes. Howells wrote, "He is distinctly a man's novelist, and as men do not need novelists apparently so much as women, his usefulness has been limited."

Always the shrewd, fresh eye, a smile at the odor of lavender and nostalgia, when we gaze so far back; even Bovary and Karenina have been blurred by wars, flappers, swingers, significant others. And most of today's novelists care nothing about the past. Nothing. In a decade every American who can write his name will call himself a writer, a poet, an artist, and fiction will be no more interesting than luncheon clubs or university faculties. The few who survive as workers not drones, stylists not scribblers, hewers of stone and drawers of blood, will look back at De Forest with a shock of recognition. His religion and morality were disintegrating around him (it seems to be an eternal process), so he was ironic and resigned, rather than passionate and militant (how few of us have escaped the same fate!); he was unsure of his own beliefs, so insufficiently stern; he tried to show the world as it was, but his half-world did not include real women. And yet he holds us. The scathing judgment, the funny anecdote, the insider's tale of corruption and failure—all those, added to more blood and guts and hunger and cowardice than any American writer had yet dared, make his *Miss Ravenel* a landmark in our literature. Later he became more "creative," and fell into various traps— grotesque minor characters, relapse into romanticism, easy and fallacious social judgments. He thrashed about, seeking an audience. In *Miss Ravenel* he was his own audience, and a real artist. He never again wrote so well, but how many among us can claim to have published even one novel of permanent value, even one novel that will occupy critics a century hence?

We must all thank the late Edmund Wilson in *Patriotic Gore* (New York, Oxford University Press, 1962), James F. Light in *John William De Forest* (New York, Twayne Publishers, 1965), and Robert H. Woodward, who did "John William De Forest" for *American Realists and Naturalists* (Detroit, Gale Research Company, 1982, ed. Donald Pizer and Earl N. Harbert). The present writer is a novelist, and not a critic or historian; is very much in these gentlemen's debt; and urges the reader to consult their works. Page references to *Miss Ravenel* are to the 1969 Charles Merrill Publishing Company facsimile of the 1867 first edition.

John William De Forest was born in 1826 in Seymour, Connecticut, and died in 1906 in New Haven, Connecticut. Selected publications: *History of the Indians of Connecticut* (1851); *Oriental Acquaintance* (1856); *European Acquaintance* (1858); *Seacliff* (1859); *Miss Ravenel's Conversion from Secession to Loyalty* (1867, out of print, except for expensive Reprint Services edition); *Kate Beaumont* (1872); *A Lover's Revolt* (1898). Posthumous: *A Volunteer's Adventures* (1946); *A Union Officer in the Reconstruction* (1948).

On Ambrose Bierce's
Tales of Soldiers and Civilians

ISHMAEL REED

SON OF A FARMER, Ambrose Gwinett Bierce was born in 1842 at Meigs County, Ohio. While a soldier, he fought in some of the key Civil War battles and participated in General Sherman's March to the Sea.

He was a prolific short story writer and essayist. His journalism appeared in Hearst newspapers, the San Francisco Examiner and the New York Journal.

He died in 1914 under mysterious circumstances. M. E. Gremander, author of *Ambrose Bierce,* speculates that he was killed in Mexico, during the battle of Ojinaga.

In order to cure his asthma, he lived in Oakland in 1888. The Victorian Oakland, California, where Ambrose Bierce lived, still exists. Mansions and public sculpture from that bustling Oakland of merchant princes and railroad tycoons, sailors and cattlemen, stands in contrast to new Oakland's functional earthquake proof buildings with their Hemingwayesque lines. To the modern reader, Ambrose Bierce's prose style may seem as gabled as those restored buildings in what is being called Old Oakland: "Without a movement, without a sound, in the profound silence and the languor of the late afternoon, some invisible messenger of fate touched with unsealing finger the eyes of his consciousness—whispered into the ear of his spirit the mysterious awakening word which no human lips ever have spoken, no human memory ever has recalled" (*The Complete Short Stories of Ambrose Bierce,* 359). But though the design may seem busy, Ambrose Bierce, in a series of short stories entitled "Soldiers," wrote about the horrors of war with insight and technical mastery. Unlike our current think-tank bureaucratic military experts, Bierce, a student at Kentucky Military Institute, knew what he was talking about.

As a participant in some of the Civil War's bloodiest campaigns, First Lt. Bierce saw the war close-up, from bush to cliff, from corpse to corpse, and writes about war with meticulous detail: "the white face turned upward, the hands thrown out and clutched full of grass, the clothing deranged, the long dark hair in tangles and full of clotted blood." Death is the companion of war ("It is the business of the soldier to kill"). And death, like war, has its advantages, its surprises: "Death has taken an unfair advantage; he has struck with an unfamiliar weapon; he has executed a new and disquieting stratagem. We did not know that he had so ghastly resources, possibilities of terror so dismal" (372).

In Bierce's war there is always the unexpected. And in one of the more absurd wars (unwilling to disobey a General's orders, Captain Ransome, of "One Kind of Officer," fires upon his own men)—a war that divided families—the enemy could be one's own blood. In "A Horseman in The Sky," Captain Carter Druse, of the Union Forces, shoots a Confederate enemy: his father. "The Affair At Coulter's Notch" ends with one of Bierce's typically impetuous young soldiers (. . . a whole battery to himself), Captain Coulter, holding his dead child and wife. His wife was a "red-hot Secessionist." But no matter what the blood ties are, the enemy is not like us. The enemy is an alien. "The soldier never becomes wholly familiar with the conception of his foes as men like himself; he cannot divest himself of the feeling that they are another order of beings, differently conditioned, in an environment not altogether of the earth" (284).

"You are bombing us as though we were from out of space," said a diplomat, recently, whose country was being destroyed by American B-52s.

Those who are heroes to some are fools to Bierce. A young officer, who risks death to scout the enemy's position, is cheered on by his troops. While they admire his bravery, Bierce takes him apart: "His saddle blanket is scarlet. What a fool! No one who has ever been in action but remembers how naturally every rifle turns toward the man on a white horse; no one but has observed how a bit of red enrages the bull of battle" (285).

Bierce strips men of their claims that they are fighting for noble abstract goals. A recent Public Broadcasting Television System documentary about the Civil War endorsed the idyllic claim that the Confederacy and its leader, Robert E. Lee, who has been given Arthurian status by some historians, fought the war to defend their homeland, or for some other romantic reason. First Lt. Bierce, the writer, is to the point: "Being a slave owner and like other slave owners a politician he was naturally an original secessionist and ardently devoted to the Southern cause," Bierce writes of Peyton Farquhar, who gets himself hanged for committing a terrorist act against the Union (307).

Throughout Bierce's work there is always a gentleman who is capable of the grisliest savagery. Bierce saw through the veneer of good breeding of the slaveowners who permitted their children to ride Negroes for fun. These characters, who always seem to be wary of offending their fellows—"I realized the brutality of my remark, but not clearly seeing my way to an apology, said nothing," one gentleman says—give little thought to shooting or hanging people. "The liberal military code makes provision for hanging many kinds of persons, and gentlemen are not excluded" (306). Indeed, the most frequent description of these men and women who commit unspeakable acts is that they are cultivated, civilized, well-bred. (The harshest word for a character in the book "detestable" is reserved for a "well bred" woman whose letter, challenging an officer's bravery, is responsible for the death of one hundred men.)

Nothing has changed. Members of "the civilized world" demonize and attribute horrible deeds to "the enemy" while they bomb defenseless populations and destroy the ancient capitals of culture with their "surgical strikes." In Ambrose Bierce's time, removing corpses from the field was called "tidying up." Today, dead people are "collateral damage." If

Truth is the first casualty of war, then language is the second. Bierce says
that war is a business in which "the lives of men counted as nothing
against the chance of defining a road or sketching a bridge" (369), echo-
ing the sentiment of a pilot returning from his tasks in the Persian Gulf:
"I don't want to see the enemy. To me, the enemy is a blip on my radar
screen and all I want is to make that blip go away. I don't want to know
my enemy."

For Bierce, humanity is capable of bestial acts and in one of Bierce's
most famous stories, "The Eyes of the Panther," a woman is transformed
into a panther. Men are beasts and Happiness is a woman who eludes
them. Tantalizes them. The Hermit in Bierce's "Haita, the Shepherd,"
says that he has only known Happiness twice. They cannot escape their
essential animal state, their "rathood," as Bierce might say, an expression
used in "One of the Missing," the brilliant story about Jerome Searing,
another one of Bierce's characters who has to risk his neck in order to
improve the position of his comrades. He ends up being threatened by
the very rifle he has loaded for the purpose of killing the enemy and in
one of those twists of fate of which Bierce is so fond, his corpse is discovered but not recognized by his brother.

What Bierce refers to as "The Power" is a trickster given to such cruel
coincidences. Learning of his wife's infidelity, Captain Armisted in "An
Affair of Outposts" enters the service (because none in his family has
committed suicide) only to protect a Governor who is his wife's lover.

But it was decreed from the beginning of time that Private Searing was
not to murder anybody that bright summer morning, nor was the Confederate retreat to be announced by him. For countless ages events had
been so matching themselves together in that wondrous mosaic to some
parts of which, dimly discernible, we give the name of history, that the
acts which he had in will would have marred the harmony of the pattern.

Some twenty-five years previously the Power charged with the execution of the work according to the design had provided against that mis-
chance by causing the birth of a certain male child in a little village at the
foot of the Carpathian Mountains, had carefully reared it, supervised its
education, directed its desires into a military channel, and in due time
made it an officer of artillery. By the concurrence of an infinite number of
favoring influences and their preponderance over an infinite number of

opposing ones, this officer of artillery had been made to commit a breach of discipline and fly from his native country to avoid punishment. He had been directed to New Orleans (instead of New York), where a recruiting officer awaited him on the wharf. He was enlisted and promoted, and things were so ordered that he now commanded a Confederate battery some two miles along the line from where Jerome Searing, the Federal scout, stood cocking his rifle. Nothing had been neglected—at every step in the progress of both these men's lives, and in the lives of their contemporaries and ancestors, the right thing had been done to bring about the desired result. Had anything in all this vast concatenation been overlooked, Private Searing might have fired on the retreating Confederates that morning, and would perhaps have missed. As it fell out, a Confederate captain of artillery, having nothing better to do while awaiting his turn to pull out and be off, amused himself by sighting a field piece obliquely to his right at what he took to be some Federal officers on the crest of a hill, and discharged it ("One of the Missing," 266–67).

Dwight Eisenhower said that every war is going to astonish you, and Ambrose Bierce would agree except that, for him, what startles humans doesn't startle "The Power," which is in charge of that "wondrous mosaic, we give the name of history." But Ambrose Bierce, a determinist, an absurdist, questions the judgment of "The Power." "Would one exception have marred too much the pitiless perfection of the divine, eternal plan?" he asks after the death of a reckless soldier who sacrifices himself in order to scout the enemy's position. "The Power" pushes men about as though they were toy soldiers and uses the law of probabilities to enforce its will. So "brave" is George Thurston that when ordered to "Throw down that sword and surrender, you damned Yank!" he tells a whole company of Confederate soldiers who have leveled their rifles at his breast, "I will not" (370). Thurston is killed while swinging in a child's swing.

But unlike today when a commander can entertain a group of laughing reporters by boasting about a direct pinpoint hit at the enemy, even amid the carnage of the Civil War the combatants found some way to acknowledge the valor of their opponents. Remorseful over the execution of Dramer Brune, a Confederate spy, who once saved his life, a Union officer, Captain Parrol Hartroy, commits suicide in "The Story of a Conscience." Lieutenant Herman Brayle's daring so impresses his comrades as well as his enemies in "Killed at Resaca" that the Confederates and the Union troops interrupt their battle to honor his corpse. "A generous enemy honored the fallen brave" (376).

The Civil War was the last hot war fought on American soil. In this century, Americans have never suffered the disasters that Europeans have experienced. In Berlin's War Museum I read the demographics. Starving European families living in the streets. The drastic decline in the male population. The raping of women by the invading enemy army. The burning of great cities. Visiting a cemetery, I was struck by the irony of bullet holes appearing near the grave sites of some of the most "civilized men" in the canon, including Georg Hegel's. Maybe that's why the Europeans seem to appreciate African-American culture; the culture of the Blues. They've been there.

Some have compared the joy with which some view the performance of hi-tech weapons with that of a child fascinated by his Nintendo game. "The Technoeuphoria!" a grinning anchor woman exclaimed as a missile hit a hydroelectric plant as though there were no humans inside. A commentator compared the most recent villain in War's Fairy Tale plot to a child, threatening his playmates with a gun so that he can get at the chocolates.

Though "An Occurrence at Owl Creek Bridge" is the best known of this collection, the most chilling is "Chickamauga," named for the scene of one of the Union's most devastating defeats. A child wanders through the corpses of the Union dead wielding a wooden sword, playing at war. It was fun until the child stumbled upon his dead mother. "The child moved his little hands, making wild, uncertain gestures. He uttered a series of inarticulate and indescribable cries—something between the chattering of an ape and the gobbling of a turkey—a startling, soulless, unholy sound, the language of a devil" (318). The war had hit close to home.

Bierce hated war. "Ah, those many, many needless dead!" he wrote. The Governor's lines in "An Affair Of Outposts" could have been Bierce's. "'Ugh!'" he grunted, shuddering—'this is beastly! Where is the charm of it all? Where are the elevated sentiments, the devotion, the heroism . . .'" (346). An army for Bierce is a "great brute," with "dumb consciousness."

His pen is like the best state-of-the-art film camera, and one wonders whether that ghoulish carnival of death, World War I, would have been avoided if Bierce's sharp images of war could have been broadcast with the satellite technology of today.

In the preface to the first edition of *Tales of Soldiers and Civilians* by one of our most uncelebrated American writers, who on the basis of this work certainly ranks with the best of our nineteenth century writers, Bierce once wrote: "Denied existence by the chief publishing houses of the country, this book owes itself to Mr. E. L. G. Steele, merchant of this city." The date is Sept. 4, 1891.

One could see why Bierce would be out of favor. By today's standards he is didactic, over sentimental, and his plot lines are often baffling, but when Presidents of the United States list their favorite western writers, I wish that Bierce's would appear among the names.

Ambrose Bierce was born in 1842 in Horse Cave Creek, Ohio, and disappeared in Mexico in 1914. Selected publications: *The Fiend's Delight* (1872); *Nuggets and Dust* (1872); *Cobwebs from an Empty Skull* (1873); *Tales of Soldiers and Civilians* (1891, reissued as *In the Midst of Life,* 1898); *The Complete Short Stories of Ambrose Bierce* (Page citations are to the University of Nebraska Press 1988 edition.); *Can Such Things Be?* (1893); *Beetles in Amber* (1895, poems); *The Cynic's Word Book* (1906, reprinted as *The Devil's Dictionary,* 1911); *The Shadow on the Dial,* 1909.

On Stephen Crane's
The Red Badge of Courage

JAMES COX

AS I WRITE THIS ESSAY on *The Red Badge of Courage,* we are once again at war. It is the fourth war in my lifetime in which this country has engaged in major conflict. I do not of course count the Spanish Civil War in which Americans sent significant volunteer units; nor do I count such recent paltry rehearsals for the present war in Iraq as Grenada, Libya, Panama, in which instant success was inevitable. Our last major war was in Vietnam—the longest though far from the bloodiest war we have ever fought—and the reaction to it was so negative that one would have thought we would never fight a war again. Yet here only a bit more than fifteen years later we are again at war, and many who had opposed the Vietnam war almost to the death now find themselves dusting off theories of just wars by way of explaining their approval of what in their youth appalled them. To review this history with a slight detachment (even I was in World War II) is to know how great a title Hemingway had for his first collection of short stories. *In Our Time* he named it, quoting from the Book of Common Prayer, yet with an irony that must strike any reader as little short of savage when considered in relation to the contents of those remarkable chapters that lie between the stories, forming the interchapters. The irony is even greater when the title is considered in relation to this now dying century, which seems to have given us more war than peace in our time. Not only that. We might as well realize that war, if it is not necessary, is nonetheless inevitable—that we can't do without it, that we need it, that somewhere and somehow as human beings we want it. Like hate and love, killing and birthing, living and dying, peace and war are a binary axis in the mind and heart of humanity as well as in its language. Hard pressed as we might be to define war, we know what it is. We know that far from being merely savage, it is nothing if not civilized, the civilized form of at once channeling and releasing the instincts of aggression that reside in the heart and soul—yes the soul—of humanity. Milton was well on target when he put his pure war in heaven, *not* on earth. Seeing war as the process of civilizing aggression is as essential as seeing the family as the civilizing form for the control and release of sexual energy. No wonder the craft of war—the discipline, the codes of conduct, the making of arms—is as much art as science. Any visitor to West Point has to be struck by the evidence on every hand that the institution wants to think of military art as much as it wishes to emphasize military science.

Being both civilized and instinctual, both science and art, war is at once dynamic and inertial. It carries with it all the acceleration at the command of civilization to discover new and more powerful forms of weaponry just as it forever retains the possibility of hand to hand combat. The very word arms evokes the development from club to gunpowder to rifle to bomb at the same time that it refers to the aggressive upper limbs of the body. The combination of acceleration and inertia works through the emotions attending war. War is after all a hastening toward death; it is for the young who, whether eager for it or forced into it, whether reckless or afraid, whether angry or appalled, find themselves both rushing and rushed toward an end that by the logic of peace ought to be further in their future. Given such acceleration, no wonder that the emotions of fear and anger, the twin expressions of helplessness, are forever at play beneath the soldier's burden of facing death in the form of an enemy.

Given this form, a science and an art at the heart and soul of civilization, we should not be surprised at the fierce reality it holds for our imagination. Since its essence is mortal conflict, it fatally attracts narration. We may deplore the narration we get—the censored presentations from the Pentagon, the lies and shameless exaggerations, the bureaucratic masking of violence, the banal human interest stories, the gamelike accounts of missiles hitting their targets—yet we are both galvanized and magnetized by these reports and wish to read and hear and see more and more of them. Indeed, the technology of communication is equal in its acceleration to the technology of weaponry, as if the processes of war and narration were one vast symbiosis. Here if ever is proof that the technology of language itself is equal to the technology of war; so much so, that we well could wonder whether the technology of language may have preceded the technology of war, whether the origin of language may have been a curse, whether the mouth itself were the prefiguration of the caves our ancestors once occupied. We always come out to such an uncertainty between the primacy of word or world.

There is a reason that the acceleration of both communication and weaponry have brought us increasingly disappointing accounts. Even with reporters near the front to relay stories and images *instantly* to us of soldiers in their trenches, or planes roaring off a runway, or anti-aircraft explosions making a thousand points of light over Baghdad we seem as far as ever from what we know is the truth of war; and so we settle for the observation, now proverbial, that truth is the first casualty of war. Thinking of that truth, we know that it must have at its heart fear, excitement, recklessness, hate, rage, horror, and death. Melville's lines are apt here. In a poem, "The Coming Storm," after claiming that Sanford Gifford's painting of that name served as a prefiguration of the Civil War, he concluded by relating both picture and war to the primary language of Shakespeare:

> No utter surprise can come to him
> Who reaches Shakespeare's core;
> That which we seek and shun is there—
> Man's final lore.

Surely, reflecting on the dynamic and inertial nature of war, we might well brood, in this last decade before the millenium, on the fact that the United States, claiming that it possesses the most advanced civilization and the accelerating technological weapons that accompany it, is bombing Baghdad, located at the confluence of the Tigris and Euphrates Rivers—the very place that we learned in our earliest schooling was the Cradle of Civilization. Beyond that, there is the first great image of the war disclosing the incinerated bodies being pulled from the rubble of an air shelter in Baghdad—a building that the Pentagon insists was a command and communications center. Such reflections could lead us to a larger fact: that the Middle East, which sustained the birth of three of the world's great religions, has held beneath its surface the richest oil wells in the world. Facing such a fact we know that the burning bush did indeed burn. As the dynamic force of religion has faded, or been converted, into the secular force of science, the inertial force of oil has been discovered to fuel the "advanced" nations.

All of which brings us to the Civil War—the one war that, for all its horror, has come down to us as a just war. Even Bob Dylan in his anti-war song of the Vietnam war significantly omitted it from the list of wars which were brutally conducted with "God on our side." That war, far more than any of our others was surely fought with God on our side. Beside every other war, even World War II, it has to seem to the majority of Americans a just war. At the same time it was the most total and bloody war in our history; its 700,000 dead would, in relation to our current population, be fifteen million. It was also a modern war, replete with great advances in weaponry and communications. If railroads, ironclads, submarines, and breech-loading carbines came into use, so did the telegraph, observation balloons, and hordes of reporters to file their stories. Both during and after the war it was the most *written* war that had ever been fought anywhere. There were the day to day accounts in hundreds of newspapers, there were the letters home; then came the endless post-war accounts by participants, the 128 volumes of Official Records published by the U. S. Government, the countless histories of the war that continue to be written, and finally the innumerable fictive efforts to capture the "reality" of the war.

Of all the fictions, *The Red Badge of Courage* is without question pre-eminent. In the almost one hundred years since its publication in 1895 it has incontrovertibly established itself as the greatest Civil War novel and one of the great war novels of world literature. It still seems miraculous that the novel could have been written by a twenty-four year old author who had not even been born until six years after Appomattox. From almost the moment of its publication, its striking power seemed to be grounded on two contradictory categories of life: experience and youth. Since it immediately brought Crane both popularity and notoriety, the compressed authority of its representation of battle experience was belied by the youth and art of its author. If the book brought Crane forward in this country as a Bohemian writer, it brought him recognition, particularly in England (when it was published there in 1896), from the literary establishment. A writer as strong as the young Joseph Conrad and a critic as acute as Edward Garnett immediately recognized that the element that resolved the contradiction between experience and youth was nothing less than the remarkable art of Crane's narrative. The art, in a word, was what made the book *new,* or we could say young, at the same time that it reorganized the vision of war, one of the oldest subjects to attract the narrative efforts of humanity. After all, what we consider Homer's oldest epic was the *Iliad.*

Those who focused on the youth of the author found themselves at pains to provide a literary precursor from whom Crane had descended, an effort that has continued down the years. Was it Tolstoy, or Zola, or Stendhal? Was it, among American authors, John William De Forest (*Miss Ravenel's Conversion*) or Wilbur Hinman (*Corporal Si Klegg and His Pard*)? Or was it *Battles and Leaders of the Civil War,* a series of articles by former commanders published in the *Century* magazine? Or could it have been the monumental *Official Records*? Although these questions, in the form of scholarly claims and contention, have been put forth throughout the century, the stark originality of *The Red Badge* continues to remain by far the most striking aspect of the book. The originality is, after all, at once the experience of the narrative. Small wonder that it would be classed as a work of realism, since it seemed true to what we now imagine is the *reality* of war. Or that it would be seen as naturalistic, since that classification places it in an up to date relationship with the sequence of literary movements that followed realism. Or that it would be called impressionistic, since that designation places it in graphic relation to the art of its time.

These efforts to locate the book either in relation to its author or in relation to its literary origins or to literary history are but an index to the manner of its originality. What no one would or could doubt is its identity as a war novel—and a war novel not just about any war but about the Civil War. We feel that we would know that much even if its subtitle were not *An Episode of the American Civil War*. As a matter of fact, the subtitle is usually absent in most editions of the novel. Yet here again, the hunger for more specific references has led to many speculations as to what particular battle of the war is being represented. Of the many interpretive forays in this direction, the battle of Chancellorsville has been the leading candidate, yet the book itself is utterly mute in the matter of naming either battle or state where the action takes place.

To see, in what we never doubt is a Civil War novel, just how little there is of what we traditionally associate with the historical Civil War, though it may not tell us what the novel is, will at least impress us with what it is not. Not only are there no actual place names; there are no fictive place names. If there is topography in the form of a small river or an open field or a forest, it remains utterly generalized. There is exactly one mention of Richmond and Washington. There is no Grant or Lee or Hooker or Jackson or Meade or A. P. Hill. There is not even a North or a South. Even the terms Yankee and Rebel appear only once or twice as yank and reb. There is no fight for the union or against slavery. There is not a mention of Abraham Lincoln or Jefferson Davis. There is not a hint of states' rights or the protective tariff. Even the characters themselves are barely named; they are a tall soldier, a loud soldier, and a youth before they are Jim Conklin or George Wilson or Henry Fleming. A tattered soldier and a cheery soldier, although they play significant roles in the book, have no names at all. Beyond all this absence, there is no real sense of the technology of war. We know that Henry Fleming has a rifle, that he moves through a world of bullets and exploding artillery shells, that there are horses and wagons and gun carriages, but we get no particular or detailed identity of any of the machinery. We get no mention of supply depots or howitzers. Finally, there is no romance in the book—no real girl left behind or met—no letters from home, no sense of a society behind or outside the society of the battlefield. True there is Henry's mother and a girl schoolmate Henry believes is looking at him as he readies for departure (this all stated in a few paragraphs in the first chapter), but they are left behind as completely as Aunt Charity in *Moby Dick* when the *Pequod* makes its plunge into the lone Atlantic.

To see what is left out, or better cut away, is to see how Crane achieved both reduction and concentration of his vision to the field of battle and to the single consciousness of a *private* soldier. He emerged with an incredibly short novel—shorter even than *The Scarlet Letter*—whose twenty-four short chapters stand at once as reminders of the twenty-four books of the *Iliad* and as a line of sentinels marking the violently abrupt sequence of war. The very first paragraph of the book sets the scene:

> The cold passed reluctantly from the earth, and the retiring fogs revealed an army stretched out on the hills, resting. As the landscape changed from brown to green, the army awakened, began to tremble with eagerness at the noise of rumors. It cast its eyes upon the roads, which were growing from being troughs of liquid mud to proper thoroughfares. A river, amber-tinted in the shadow of its banks, purled at the army's feet; and at night, when the stream had become a sorrowful blackness, one could see across it the red, eyelike gleam of hostile camp-fires set in the low brows of distant hills (5).

So much is done here. First there is the pathetic fallacy hard at work throughout the passage: the cold *reluctantly* passing, the fogs *retiring,* the river *purling* by day and *sorrowful* at night. Nature herself is being psychologized as if it had a human will, and at the end of the paragraph it has become an animated form containing the eyelike gleam of hostile campfires set in the *brows* of distant hills. Even more important, the natural process *reveals* the army stretched out and resting, awakening, and trembling at the noise of rumors. Yet if nature is sufficiently animated by the reportorial narration to reveal the scene, it nonetheless must be invested with the power. In such an exchange we can see at the very outset that the book is neither fully naturalistic nor impressionistic, neither deterministic nor subjective but involved in both worlds even as it is subjected to a reportorial narration that implicates both forces, glaringly mixing them together.

Naturalism and impressionism are not the only literary registers brought into focus in the text. There is also realism. No wonder W. D. Howells saw in Crane's early work—he was less enthusiastic about *The Red Badge*—a writer who was extending the range of realism into the urban streets. In *The Red Badge,* Crane extends realism down into the society of soldiers. They are invariably middle class soldiers, speaking an American vernacular that could be either urban or rural. The narration is clearly committed to erasing any distinction that could be made between the two. Crane, who had written *Maggie, a Girl of the Streets,* could clearly have made such a distinction, but here he wants merely to mime an informal language characterized by its deviation from formally "correct" speech yet not individuated to city or region. More important, the language is not discriminated in terms of character. The youth, the tall soldier, the loud soldier all speak alike. If they are privates they none-theless speak a "general" vernacular—a representative language of their society—an ungrammatical, slightly deviant, and unschooled language, yet not one to evoke sympathy so much as to express a unity, directness, and informal simplicity of background. Just as their designation as tall soldier, loud soldier, and youth takes precedence over their individual names, their language designates their identity as soldiers rather than individuals.

For all that they are soldiers, their world is not in any strict sense mili-tary. True they are subject to orders from the officers, but there is nothing in this beginning that stresses the abuse and repression so familiar in nar-ratives of military life. Indeed these private soldiers seem wonderfully free in their informality. Instead of being called to attention or suffering under high handed officers, they are subject to the vanity, skepticism, and restiveness that come from the boredom of waiting for action. When the tall solidier, whose name is later revealed to be Jim Conklin, brings a new rumor of a military action, he "swells" with the importance of his narration but is greeted with such scoffing disbelief from a loud soldier that their exchange threatens to descend into anger. Then a corporal be-gins to swear at the thought of moving from the comfortable quarters he has constructed for himself. Finally the company joins in a "spirited de-bate" replete with arguments about strategy. The entire discussion re-sembles nothing so much as a small town cracker barrel discussion. What is uppermost in the representation is the *ordinariness* of the participants. They have no real distinction, yet if their foolishness and pretensions are exposed by the narration, they are not belittled. The informal, un-schooled ordinariness of these soldiers is the very stamp of Crane's realism.

From this introductory scene and action, accomplished in less than two pages, the narration moves to a "youthful private" who is listening to the "words of the tall soldier," and we are brought abruptly in relation

51

to the consciousness of the central figure of the book. The relation between the narration and Henry Fleming's consciousness is not so much one of invasion as it is of concentrated attachment. The consciousness of Henry Fleming is, after all, his *private* thoughts. The thoughts of the privates we first see are their public thoughts—what they can say to each other.

Upon hearing them, Private Fleming retires through an "intricate hole" into the privacy of his hut—it is not a tent—"to be alone with some new thoughts that had lately come to him" (6). The narrative rarely leaves that consciousness but reports it in such a way that there is always detachment in its attachment. Thus there is always a gap between the report and the thoughts, sensations, and responses of this youth. The essential nature of the gap is one of irony, an irony that results in exposure as much as disclosure. If we see what Henry is thinking and feeling, we also see the illusory nature of his thoughts in relation to the field of battle in which he finds himself. The great force of the narrative rests in its capacity to render the reality of his experience as well as the external nature of battle. His experience of course colors the battle, but the battle colors his experience. His thoughts always at war with each other, he is himself embattled; at the same time, he is in a battle. To see so much is to see both the nature and violence of civil war.

The best way to see that violence is to sketch the action from the moment the narrative attaches itself to the consciousness of this youth. First of all there is the fact that Henry had "of course dreamed of battles all his life" and had enlisted in the army. If he had dreamed of war, his waking consciousness had feared that wars, the "crimson splotches on the pages of the past," were the vividly red moments of history that were now as bygone as crowns and castles. "Secular and religious education had effaced the throat-grappling instinct, or else firm finance held in check the passions" (7). Disappointed at his mother's objections to, rather than her support of his enlistment, he had nonetheless volunteered, had then felt a pang at his mother's helpless assent to his departure and her gift of blackberry jam, and had even felt shame at looking back at her tear-stained face as she knelt among the potato parings; but he had felt a thrill of self-importance in the village as he thought he saw a feminine schoolmate looking upon him as his company assembled.

The narrative gives but the briefest moment to this recapitulation of his boyish fantasies of Homeric battles—as an inner life they are every bit as ordinary as the public language of the solders—before launching its report of the move into battle. Throughout the brief march toward the conflict, replete with the soldiers' inveterate complaints and their continuing arguments about strategy, Henry remains silent with his own continuing doubts. Afraid to reveal them, he is astonished when, at the threshold of battle, Wilson, the outwardly brave and loud soldier, sobbingly announces his belief that he is to die and gives Henry a packet of letters to be sent home. In the ensuing battle, Henry manages to stand his ground against the first attack, forgetting himself in the rage of action; but in the very throes of luxuriating in his accomplishment the enemy attacks again. Seeing men beside him waver and run, Henry joins in a fight as blind as his battle stand had been. His flight brings him to a point behind the lines from which, watching artillerymen mechanically serve their battery, he discovers that the blue line has held. Afflicted with this new knowledge, he feels like a criminal and, rationalizing his behavior, begins to justify his flight as an instinctive effort at self preservation. This line of thought, figured in a full retirement from the field, leads him to the isolated depths of a forest, where "the high arching boughs made a chapel" (41–42). Pushing the boughs aside and entering, he confronts the eyes of a rotting corpse.

Recoiling from this ultimate reach of his retreat, he stumbles into a column of wounded soldiers making their way to the rear amid the rush of horse teams bringing reinforcements to the front. Two figures, a spectral soldier and a tattered soldier, galvanize his attention, and, in a true shock of recognition, he realizes the spectral soldier to be Jim Conklin. Stricken with anguish, he listens to Jim's supplications for protection and then watches him spectacularly die. When the wounded tattered soldier, who has reappeared to watch Conklin die, renews his questions about where Henry is wounded (questions which had made Henry try to escape him), Henry feels his questions like knife thrusts. Fearing that he is about to witness another death and distraught at the tattered soldier's delirium, he tears himself away from such a gruesome possibility.

He then finds himself rounding a little hillock, from which he can see retreating soldiers coming from the front in disarray and being met by another column advancing toward the front. That scene, an objective correlative of his conflicted state of mind, mirrors his wish that the army will be defeated so as to hide his cowardice as well as his shame at his own flight. When the advancing column suddenly bursts upon him in full retreat, he accosts a fleeing soldier with the all but inarticulate question of "Why—why—" only to be smashed in the head with the impetuous soldier's gun. Stunned and bloodied, he struggles through the littered battlefield in confusion until a cheery soldier, whose face he never sees, miraculously leads him back to his regiment.

Reunited with his company, he is treated with great solicitation by Wilson, who, after a time, sheepishly asks for his bundle of letters. If Wilson's kindness lacerates the inner sore beneath Henry's wound, his shamed request for the letters gives Henry a privileged stance of superiority. The battle continuing on the following day, he and Wilson—both goaded to rage at an officer's referring to the company as mule drivers—perform with distinction not only in a first but also in a second engagement. So the battle ends on a successful note for Henry Fleming, and he once again indulgently luxuriates in his achievements.

This brief summary of the action provides what we might call a dead line along which to chart the sequence of Henry's emotions. Out of the most basic adolescent fantasies that bring him to the ground of battle, there are first the private doubts that isolate him, then the helpless rage of battle, then the pride of having survived without fleeing, then abject fear and flight, then a shame that produces defensive rationalizing, then the recoil from the ultimate horror of death (the images of the rotting dead soldier and the dying Jim Conklin), then more rationalization combining fear, shame, doubt; then the blow, the wound—both false and true—reducing him to a hopeless, helpless, and lost wanderer whose one instinct is to keep on his feet; then the reunion with his company, bringing with it a mixture of relief and guilt; then Wilson's shamefaced request for a return of the letters, producing a triumphant superiority and aggression; then the rage of battle once more and a fuller sense of triumph when his actions receive praise, and finally a self-satisfied pride in accomplishment resting yet uneasily on the lie of his wound, his red badge of courage.

This abrupt sequence of emotions forms the ground of Henry's action, determining his behavior more than the orders of his officers. Crane's achievement is to displace the technology of war, its accelerating machinery, with an acceleration of emotions running between the poles of fear and rage. Fear is flight from death, rage the assault upon it. Death is, of course, the enemy, at once the feared and fated end of the natural process of living, and, in battle, the hated and feared living enemy determined to kill. It is no accident that the word courage—designating the chief virtue of the soldier—contains within it the word rage, the aggression of the heart and mind. Both fear and rage are all but blind, instinctual, and both generate the lines of energy that society—in this instance civilian society at war with itself—transforms into shame and honor, cowardice and courage, with all the feelings that attend them. Henry Fleming's inner civil war is his violent experience of these emotions at war within himself. Crowded together in the closest proximity, they are always at the point of conflict and collision.

But there is the outer war, whose external reality we never doubt. If it is an expression of Henry's inner conflicts, he is equally an expression of its intensity. It is, as I have noted, the objective correlative of his inner turbulence, but the point is that it *is* objective. Its essential nature is violent *civil* disorder—a melee of discordant sounds, as if civil society and speech were themselves dissolving into roars and curses even as the machinery of war assumes the role of civil discussion. Thus artillery opens with a "furious debate," musketry "sputters," cannons "enter the dispute," guns "argue with abrupt violence," shells hurtle overhead in "long wild screams," cannon are engaged in a "stupendous wrangle," artillery "assembles as if for a conference." At the same time the speech of soldiers increasingly descends into incoherence, emanating in curses, oaths, screams, bellowing, yells, roars. Chapter XI concludes with this description of Henry Fleming: "He was a slang phrase" (58). Battle utterances are characterized by incomplete utterances. A good example—one among many—occurs late in the book when the lieutenant rallies his men:

> As they halted thus the lieutenant again began to bellow profanely. Regardless of the vindictive threats of the bullets, he went about coaxing, berating, and bedamning. His lips, that were habitually in a soft and childlike curve, were now writhed into unholy contortions. He swore by all possible deities.
>
> Once he grabbed the youth by the arm. "Come on, yeh lunkhead!" he roared. "Come on! We'll all git killed if we stay here. We've on'y got t' go across that lot. An' then"—the remainder of his idea disappeared in a blue haze of curses (88–89).

55

That blue haze of curses brings us to the matter of color. Just as Crane's sounds of war veer always between curses and roars, his colors are boldly primary. The brown and green of the opening paragraph set the tone. There we see the process of nature revealed not in gradual but bold change. And we see that process again startlingly shown in the description of the dead soldier in the green forest chapel:

> He was being looked at by a dead man who was seated with his back against a columnlike tree. The corpse was dressed in a uniform that once had been blue, but was now faded to a melancholy shade of green. The eyes, staring at the youth, had changed to the dull hue to be seen on the side of a dead fish. The mouth was open. Its red had changed to an appalling yellow. Over the gray skin of the face ran little ants. One was trundling some sort of bundle along the upper lip (41).

The strength of the passage gives the corpse a life of its own, which indeed it has, since it is still in the process of nature's change; the youth is the one who is arrested in the face of those startling eyes.

But the more memorable presence of color comes about when Crane seems to have almost violently asserted it by abruptly and visibly thrusting it on objects. A sort of index to the process is disclosed in the final battle sequence when Henry, resting on the laurels he feels he has won, recalls "bits of color that in the flurry had stamped themselves unawares upon his engaged senses" (95). This stamping of color is evident in the very title of the book. Even more telling are the "crimson splotches" that, in Henry's mind, constitute the wars on the pages of history. Then there is the red god of battle. Rage, like new blood, is red, though like old blood it can also be black. Flames of musketry are seen as yellow tongues. This flash and splash of color is seen in the red badge itself that Henry wishes for when he enters the column of wounded men; and later, angry at being called a mule driver, he pictures "red letters of revenge" to be written to the insulting officer. Though a search for color will actually disclose that sound is actually much more present in the prose, the instances of color have a vivid force. The title of the book has its own finality, reminding us almost helplessly of those other American titles, *The Scarlet Letter* and "The Masque of the Red Death," and reminding us too that Hawthorne and Poe are deeply inscribed in this book. Given other Crane titles—"The Blue Hotel," "The Bride Comes to Yellow Sky," *Black Riders* and *The Third Violet*—possibilities of color begin to haunt the mind. It is possible, of course, to pursue these colors into patterns of meaning and symbolism, yet such pursuits inevitably evade the much more important fact that the violent *presence* of color abruptly converts meaning into vivid images that annihilate prior symbolic reference. Henry Fleming is both enacting and fulfilling this instantaneous process of conversion when, in his triumphant red rage of charging the enemy lines, he becomes the color bearer of his company.

Finally there is the primary quality of form itself. The images in *The Red Badge* violently assert deformity. Corpses are twisted, bodies writhe, faces are contorted, dead soldiers lie upon the field as if they had been dumped from the sky, a dying soldier is seen "thrashing about in the grass, twisting his shuddering body into many strange postures," soldiers in battle are stretched on the ground or on their knees "as if they had been stricken by bolts from the sky." All the qualities of sound, color, and deformity are concentrated, at almost the exact center of the book, in the description of Jim Conklin's death:

> His spare figure was erect; his bloody hands were quietly at his side. He was waiting with patience for something he had come to meet. He was at the rendezvous. They [Henry and the tattered soldier] paused and stood, expectant.
>
> There was a silence.
>
> Finally, the chest of the doomed soldier began to heave with a strained motion. It increased in violence until it was as if an animal was within and kicking and tumbling furiously to be free.
>
> This spectacle of gradual strangulation made the youth writhe, and once as his friend rolled his eyes, he saw something in them that made him sink wailing to the ground. He raised his voice in a last supreme call.
>
> "Jim—Jim—Jim—"
>
> The tall soldier opened his lips and spoke. He made a gesture. "Leave me be—don't tech me—leave me be—"
>
> There was another silence while he waited.
>
> Suddenly, his form stiffened and straightened. Then it was shaken by a prolonged ague. He stared into space. To the two watchers there was a curious and profound dignity in the firm lines of his awful face.
>
> He was invaded by a creeping strangeness that slowly enveloped him.

For a moment the tremor of his legs caused him to dance a sort of hideous hornpipe. His arms beat wildly about his head in expression of implike enthusiasm.

His tall figure stretched itself to its full height. There was a slight rending sound. Then it began to swing forward, slow and straight, in the manner of a falling tree. A swift muscular contortion made the left shoulder strike the ground first.

The body seemed to bounce a little way from the earth. "God!" said the tattered soldier.

The youth had watched, spellbound, this ceremony at the place of meeting. His face had been twisted into an expression of every agony he had imagined for his friend.

He now sprang to his feet, and, going closer, gazed upon the pastelike face. The mouth was open and the teeth showed in a laugh.

As the flap of the blue jacket fell away from the body, he could see that the side looked as if it had been chewed by wolves.

The youth turned, with sudden, livid rage, toward the battlefield. He shook his fist. He seemed about to deliver a philippic.

"Hell—"

The red sun was pasted in the sky like a wafer (49–50).

There it all is. The violent heaving, the strained motion, the animal action, Henry's sinking wail and unfinished supreme call, the muscular contortion, the pastelike face fixed in a frozen laugh, the wolf-like wound, the truncated philippic, and the final sentence sealing the passage in the color of the red sun.

It is hardly surprising that this striking final sentence of the chapter has arrested critics in search of meaning. Robert Wooster Stallman took the wafer to refer to communion and Jim Conklin—with his initials, his wound in the side, and the tattered soldier's accompanying passionate cry, "God"—to be the Christ. Stallman has been sufficiently flogged for his interpretation, so I shall not join the host of his detractors other than to note that he, like those seeking for literary precursors, actual battle sites, and color symbolism as literary, historical and symbolic subtexts of the narrative, was yearning for a religious subtext. The point is that all these subtexts have been blown away by the violence of battle. Henry's philippic breaks off with but one word—hell. Hell in this text has utterly lost its theological sense; it, like all the other curses, is but the expression of present rage springing from the annihilation of traditional religious meaning. The wafer of the final sentence is, as others have seen, like the molten wafer of wax used to seal a letter. Whether it comes from Kipling's *The Light that Failed,* which Crane had surely read, is beside the point. Just as a wax wafer is pasted on a letter to seal it, so is the sun, as if it had been passed over Conklin's pastelike dead face, pasted in the sky.

The force that pastes the sun in the sky is of course the sentence itself. The entire passage shows just how, even as Henry's voice is unable to complete sentences, the narrative does nothing but complete them. Sentences in this book are the units of force effacing and displacing the author behind them with their own authority. They both report and execute the action. They literally sentence Henry Fleming to the war he has dreamed of all his life. They boldly and visibly stand forth, in the manner that Emerson spoke of his own sentences, as infinitely repellent particles. They all but annihilate paragraphs in their determination to stand alone. Of course they are in sequence, but they expose the discontinuity as much as the continuity of sequence. Their conclusiveness has sufficient finality to transform the silence between them into an abrupt gap of stillness as astonishing as the grotesque images they assert. That astonishment is really the ultimate emotion of battle—more violent than mere surprise. It is an emotion that *excessively* fulfills the anxiety and curiosity of suspense, those emotions on which novelistic narration so much depends.

That is why these sentences not only threaten to annihilate paragraphs; they threaten the plot and suspense of traditional novelistic narrative. They are as determined to conclude action as they are to continue it. All but equal to each other in their declarative brevity, they have a genuinely democratic order, transforming turning points and climaxes of narrative into a continuum of violent intensity and at the same time annihilating the distinctions of military hierarchy and rank. The officers speak the same informal, ordinary, and violent language as the privates; Henry and the lieutenant are utterly equal in their united bellowing appeals for the men to charge. Higher battle strategy, like the battle lines that dissolve in the violence of battle, disintegrates into the soldiers' arguments about strategy.

Still, this book is a narrative, and the conventions of narrative, like all the traditional meaning and symbols of history and religion are, like the enemy, threatening a counterattack. That threat indicates that there is also a civil war in the very form of the book. That pressure is very much in evidence as the concluding movement of the novel. In the midst of Henry's heroic charge when men, "punched by bullets, fell in grotesque agonies," and the regiment "left a coherent trail of bodies," we are given this passage:

> It seemed to the youth that he saw everything. Each blade of grass was bold and clear. He thought that he was even aware of every change in the thin, transparent vapor that floated idly in sheets. The brown or gray trunks of the trees showed each roughness of their surfaces. And the men of the regiment, with their staring eyes and sweating faces, running madly, or falling, as if thrown headlong, to queer, heaped-up corpses— all were comprehended. His mind took mechanical but firm impression, so that afterward everything was pictured and explained to him, save why he himself was there.
>
> But there was a frenzy made from this furious rush. The men, pitching forward insanely, had burst into cheerings, moblike and barbaric, but tuned in strange keys that can arouse the dullard and stoic. It made a mad enthusiasm that, it seemed, would be incapable of checking itself before granite and brass. There was the delirium that encounters despair and death, and is heedless and blind to the odds. It is a temporary but sublime absence of selfishness. And because it was of this order was the reason, perhaps, why the youth wondered, afterward, what reasons he could have had for being there (86–87).

The delirium that encounters despair and death is, then, the sublime absence of selfishness. Here the novel hovers at the threshold of ennobling Henry's "heroism" and we might well be lulled into seeing the narrative, which is so much in the convention of the *bildungsroman,* as a register of Henry Fleming's moral growth toward maturity. The book's conclusion, with the regiment retiring from the battlefield and Henry once more luxuriating in a feeling of accomplishment, can be seen to reinforce such a vision of growth. Nearing its end, the narrative boldly asserts, "He was a man."

Yet to conclude moral growth and maturity from this sentence is to displace the iron irony of the narrative with blatant sentimentality. Although Crane cut some passages from the concluding chapter which expose the same complacent self satisfaction, there is sufficient irony remaining to indicate that his asserted manhood is no more secured than it was after his first battle when the narrative asserted the same thing. He is really no better or worse than he was then nor is there evidence he is better or worse than all the men who were killed or who survived. He could just as well have been killed, but that end would truly have made the book sentimental. Crane did better to keep him alive, letting all that selfishness, which had been for a moment sublimely absent, return in the form of pride.

This does not mean that there was nothing to Henry's bravery. He did fight as blindly as he ran, and presumably he killed some of the enemy when he kept blindly firing after his company had retreated, though we are spared actually seeing him in the act of killing. His distinction in battle comes from the excessive rage that is within him if it comes from anything. He had *of course* dreamed of battles all his life, and he just as arbitrarily of course fought out of the rage and dream that was in him. If war is an expression of death and grotesque disorder, it is nonetheless the sentence of existence, as near as the rage and dream that are always in us. The sentence of war was always in Crane, evident in the violence of *Maggie* with its opening on a street fight and in *George's Mother* opening with a woman battling with pots and pans in a kitchen. In *The Red Badge* he made it fully and exclusively *present,* so present that he could do little afterward except pursue it over the world as a reporter.

Grotesque and terrible as war may be, Crane does not write *against* war; he writes through it. His sentences, flattening perspective in their bold and visible presence, have the strength of line and form that we see in a Cezanne painting. They possess the "curious and profound dignity in the firm lines of [Jim Conklin's] awful face." If George Wyndham, who reviewed the book when it appeared in England and who himself had been a soldier, felt that it perfectly expressed his past experience of battle action, Ford Madox Ford, who fought in World War I, felt that it perfectly foretold the experience of that war too. It retains to this day a remarkable modernity.

Joseph Conrad was good, in his memoir of Crane, to leave us his remembered image of Crane sitting at a table with a half-empty glass of beer gone flat, writing by hand in a steady deliberation. No one who reads *The Red Badge* can doubt that that hand—the inertial hand that writes writing about the hand that fights—was possessed of true courage.

Stephen Crane was born in 1871 in Newark, New Jersey and died in 1900 in Badenweiler, Germany. Selected publications: *Maggie: A Girl of the Streets* (1893); *The Red Badge of Courage: An Episode of the American Civil War* (1895, many editions in print; page citations are to the Norton edition); *The Black Riders* (1895, poems); *The Little Regiment and Other Episodes of the American Civil War* (1896); *The Open Boat and other Adventures* (1898); *War Is Kind* (1899, poems); *Wounds in the Rain: War Stories* (1900); *Great Battles of the World* (1901).

On Ellen Glasgow's
The Battle-Ground

R. H. W. DILLARD

ALTHOUGH ELLEN GLASGOW's major later novels and especially *The Sheltered Life* (1932) seem to be safely and at long last in the process of intelligent rediscovery, only *Virginia* (1913) among her earlier novels is receiving anything like the critical reassessment it deserves. Neither *The Battle-Ground,* Glasgow's only Civil War novel, nor *The Deliverance* (1904), a quite important novel set in the post-war years of the Reconstruction, have received the critical attention required to allow them the possibility of new understanding (or new readers).[1] I hope in these notes and speculations on Ellen Glasgow's fourth novel, *The Battle-Ground* (1902), to suggest and encourage new readings of the novel and, by association, of her other early (and other historical) novels as well.

In *The Battle-Ground,* Miss Lydia, a stereotypical Southern maiden aunt who has accepted (as appropriate to a spinster) a life without freedom in her father's house while at the same time granting to men a life of moral license, "read Scott and enshrined in her pious heart the bold Rob

Roy."[2] Glasgow's ironic association of Sir Walter Scott, who originated and established the form of the historical novel, with Miss Lydia suggests that Monique Parent's thumbnail description of *The Battle-Ground* as "*Un vrai* civil war novel, *rempli de'héroïsme et de pétales de roses*"[3] even though it is the generally accepted critical opinion of the novel may not be entirely correct, and that Louis D. Rubin, Jr.'s scornful dismissal of the novel as "a conventional love story" containing "little impressive realism" in which Glasgow's "picture of the life 'before de Wah' is in roseate colors, and the war is important only as it destroys the old society"[4] may be just as much off the mark.

After a fresh encounter with *The Battle-Ground*, I believe that the irony of Glasgow's connecting the novels of Scott with Miss Lydia—novels which were much admired and even revered in the Old South, with a woman who is a willing victim of that "old society"—may be read as a sign of the distinctive nature of this novel: that it is not a romantic novel in the traditional mould of Scott (or, at least, of Scott as he was perceived in the American South), but that it is rather an appropriation of a literary form still respected and widely read among adherents of the Southern Old Order, designed to function as a systematic critique of the dominant project of the traditional historical novel (to romanticize and idealize the Old Order), endeavoring to analyze and subvert the values of that very order, and in particular to reveal the sources and transformations of power within the Old Order as it passed through the Civil War.

THE SPECIAL QUALITIES OF *The Battle-Ground*

Early in *The Battle-Ground*, a group of children watch a wagon filled with women pass by on a country road in the Valley of Virginia (4–5). The women are slaves who have been sold after the death of their master and are on their way to a new home. They are standing and singing the slave's farewell—"Gawd A'moughty bless you twel we / Meet agin," and only one of them is crouching and weeping. "Excitement gripped them like a frenzy—and a childish joy in a coming change blended with a mother's yearning over broken ties."

It reveals a great deal about Ellen Glasgow and the special qualities of her Civil War novel that she equates the powerlessness of these slaves to that of both children and mothers: children, who in their timeless and heartless innocence can see only the positive benefits and opportunities of change, and mothers, who from the time of their initial leaving home after marriage, through the *partum* of giving birth, to the loss of children to their own adult lives (or children and husbands to death), know the nature of broken ties most intimately. Slaves, children and mothers, to Glasgow, all constitute categories of people who, because of age, biology, and/or social convention have been denied freedom of choice. The only man in the scene is also a slave, and the only advice he can offer to the women in the wagon (and metaphorically to those other powerless groups) is to "set down . . . . You'd feel better. Thar, now, set down and jolt softly."

Contrary to what one unaccustomed to Ellen Glasgow's ironic fiction might suppose, the white men in the novel are also relatively powerless. True, many of them own plantations and have the power to buy and sell slaves and to make all of the significant decisions in regard to life in their homes and in their community, but their homes are in the western Valley of Virginia and not the state's Tidewater and Piedmont centers of power. And they are not the men making the major decisions for the state or the nation: they are older men whose time has past like the ex-soldier, Major Lightfoot, and the former governor of Virginia, Peyton Ambler, or they are affluent young men who have yet to assume power like Champe Lightfoot and the central male character of the novel, Dan "Beau" Montjoy, or they are disenfranchised poor whites, such as the tall young mountaineer soldier nicknamed "Pinetop," who, Dan Montjoy comes to realize, is "a victim to the kindly society in which he himself had moved—a society produced by that free labour which had degraded the white workman to the level of the serf" (442).

Those who are truly in power appear in the novel only as names in news reports or on the lips of those who share their political views. Governor Ambler still has some authority and power as he travels the state speaking against secession, but once secession does occur, he takes a general's commission and becomes just another relatively minor figure who dies in the war. Even those Confederate generals who were to assume mythic proportions after the war appear in *The Battle-Ground* only fleetingly: Stonewall Jackson, who rides by his suffering men on the freezing road to Romney, "glanced quietly over them, and passed on, his chest bowed, his cadet cap pulled down over his eyes" (344), and Robert

E. Lee, whom Dan manages to approach after the surrender at Appomattox "only in time to see him ride onward at a walk, with the bearded soldiers clinging like children to the stirrups" (483). The soldiers, who have borne the brutal suffering of the war, remain in the powerless position of children even when their leaders have surrendered power over them. Pinetop, the yeoman soldier who, among the novel's major characters, comes closest to Lee in this scene and hears him say that "I've done my best for you," is metaphorically put in his place in relation to Lee and the power he represents when he reports that "I kissed old Traveller's mane" (483).

In certain very important ways, nothing was really changed in the passing of the Old Order at the end of the novel and at the end of the war; the power, even when it has been diminished by the defeat, remains in the hands of those who formerly wielded it, especially in relation to those at the very bottom of the social order. The Lightfoot plantation, Chericoke, has been burned to the ground, but the "Ole Marster and Ole Miss" (503) are living safely in the overseer's house, and their slaves, now freed, continue to take care of them because they have neither the means nor the knowledge to survive anywhere else or in any other way. And Pinetop, the poor white mountaineer, recognizes that the democratic spirit among the soldiers will not last and that his friendship with Dan Montjoy will only be possible after the war if Dan should become an outlaw and forfeit his position in the social hierarchy:

> I reckon you'll go yo' way an' I'll go mine . . . for thar's one thing sartain an' that is our ways don't run together. It'll never be the same agin—that's natur—but if you ever want a good stout hand for any uphill plowing or shoot yo' man an' the police git on yo' track, jest remember that I'm up thar in my little cabin. Why, if ever officer in the county was at yo' heels, I'd stand guard with my old squirrel gun and maw would with her kettle (488).

"Although *The Battle-Ground* is not a romance," Glasgow was to say much later in her life when she was preparing the prefaces to the Old Dominion edition of her novels, "it is, nevertheless, the work of romantic youth,"[5] but she also went on to defend the novel's romantic qualities by concluding that "If I have dealt with the spirit of romance, it is because one cannot approach the Confederacy without touching the very heart of romantic tradition. It is the single occasion in American history, and one of the rare occasions in the history of the world, when the conflict of actualities was profoundly romantic. For Virginia, in that disastrous illusion, the Confederacy was the expiring gesture of chivalry" (CM 24–25).

The Battle-Ground is avowedly a portrayal of "the last stand in Virginia of the aristocratic tradition" (CM 13), but it is not a romantic novel. It was, by Glasgow's own account, written amid "a babel of costume romances and a literary epidemic of curled wigs and lace ruffles" (CM, 16), and it was written by an independently minded young woman whose previous work had consisted of two naturalistic novels, *The Descendant* (1897) and *Phases of an Inferior Planet* (1898), and a political novel, *The Voice of the People* (1900). When she was twenty-three, she had travelled to London and had laid a rose, not on Chaucer's grave as some of her acquaintances expected, but on Charles Darwin's.[6] She was later to say that "the book that influenced my mind most profoundly in youth was *The Origin of Species;* and it was in response to this benign and powerful inspiration that I conceived my first novels" (CM, 58). She also claimed proudly that "I studied *The Origin of Species,* until I could have passed successfully an examination on every page" (WW 88). Given her close attention to Darwin's thought, it is only natural that her characters were in many ways powerless in the face of larger forces that define and manipulate them. She was also confirmed in her understanding of the limitations of individual freedom by her reading of Henry George's analysis of world poverty in his *Progress and Poverty,* to the point of becoming briefly a "Fabian socialist" (WW 81).

Darwin, George, and the naturalistic fiction of Guy de Maupassant and Hamlin Garland, along with her own acute analysis of the position of women in a male-dominated culture, all shaped her early fiction and set it apart from the romantic Southern fiction of the day. No wonder, then, that her Civil War novel is not just another mythic Valhalla of the Old Order, but is rather a complex study of the violent destruction of a deadly illusion of power and order, and especially of the effects of the illusion and its loss on a varied group of people who had always lived in its grip. It was Glasgow's unusually tough-minded and analytic approach to fiction in her first three novels that led Stuart P. Sherman to assert in

1925 that "Realism crossed the Potomac twenty-five years ago, going north,"[7] but my reading of her Civil War novel, as well as the apt nature of his metaphor, makes it seem to apply just as much to *The Battle-Ground*.

THE STORY OF *The Battle-Ground*

The Battle-Ground is, as Glasgow suggested, "not literally a novel of war, but a chronicle of two neighboring families, the Amblers and the Lightfoots, who had lived through a disastrous period in history" (CM 19). Major Lightfoot is a fire-eating secessionist whose political beliefs reflect his hot-tempered nature; Governor Ambler is a smaller and quieter man, who believes in the preservation of the union. Lightfoot's grandson, Dan Montjoy, the product of a romantic elopement of the Major's daughter with Jack Montjoy who later abandoned her and her son, is the primary male character of the novel, and the Governor's daughter, Betty, a red-headed young woman who does not fit the mold of the southern belle in any way, is the most important female character. Betty's older sister, the raven-haired Virginia, is a classic romantic beauty, and it is she that both Dan and his cousin Champe think that they love. Dan and Betty come to love each other, and finally earn each other's mature love after passing successfully through the crucible of the war. Virginia marries Jack Morson, but dies in childbirth after desperately searching for her husband among the wounded in the Richmond hospitals during the battle of Seven Pines.

The first half of the novel is primarily Betty's, but the war and Dan's active involvement in it as a foot soldier give the second half of the book to him. Dan is wounded and loses two fingers on his left hand, but he does shed the illusions of the Old Order and comes to terms with his own weakness, realizing that

> The years had taught him nothing if they had not taught him the wisdom most needed by his impulsive youth—that so long as there comes good to the meanest creature from fate's hardest blow, it is the part of a man to stand up and take it between the eyes (493–494).

The future, however, seems to belong to (and to depend heavily on) Betty. The war has not taught her the truth about herself so much as it has allowed her to express in action what she has already known. "You are very strong, my child," her mother tells her, "and I think it makes us all lean too much upon you" (455). It is important to what Betty represents—the newly freed woman who will take perhaps more than an equal share of the burdens of the future—that she (red hair, active nature, and all) survives when her passive and ideally perfect sister doesn't, and that she and Dan turn away from the unharmed Ambler plantation house and walk through "battle-scarred elms," a "ruined gate," a "twisted tree," a "crumbled wall," "scattered stones," and "a broken urn" to the "ashes of Chericoke" before they make the important promise to "begin again together" (511–512) that closes the book.

GOOD AND BAD BLOOD

Dan Montjoy is the son of "good" and "bad" blood, the product of Jack Montjoy's elopement with Jane Lightfoot, and he is a creature of pride even as a child, "dumb, yet disdainful, like a high-bred dog that has been beaten and turned adrift" (28). When Betty first meets him (at night on the road where she has come to bury a frog's leg given to her by a conjure woman in a vain effort to turn her unfashionable red hair black like Virginia's), she mistakes him for the Devil. His grandfather treats him like a Lightfoot (and spoils him), but he is also aware of his "bad" Montjoy blood which he fears weakens him.

The idea of good and bad qualities as the product of blood is not, of course, solely the product of romantic Southern ideas about breeding, for Darwin himself gave authority to this belief, too:

> There is not the least inherent improbability as it seems to me, in virtuous tendencies being more or less strongly inherited; for, not to mention the various dispositions and habits transmitted by many of our domestic animals to their offspring, I have heard of authentic cases in which a desire to steal and a tendency to lie appeared to run in families of the upper ranks; and as stealing is a rare crime in the wealthy classes, we can hardly account by accidental coincidence for the tendency occurring in two or three members of the same family. If bad tendencies are transmitted, it is probable that good ones are likewise transmitted.[8]

The battle-ground of the title, then, refers to more than the state of Virginia during the Civil War, for Dan Montjoy is himself a Darwinian battle-ground upon which the good and bad elements of his nature struggle. "The boy's kind heart will save him," the Governor says of young Dan, "or he is lost" (66), and Dan eventually comes to recognize and despise his weakness:

> "A man!" he appeared to snap his fingers at the thought. "I am a weather-vane, a leaf in the wind, a—an ass. I haven't known my own mind ten minutes during the last two years, and the only thing I've ever gone honestly about is my own pleasure . . . . I've been ruined, and it's too late to mend me" (168).

But what is exactly his "bad" blood and what his "good" becomes more difficult for Dan to perceive during the war. The familiar naturalistic novelist's atavistic "beast in man" ironically becomes the agent of valor in battle as Dan depends upon his "good" Lightfoot blood:

> The hot old blood of his fathers had stirred again and the dead had rallied to the call of their descendant . . . . As he bent to the fire, the fury of the game swept over him. All the primeval instincts, throttled by the restraint of centuries—the instincts of blood guiltiness, of hot pursuit, of the fierce exhilaration of the chase, of the death grapple with a resisting foe—these awoke suddenly to life and turned the battle scarlet to his eyes (312).

Later, during Jackson's mountain campaign, Dan is tested fully by war and emerges victorious over his "bad" blood:

> Dan, sitting watchful by the fire, fell into the peculiar mental state which comes only after an inward struggle that has laid bare the sinews of one's life. He had fought the good fight to the end, and he knew that from this day he should go easier with himself because he knew that he had conquered. The old doubt—the old distrust of his own strength—was fallen from him (346–347).

But the more interesting and valuable "blood" victory comes when Dan learns of his father's brave death on the surgeon's table after a battle and comes to terms with his "bad" Montjoy blood:

> It was as a braggart and a bully that he had always thought of him; now he knew that at least he was not a craven—that he could take blows as he dealt them, from the shoulder out. He had hated his father . . . and he did not love him now . . . . There had been war between them to the grave, and yet, despite himself, he knew that he had lost his old boyish

shame of the Montjoy blood . . . . For the first time in his life there had come to him, like an impulse, the knowledge that he must not lower his father's name (376–377).

Dan's experiences in the war and his discoveries reveal the failings both of the Old Order's blood-based social hierarchy and of a strictly deterministic interpretation of Darwin as well. Glasgow insists on the primacy of individual moral experience even in the face of biological and social orders that diminish both individual freedom and power. Dan loses the comfort of being able to attribute his successes to his "good" blood or to blame his failings on his "bad" blood, but he gains the moral freedom that will enable him to start a new life with Betty by realizing that his blood, for all its inherited tendencies, is his own—a truth that Betty had known all along when she realized that Dan was at his best when he was neither Lightfoot nor Montjoy, just himself. She had once tried to teach him what she knew when he was complaining about his "bad" Montjoy blood by simply saying to him, "Your blood is good" (171).

THE CIVIL WAR ITSELF

In an essay written late in her life and published in 1938, Ellen Glasgow's dark Darwinian view of human biological necessity led her to define war as the result of a "deep destructive instinct" which is unavoidable.[9] She goes on to say:

> Having lived through one world war, I can remember that the worst of such hostilities was not the thought of death in battle; it was not even the thought of the young and the best who were sacrificed: but it was the pleasurable excitement with which so many men, and more especially so many women, responded to the shock and the hatred and even the horror. For I still think, as I thought then: the worst part of war is that so many people enjoy it (EGRD 241).

She adds that in her childhood she "was accustomed to hearing decorous Southern pillars of society declare that the happiest years of their lives were the four years in which they marched and fought and starved with the Army of Northern Virginia."

In *The Battle-Ground*, Major Lightfoot, the old soldier, profligate gambler, and strong believer in the rightness of slavery, is the spokesman for the war-lovers, and he says at one point during the secession debates that "my honest opinion is that there are not fifty men in Virginia with the spirit to secede—and they are women" (274). Once the war starts, he and his kind remain true to their beliefs, but they lose narrative privilege in the novel as the horrible discoveries of Dan at the front and Betty at home dominate the narrative's progression. Glasgow makes sure that even her readers may enjoy the book, but not the war.

The young soldiers in camp waiting for what they predict will be a war of only two weeks (in a chapter called "How Merry Gentlemen Went to War") share the Major's enthusiasm, but once they have been through the confused violence of the First Battle of Manassas (in a chapter called "The Reign of the Brute") and especially after the suffering during the winter march to Romney, they lose their taste for war. Dan's masculine Lightfoot nature responds to the excitement of the battle and "the savage smell of the discolored earth" after the fighting has ceased at Manassas, but it is overwhelmed by "the peculiar sensitiveness which had come to him from his childhood and his suffering mother" (326). That sensitivity which arises from the loss of personal power caused by the desertion of his father and from his identification with his mother's suffering allows Dan to see the reality of war far more clearly than his grandfather, who is caught up in the disastrous illusion of power, ever could.

In a scene clearly drawn from Glasgow's study of the battlefield photographs of Alexander Gardner, Dan awakens early in the rainy morning following the battle and looks at his sleeping fellow soldiers, but he sees instead the truth of war:

> Then a shudder followed, for he saw in the lines of gray men stretched beneath the rain some likeness to that other field beyond the hill where the dead were still lying, row on row. He saw them stark and cold on the scorched grass beside the guns, or in the thin ridges of trampled corn, where the gay young tassels were now storm-beaten upon the ripped-up earth. He saw them as he had seen them the evening before—not in the glow of battle, but with the acuteness of a brooding sympathy—saw them frowning, smiling, and with features which death had twisted into a ghastly grin. They were all there—each man with open eyes and stiff hands grasping the clothes above his wound (325).

72

At home, Betty and Virginia suffer through the women's part in the war. Alone in the room where she and Virginia sleep, "within the four white walls she [Betty] moved breathlessly to and fro like a woodland creature that has been entrapped" (329)—a description which is particularly telling because Betty has been presented throughout the early part of the novel as the freer of trapped animals and the defender of all woodland creatures. Betty feels the blood call to battle as strongly as Dan so that she cannot bear "the folded hands and the terrible patience that are the woman's share of war" (329). It is, of course, while playing the woman's traditional role that Virginia loses her child and her life, as much to her fears for the safety of her wounded husband and her vain efforts to find and help him as to the actual fatal trauma of the childbirth.

Betty does eventually get her war directly, both when she faces down a deserter who has "penetrated into Betty's chamber" (433) with a revolver she keeps on her dresser and, more importantly, when she carries an increasingly heavier and heavier share of the burden of feeding and caring for both the Lightfoot and Ambler families. Betty, like Dan, comes to see the grim fact of war; when her mother murmurs wonderingly, "I see a great light on the road," it is Betty who glances "to the mountains huddled against the sky" and announces calmly that "It is General Sheridan going up the valley" (460–461).

AN IMAGE

Among Ellen Glasgow's great strengths as a novelist is her ability to forge powerful images which define large social conditions with precision and imaginative power. In her fifth novel, *The Deliverance* (1904), she sums up the desperate lie that informed much of Southern life during the Reconstruction with the image of a blind old woman who sits alone in her empty, poverty-stricken home, protected by her family from the truth of her condition:

> She lived upon lies . . . and thrived upon the sweetness she extracted from them. For her the Confederacy had never fallen, the quiet of her dreamland had been disturbed by no invading army, and the three hundred slaves, who in reality scattered like chaff before the wind, she still saw in her cheerful visions tilling her familiar fields. It was as if she had

fallen asleep with the great blow that wrecked her body, and had dreamed on steadily throughout the years. Of real changes she was as ignorant as a new-born child . . . . Wonderful as it all was . . . the most wonderful thing was the intricate tissue of lies woven around her chair. Lies—lies— there had been nothing but lies spoken within her hearing for twenty years.[10]

In *The Battle-Ground,* she describes another domestic scene which defines the absurdity and waste of a society which is dependent upon slavery with quiet economy. Mr. Bennett, a serious young tutor from the North who has been hired by Major Lightfoot to teach Champe and Dan, observes the life of a small Lightfoot slave, Mitty, "whose chief end in life was the finding of Mrs. Lightfoot's spectacles":

> He was an earnest young man, but he could not keep his eyes away from Mitty when she was in the room; and at the old lady's, "Mitty, my girl, find me my glasses," he felt like jumping from his seat and calling upon her to halt. It seemed a survival of the dark ages that one immortal soul should spend her life hunting for the spectacles of another (68).

A PORTRAIT, A WEDDING DRESS, AND A FLAG

Women, idealized and realistically powerless, became, in the disastrous illusion of the Old Order, veritable icons of the Old Order itself. In *The Battle-Ground,* the portrait of Great Aunt Emmeline offers, of course, the clearest example of that symbolic equivalence. That her portrait is saved from the burning Chericoke and hung in a place of honor in the overseer's house represents, ironically and importantly, the defeated South's clinging to its idealized image of itself—to the disastrous illusion that blinded it to the effects of slavery and led directly to its downfall.

The Lightfoots may keep Aunt Emmeline's portrait on the wall as a sign of their holding to the old ideals and values, but for the South in general, the Confederate battle flag takes on (and still retains) all of the symbolic values once imbued in the idealized image of the woman and invests it with the further romantic symbolism of the Lost Cause. In *The Battle-Ground,* Glasgow tracked the symbolic transformation of Old Order to Lost Cause, of Woman to Flag in a particularly subtle and interesting way.

After First Manassas, Betty's frustration with her not being a part of the war leads her to collect silk from which to make battle flags. Mrs. Lightfoot offers her wedding dress to the cause in a chapter infused with romance: cavalrymen galloping by, a copy of the *Morte d'Arthur,* "the peculiar feeling of kinship which united the people of the South" (335–337). But before the dress can be made into a flag, Virginia borrows it to marry Jack Morson, taking on herself thereby the role of icon of the Old Order. Virginia dies during the Battle of Seven Pines, and with her the iconic role of the Southern Woman—both victims of the realities of the war. Then, long after Virginia's death, at the last battle of the war in Virginia, Sailor's Creek, Dan rescues a fallen battle flag—"the helpless flag he had loved and followed for four years" (473). The flag has already come to represent both the Old Order and the Lost Cause:

> The cause for which he had fought, the great captain he had followed, the devotion to a single end which had kept him struggling in the ranks, the daily sacrifice, the very poverty and cold and hunger, all these were bound up and made one with the tattered flag upon his arm (473).

At Appomattox, after the surrender, the final symbolic transformation of the wedding dress occurs. Dan cuts the flag into little pieces, passing it out to his fellow soldiers, keeping the last fragment for himself. It has now become a holy relic of the Lost Cause.

But for Ellen Glasgow, this last relic of the Old Order, of the disastrous illusion, has no power. Hers is certainly not the vision that was a century later to produce the "Fergit, Hell" version of the Southern icon. The wedding dress, for all its idealization and entrapment of the woman in a powerless symbolic role, was also a sign of the renewal of life and the future; the cut-up battle flag represents only loss and defeat, leading not to the future but only continually back to the past:

> This was the end of the flag for which he was ready to give his life three days ago. With his youth, his strength, his very bread thrown into the scale, he sat now with wrecked body and blighted mind, and saw his future turn to decay before his manhood was well begun. Where was the old buoyant spirit he had brought with him into the fight? Gone forever, and in its place he found his maimed and trembling hands, and limbs weakened by starvation as by long fever. His virile youth was wasted in the

slow struggle, his energy was sapped drop by drop; and at the last he saw himself burned out like the battle-fields, where the armies had closed and opened, leaving an impoverished and ruined soil (478).

The bit of flag is never mentioned again in the novel, for Dan and Betty, who have experienced the war and its multitude of losses, must find their strength in the future and not in the past to which the flag must forever point.

MISSING WOMEN

Betty Ambler, red-headed, independent-minded and intelligent, in a context of dark-haired, submissive, and artificially ignorant (to use Frederick P. W. McDowell's phrase) women, is the central female figure in the novel and a very active force in its narrative development. But it should come as no surprise that in a novel concerned with a society that idealized and abstracted women, the absence of several women helps define the parameters of the world of the novel almost as much as the active presence of Betty and the other women characters.

Dan's Great-great-aunt Emmeline is the "abiding presence" of Chericoke, the seat of the Lightfoots, where there is "an ottoman . . . covered with a piece of her wedding dress," a spray of English ivy she "set out with her own hands" that has grown across a window in which she once wrote with her diamond ring the words "Love is best" which can still be seen "faint against the ivy that she planted on her wedding day" (30–31). Her beauty sets the standard by which all other women are judged, and her portrait dominates the house, an iconic representation of the Old Order's romantic (and disastrous) illusions concerning itself. When Betty and Virginia are tested against the ideal of Aunt Emmeline, Virginia's passing the test places her symbolically within the paradigm of the Old Order, while Betty's failing to live up to Emmeline's standards places her outside the Old Order and frees her to a considerable degree from its illusions.

The death of Aunt Emmeline's surrogate, Virginia, along with her baby, during the Battle of Seven Pines ends symbolically the "old society" as well, and it is important, then, that only Aunt Emmeline's portrait is saved from the ruins of Chericoke during the war. The portrait, at the end of the novel, comes to represent the absurd survival of the Old Order's ideals even in a context of poverty and destruction. Before the war, Aunt Emmeline stood for romantic illusion in a society that lived by and for that illusion, and after the war, when the society has been permanently changed, she continues to represent a vision of that lost society as edenic—a vision that gave birth to all the romantic plantation and Civil War novels of Thomas Nelson Page and his ilk that *The Battle-Ground* is subtly exposing and subverting.

Dan's mother, Jane Lightfoot Montjoy, is another important missing woman in the novel, eloping into romantic legend with Jack Montjoy, but in reality only into a brutally bad marriage and an early death in childbirth fewer than a dozen years later. The memory of her suffering and the fact of her absence shapes Dan's character and gives it a feminine sensitivity that saves him from the submission to the atavistic violence of both his "good" Lightfoot blood and his "bad" Montjoy blood, and that enables him to survive the war without becoming a futureless diehard partisan who continues to fight the war long after it is over or a sentimental romanticizer of the past who can never even imagine a vital future that is different or better.

In Betty, Dan finds the active promise of the future, but he also finds the long-missing comfort of his mother as she draws "him to her bosom, soothing him as a mother soothes a tired child" (511). Only after finding his missing mother in Betty (and coming to terms thereby with both his memories of her suffering and his actual suffering in the war) does he find the personal strength that he feared the war had taken from him. Only then does he realize that he no longer needs his lost mother (or the Lost Cause), and, instead of merely shaking hands with Betty as he had done at his homecoming earlier, he catches "her from the ground as he had done that day beside the cabin in the woods, kissing her eyelids and her faithful hands" (511). Betty and Dan are able to establish a relationship that is not based upon dependency—either of willingly weak wife on strong husband or of wounded soldier/child on surrogate mother. They find no need for a hierarchical relationship and, as Betty (who has the last word) says, "begin again . . . and this time, my dear . . . begin together" (512).

The third missing woman whose absence haunts the book is Sarindy, the wife of a freed slave, Levi, who tells Betty that "she warn' nuttin' but a fiel' han', young miss, en I 'uz Marse Bolling's body sarvent, so w'en dey sot me loose, dey des sol' Sarindy up the river. Lawd, Lawd, she warn' nuttin' but a fiel' han', but she 'us pow'ful likely" (149). When, late in the war as Sheridan was devastating the Valley of Virginia, Levi brings Betty a basket of eggs to help her feed her mother, Betty feels "a compassion as acute as pain" and remembers "the isolation of his life, the scornful suspicion he had met from white and black, and the injustice that had set him free and sold Sarindy up the river" (460). The pledge of friendship between these outsiders, the freed black man and the independent white woman (and, on her word, the independent white man, Dan, as well) testifies to the emotional power of the missing Sarindy which, along with the suffering of Jane Lightfoot, may ultimately prove of greater force than the portrait of Emmeline and all that it represents.

The memory of Emmeline as the icon of the Old Order and its values, is, like her portrait, preserved after the war, but that memory is revealed by the narrative to be hollow and, like the flag of the Lost Cause, to lead only to the past. On the contrary, the memory of Jane Lightfoot, the white woman who was betrayed and victimized by the "disastrous illusion" of the Old Order, and of Sarindy, the black woman who was casually sold away from her husband by that same Old Order, is privileged by the narrative and opens, through Betty and Dan, into the possibilities of the future.

SLAVES AND POOR WHITES

The slaves in *The Battle-Ground* peacefully accept their condition, having been kept in a child-like condition of absolute dependence upon their white masters even as the society that enslaved them depends absolutely upon them for its very existence. The night of John Brown's raid, fear of a slave revolt sweeps through Virginia and infects Governor Ambler—fear of "an enemy that crept upon him unawares" and "of a hidden evil which might be even now brooding at his fireside" (246). The slave revolt never develops, but the Governor discovers in himself an awareness of the source of the evil of the night in the evil at the heart of the society in which he lives and which he once governed:

> And yet with it all, he felt that there was some wild justice in the thing he dreaded, in the revolt of an enslaved and ignorant people, in the pitiable and ineffectual struggle for a freedom which would mean, in the beginning, but the power to go forth and kill. It was the recognition of this deeper pathos that made him hesitate to reproach even while his thoughts dwelt on the evils . . . (247).

The slaves do not revolt, and, in the course of the war, they continue to support the lives and families of their white masters. Dan's slave Big Abel appropriately bears the name of the first victim of biblical history, and he makes no effort to take up "the power to go forth and kill" of Cain. Rather, he faithfully follows Dan through the war, saves his life, and helps him home after the war. The change in white consciousness represented by Governor Ambler, Dan and Betty may ultimately offer them a chance for freedom and empowerment, but at the end of the novel (and the war) they remain dependent and powerless like children and, to a lesser degree, white women.

The situation of the poor whites is much the same as that of the blacks. The only rewards their lives give them would seem to be what Dan saw in the sallow, ugly face of Mrs. Hicks, the wife of a poor tavern keeper: "the dignity with which suffering had endowed this plain and simple woman" (241). The mountaineer Pinetop does not fight and risk his life in the war to protect slavery or even the Old Order that lived by and on slavery. He speaks of his attitude toward slavery (and reveals the racism of the poor whites that was to plague the South for more than a century to follow): "If these folks have come arter the niggers, let 'em take 'em off and welcome . . . . I ain't never owned a nigger in my life, and, what's more, I ain't never seen one that's worth owning" (323). He simply fights for the Virginia that has disempowered him, but which he sees as his home and not, therefore, to be invaded—illustrating thereby Glasgow's belief that "men will fight desperately, provided an emotion or an instinct responds, to perpetuate systems and institutions which will work only to destroy their defenders" (CM 22).

In the novel, freed blacks and white women may act in league to nurture and protect life after the war (as Levi and Betty do with the eggs (460)), just as freed blacks and enlightened white men may also forge new bonds of mutual understanding and assistance (which Glasgow indicates with Dan's borrowing of Levi's lantern to light his solitary way in the darkness (221–222)), but the former slaves and the poor whites are unable, because of their enforced ignorance and poverty, to see past their old habits of behavior and their prejudices to form an alliance against the weakened but still powerful Old Order and the reimposition of its "disastrous illusion."

A FINAL NOTE

On the road to Romney, Dan observes the sleeping, snow covered soldiers around him and catches his breath "as a man might who had waked suddenly among the dead":

> Even the wintry sky borrowed, for an hour, the spectral aspect of earth, and the familiar shapes of cloud, as of hill, stood out with all the majesty of uncovered laws—stripped of the mere frivolous effect of light or shade. It was like the first day—or the last (346).

With an apocalyptic fury, the Civil War, to Glasgow, uncovered the laws that governed the society of the pre-war South. The war revealed a ruling class that empowered itself at the expense of enslaved blacks, economically and socially repressed poor whites, and idealized but powerless women, and that shielded and protected itself with the "disastrous illusion" of Southern chivalry and the myths of the Old Order. But, unfortunately, the war and its aftermath also revealed the awesome force of that illusion, which continued to empower the old ruling class at the expense of blacks, poor whites, and women.

In *The Battle-Ground,* Dan and Betty mark a new beginning, the "first day" of a new order based on a realistic vision born of the suffering of the war, but Glasgow's ironic intelligence would not allow her to romanticize that new beginning. Transformations of power had begun, but the old power was still very much in evidence—the "first day" was not to be the "last day" of the Old Order. Even as Dan and Betty walk toward a new life (and the implicit promise of a new wedding dress), the portrait of Aunt Emmeline hangs on the Lightfoots' wall, the freed slaves are still serving their old masters, the poor whites have returned to their isolation in the mountains, and the fragments of Dan's battle flag are preserved by Dan's fellow soldiers all over the new south. And, with appropriate irony, Ellen Glasgow's complex, intelligent novel continues to be ignored by critics and readers alike who have been misled by its appropriation of a familiar and conventional literary form and have therefore failed to discover the genuine significance of what it enabled that form to do and say.

Among the many romantic novels of the Old South and the Civil War which were popular at turn of the century, *The Battle-Ground* sat up in 1902 and looked around as one might "who had waked suddenly among the dead." I can only hope that modern readers will discover it among the dead and honor its vitality anew.

1. Glasgow specialists have, of course, written intelligently about *The Battle-Ground* in monographs on her work, and I should like to mention especially Frederick P. W. McDowell's *Ellen Glasgow and the Ironic Art of Fiction* (Madison: University of Wisconsin Press 1960), Monique Parent's *Ellen Glasgow, Romancière* (Paris: A. G. Nizet 1962), Joan Foster Santas' *Ellen Glasgow's American Dream* (Charlottesville: University Press of Virginia 1965), and, most fully, J. R. Raper's *Without Shelter: The Early Career of Ellen Glasgow* (Baton Rouge: Louisiana State University Press 1971).

2. Ellen Glasgow, *The Battle-Ground* (New York: Doubleday, Page, 1902) 52. Further references will be noted parenthetically.

3. Parent 507.

4. *The Curious Death of the Novel: Essays in American Literature* (Baton Rouge: Louisiana State University Press, 1967) 192–193.

5. Ellen Glasgow, *A Certain Measure: An Interpretation of Prose Fiction* (New York: Harcourt, Brace, 1943) 5. Further references will be noted parenthetically as CM.

6. Ellen Glasgow, *The Woman Within* (New York: Harcourt, Brace, 1954) 120. Further references will be parenthetically noted as WW.

7. *Critical Woodcuts* (New York: Scribner's, 1926) 76.

8. Charles Darwin, *The Descent of Man* (New York and London: Merrill and Baker, 1874) 140.

9. *Ellen Glasgow's Reasonable Doubts: A Collection of Her Writings,* ed. Julius Rowan Raper (Baton Rouge: Louisiana State University Press, 1988) 240. Further references will be noted parenthetically as EGRD.

10. Ellen Glasgow, *The Deliverance* (New York: Doubleday, Page, 1904) 74.

Ellen Glasgow was born in 1873 in Richmond, Virginia, and died there in 1945. Selected publications: *The Descendant* (1897); *The Battle-Ground* (1902, out of print); *The Deliverance* (1904); *Barren Ground* (1925); *The Romantic Comedians* (1926); *The Sheltered Life* (1932); *Vein of Iron* (1935). *A Certain Measure* (1943, essays); *The Woman Within* (1954, autobiography); *The Collected Stories of Ellen Glasgow* (1963).

On Mary Johnston's
The Long Roll

George Garrett

I

WHEN THE LIFE AND WORK of Mary Johnston (1870–1936) are discussed at all, there are several things that are usually said. About her life it is usually noted that she was a wonderfully well-read writer, though except for the briefest of periods (three months) never formally in school. She was privately tutored and self-educated. It is remarked that by the age of nineteen, following the death of her mother, she assumed the parental responsibility for her younger brothers and sisters and likewise served her father, John William Johnston, as companion, hostess and housekeeper, until his death in 1905. After which she looked after herself and the others in the family, earning her living chiefly as a novelist.

Born in Buchanan in the Shenandoah Valley, close by the James River and at the edge of the Blue Ridge Mountains, she lived in Birmingham, Alabama, New York City, and Richmond, Virginia, and travelled with her father to England, Scotland, Ireland, France and Italy. Later travels took her all over Europe and to Egypt, an amazing itinerary for a young woman of that age and of her background. A few years after her father's death, she bought, built, and lived in a large house, "Three Hills," beautifully situated on a high hilltop in Bath County near Warm Springs. With her advances and earnings as a novelist she held on to this mansion for the rest of her life; though, in order to save it, she felt forced to change publishers (from Houghton Mifflin to Little, Brown, both Boston firms) and, as well, to take in boarders from time to time to make ends meet. "Three Hills" is still there, privately owned and serving as an inn and restaurant.

The intellectual life and development of Mary Johnston is interesting enough to divert attention from her art. She was a leader in the Equal Suffrage movement and was instrumental in the formation of the Equal Suffrage League of Virginia. She was more than casually interested in Socialism and studied its literature and attended some Socialist party meetings. During World War I she was at least allied with those who were part of the pacifist movement. She studied science and was fascinated by many aspects and applications of evolutionary theory. In her mature years she became deeply interested in psychic phenomena and mysticism.

Her literary life and career are interesting and even unusual in a number of ways. Beginning in 1898 with *Prisoners of Hope* she was the author of some twenty-two works of fiction, one nonfiction book, a published drama written in blank verse (*The Goddess of Reason* 1907). A number of her works were successfully translated into film, several, early and late, proved to be best sellers, and one, her second novel, published in her thirtieth year, *To Have and To Hold* (1900), a novel concerned with the Jamestown settlement, was an enormous popular and commercial success, a true "blockbuster" before that term was invented, reportedly selling something in the neighborhood of 500,000 copies in hardcover. She was certainly, from that moment on, a "known" writer, for better and worse. Well and widely read in her own American literature—she was moved and influenced, one way and another, by James, Cooper, Hawthorne, Emerson, and Whitman. She also knew Thomas Hardy and J. M. Barrie of the British older generation; was both friend and correspondent to her colleagues Ellen Glasgow and Evelyn Thomson; and, by attending a number of conferences, she at least met some of the younger generation of moderns. For example, in the fall of 1931 she was one of the thirty-three southern writers who assembled, at the invitation of Ellen Glasgow and Professor James Southall Wilson, at the University of Virginia for a conference of several days. Among those who were also present were DuBose Heyward, Paul Green, Allen Tate, Carolyn Gordon, Donald Davidson, Laurence Stallings, James Boyd, Struthers Burt, Josephine Pinckney, and others, including Alice Hegan Rice, author of the highly popular *Mrs. Wiggs of the Cabbage Patch.* Another writer who was visibly and actively present both at the formal and purely social sessions (his first recorded words on arriving in Charlottesville were: "Know where I can get a drink?") was William Faulkner.

It is hard to believe, harder to understand how someone as much a part of the American literary scene, certainly from her first book to her last, *Drury Randall* (1934), could have been so quickly forgotten, so largely ignored ever since, especially in view of the recent rediscoveries and acts of rehabilitation performed by feminist critics and scholars. This is also something that is usually said; though, reflexive or not, it still needs to be said.

Finally, and most pertinently, another notion about Mary Johnston needs to be reiterated. If she had done nothing else whatsoever except for her two Civil War novels—*The Long Roll* (1911) and *Cease Firing* (1912)—she has earned honor and recognition for some of the most ambitious and successful writing about that terrible period in our national history. That a large and crucial part of both books consists of extraordinarily vivid and authentic (almost cinematic in a documentary sense) writing about combat is nothing less than remarkable. True, she had had the stories of her father, a Major of Artillery of the Confederate States of America, and her kinsman the distinguished General Joseph E. Johnston (it is to the memory of the two of them that the two books are dedicated) to listen to; and we know from her papers that she mastered and made full use of all the primary and secondary sources available at the time; and that she went beyond that, walking the roads and exploring the terrain of the battlefields, seeking to make her story as factually accurate as it could possibly be. But none of this prepares the reader for the overwhelming impact of some of the finest writing about combat by any American before or since. That it should have been the work of a woman novelist in an age marked by habits of literary gentility and by the fashions of historical romance, fashions which she, herself, had earlier mastered and exploited to the fullest extent and success, is a stunning tribute to the power of focused imagination. This latter point, how she turned away about as far as she possibly could have from the acceptable literary tropes which had helped, thus far, to make her career and her living, is no indifferent matter. Literary habits and mindset, both for writers and readers, are extremely difficult to shed or to transcend even when they are fully known and recognized. And beyond the difficulty lies the great risk. The writing of *The Long Roll* and its companion, *Cease Firing,* demanded an act of great artistic daring, faith really, from Mary Johnston. On the strength of her ambition and daring alone she fully deserves to be remembered with honor. It is hard to make simple claims for the influence of these works. Who knows which, if any, of the writers of the wars that have been the continuing affliction and subject of the twentieth century, may or may not have opened either of her books or have ever even heard of Mary Johnston? But there are certain works which serve to change things, to alter our ways of seeing and being and thinking about things, including our past, ever after.

It is easier to make this point by analogy, easier to see in social and political thought than in literary art. But the matter is analogous. In 1638 a very young Englishman, fighting for his life alone in the Court of Star Chamber said something passionate about how things relate to one another, about how things are linked for good and for ill:

> For what is done to any one may be done to every one: besides, being all members of one body, that is, of the English Commonwealth, one man should not suffer wrongfully, but all should be sensible, and endeavor his preservation; otherwise they give way to an inlet of the sea of will and power, upon their laws and liberties, which are boundaries to keep out tyranny and oppression; and who assists not in such cases, betrays his own rights, and is overrun, and of a free man made a slave when he thinks not of it, or regards it not, and so shunning the censure of turbulency, incurs the guilt of treachery to the present and future generations.

The young man was Freeborn Jack Lilburne, and the words he spoke to the judges at Star Chamber have been taken over to form the motto of the American Civil Liberties Union. And at his death, on one finger, Thomas Jefferson wore a ring with "Lilburne" on it, in honor of the ideas and ideals of Freeborn Jack.

I do not propose that we should wear rings in honor of the words of Mary Johnston. But I do suggest that among those of us, American writers, who have come along after her, we owe her something, a large debt, in whatever we may choose to write (or film) about the Civil War in particular and all war, combat, in general. I doubt if Shelby Foote owes her much of anything directly; yet her two novels helped to form the climate which allowed him to conceive of and to achieve his masterpiece—*The Civil War: A Narrative.* And without Shelby Foote there would have been no Public Television program—"The Civil War." I seriously doubt if Norman Mailer, for example, or, to be more recent, Tim O'Brien have ever glanced at or even heard of Mary Johnston's Civil War books. But they owe her something whether they know it or not, as do we all. She prepared the way. And there are moments, passages and sequences in both *The Long Roll* and *Cease Firing* which are better writing about men at war than anything in *The Naked and the Dead* (or anything in James Jones for that matter) or the work of Tim O'Brien.

There. Some things which are *not* usually said about the work of Mary Johnston.

II

Like a lot of books of the early years of this century, *The Long Roll* has illustrations. (It also has advertisements, but that convention surprises only contemporary readers who, though bombarded from all sides by advertisements, are somewhat disconcerted by this lapsed convention.) The end papers are maps, of "The Valley and Piedmont Virginia" and, on a large scale the "Region of the Seven Days' Fighting." Nothing could be more appropriate for a book about a war than the empty and innocent and abstract maps soon to be filled with soldiers of both sides, soon to become places of human suffering, wounds and death. The book begins before the war and then divides itself between the early Valley campaigns and the larger battles fought in the east around the Richmond area, ending with Chancellorsville. Each book has four color illustrations by N. C. Wyeth, a frontispiece and three others, scattered through the text and, yes, *illustrating* its line and development.

The sequence of the internal illustrations in *The Long Roll* follows the direction and sequence of the story, then, and offers direct support to the narrative. The first, "The Lovers," might well be a jacket cover for an historical romance, two beautiful young people, a well-dressed young lady and a splendidly uniformed Confederate officer standing in a gentle embrace, perhaps at the moment of parting, in an attractive sylvan scene. The second, a couple of hundred pages later, "The Battle," is a swirl of smoke and fog and confusion. In the background, only partly visible, a torn and tattered Confederate stars-and-bars battle flag. In the foreground several hatless, deadly serious men armed with muskets, one firing at close range, another evidently hit and falling down. The last, near the end of the book, a fully dressed horseman—high boots, overcoat and cape, visored cap, with a drawn revolver, alone and alert among leafless trees in a snow-dusted wintry setting. "The Vedette" (Vedette was the term for a mounted sentinel out in front of the pickets) is a cold and menacing vision of a veteran soldier, a survivor. He is nothing else, neither more or less, than a soldier. The frontispiece of *The Long Roll* is a picture of Stonewall Jackson, with his horse Little Sorrel, Jackson standing on a high place, very stern and somehow ungainly, looking down, brooding about something. Brooding about all that follows. This is singularly apt; for *The Long Roll* soon enough becomes (among a good number of other things) the unfolding of the brief and brilliant story of Stonewall Jackson, that awkward and enigmatic man, who was, in the view of many and of this book, the South's great warrior. Its last pages give us his now-famous last words—"Let us cross over the river, and rest under the shade of the trees." And the book ends with the historical scene of Jackson lying in state in the Virginia Hall of Delegates in the Capitol of the Confederacy.

Although Jackson is talked about by some of the fictional characters in the early stages of the narrative, the days leading up to the actual outbreak of the war, he does not appear in person until the sixth chapter of the book, "By Ashby's Gap," some 60 pages into the 683 page story. He is viewed and judged, in first and untested impression, by the narrator, a collective speaker and general point of view for all the characters we have come to know so far:

> An awkward, inarticulate, and peculiar man, with strange notions about his health and other matters, there was about him no breath of grace, romance, or pomp of war. He was ungenial, ungainly, with large hands and feet, with poor eyesight and a stiff address. There did not lack spruce and handsome youths in his command who were vexed to the soul

by the idea of being led to battle by such a figure. The facts that he had fought very bravely in Mexico, and that he had for the enemy a cold and formidable hatred were for him; most other things against him. He drilled his troops seven hours a day. His discipline was of the sternest, his censure a thing to make the boldest officer blench. A blunder, a slight negligence, any disobedience of orders—down came reprimand, suspension, arrest, with an iron certitude, a relentlessness quite like Nature's. Apparently he was without imagination. He had but little sense of humour, and no understanding of a joke. He drank water and sucked lemons for dyspepsia, and fancied that the use of pepper had caused a weakness in his left leg. He rode a rawboned nag named Little Sorrel, he carried his sabre in the oddest fashion, and said "oblike" instead of "oblique" (first edition, 60–61).

This is all in the public, historical narrative voice, one of a wide variety of voices she uses to create a chorus for her story. But two things are worthy of noting. First, that everything in that straightforward block of information pays off later in action, in plot, in the story. Nothing, not a word or a thing mentioned proves to be idle or irrelevant. The only other writer I've encountered who can do the same thing so effectively—the throwaway passage of detailed description or exposition which proves to be in each detail of the utmost importance, one way and another—is Nabokov. Secondly, this was and is a daring bit of narrative strategy. It challenges the reader with a strong first impression to *unlearn* acquired responses. Truth is, we learn that Jackson's widow, and others among his coterie of dedicated admirers who were still alive to read this far (evidently they read not much farther than his earliest appearances in the narrative) were very angry and upset. No matter. Johnston knew where she was going with his character and her story. She plunges us into the time and its quick, easy, ignorant, finally innocent judgments, making us contemporaries. A little later, after Jackson has begun to prove himself as a leader of men in combat, a leader capable of bringing courage and endurance, the best, out of them, that same collective narrator's voice offers another evolving judgment:

In peace, to the outward eye, he was a commonplace man; in war he changed. The authority with which he was clothed went, no doubt, for much, but it was rather, perhaps, that a door had been opened for him. His inner self became visible, and that imposingly. The man was there; a firm man, indomitable, a thunderbolt of war, a close-mouthed, far-seeing, praying and worshipping, more or less ambitious, not always just, patriotically devoted fatalist and enthusiast, a mysterious and commanding genius of an iron sort (144).

Then we are allowed to see the great man earn his greatness, become a myth and at the last a monument. Something not lost on an educated private soldier ("a young man like a beautiful athlete from a frieze, an athlete who was also a philosopher") who speaks out loud to the corpse in the bier: "Hail, great man of the past!" he said. "If today you consort with Caesar, tell him we still make war."

This speaker speaks also for us. And, in the story and in his own time, he speaks more presciently than he can possibly know. For with Jackson's death, in Mary Johnston's version of the war, the South has already reached its high tide and that tide has now turned against the South. *Cease Firing* will follow, devoted to defeat, the unravelling, the ebb tide.

Between the beginning and the ending of *The Long Roll* there is a blended mixture of real and fictional characters. Among the historical characters who appear with more dimension than mere expository mention are Robert E. Lee and Jeb Stuart, Jefferson Davis, Fighting Joe Hooker, A. P. Hill and many others with what we have come to call cameo roles.

Meanwhile the fictional characters are entrapped in plots and subplots which could, in another context, turn this story into a more conventional historical romance. Part of the suspense of the narrative, for the reader who was familiar with the literary fashions of the age and, perhaps as well, with Johnston's earlier work, was just how seriously to take and to respond to these elements. There could be little or no suspense, finally, about the outcomes of battles and the end of things. But the shape of the story, itself, could be used to surprise the reader even as the characters are surprised. Moreover the narrative is an implicit critique of the truth of the world of historical romance, a world which is broken to pieces against the edges of hard facts. Among the fictional characters, each with a personal story and with personal problems and difficulties to be resolved, are a romantic triangle: Richard Cleave, Judith Cary, and Maury Stafford. These are upper class people. They have the usual southern, extended network of family, kinfolk, friends, etc. There are other central characters—for example, Billy Maydew, the mountain man, and Allan Gold, the schoolmaster. And there is a wonderfully realized cowardly lowlife, a character who fits into a more contemporary literary fashion, Steve Dagg, a *miles glorioso* right out of Shakespeare, only with a southern accent and dialect. He goes to great trouble to try to keep skin and bones intact in all situations. There are also the women and there are the slaves.

All have different points of view and each has a slightly different language. The slaves alone speak in phonetic dialect, something now routinely acceptable only from African-American writers. In Johnston's favor it should be said that in her use of this convention, widely popular at the time, she is very seldom condescending to the speakers or simply cute. There are the languages of the various classes, high and low, expressed in narration as well as in dialogue; and for the most part Mary Johnston's dialogue is excellent and authoritative. There are various levels of narrative rhetoric as well, ranging from an occasional voice close to that of straightforward textbook history and, from time to time, of real and imaginary documents, to song lyrics (and in one case, page 275, the musical notation for a bugle call). Above all she is superbly the master of a remarkable range of points of view, shifting back and forth from the limited visions of individuals to complex expressions of collective points of view of collective actions. It is not done in a crudely schematic way, but gradually the collective vision and its point of view overwhelm and finally replace the individual points of view and, to a large extent, the individual problems which come out of the individual particularities and peculiarities of character and out of the complexities of what was once plot, an expendable pattern of desires and events no longer of much importance measured against the huge and simple course of the war.

The war, itself, becomes something like an inhuman character with a life and a death of its own. One is reminded of an image near the end of Mary Lee Settle's memoir of her own service in World War Two, *All the Brave Promises,* where, finally discharged from the British WAAF, late in the War, she goes to London to work for the Americans. She writes that "I was on the way to the American Office of War Information in London, the cocktail parties, the conferences, the PX cigarettes, the frenetic turmoil of the people who had names and thought they were running the juggernaut of war, which was only spending itself toward its own death like a great tiring unled beast." Never completely—it will be more complete in *Cease Firing*, the War takes over from its managers, the generals on both sides, and from its performing victims in *The Long Roll*. Here, for example, is the collective viewpoint and language, developed out of a passage which began with a badly wounded soldier desperately searching for a drink of water, in which the suffering perceiver is no longer that single soldier but everyman, then and now, including the reader. The situation is an artillery "exchange" between Federal and Confederate batteries (459).

> The sound was enormous, a complex tumult that crashed and echoed in the head. The whole of the field existed in the throbbing, expanded brain—all battlefields, all life, all the world and other worlds, all problems solved and insoluble. The wide-flung grey battlefront was now sickle-shaped, convex to the foe. The rolling dense smoke flushed momently with a lurid glare. In places the forest was afire, in others the stubble of the field. From horn to horn of the sickle galloped the riderless horses. Now and again a wounded one among them screamed fearfully.

The movement of the whole passage is from small to large, from particular to general, from concrete to abstract (geometry). Then, at the end, that rush of riderless horses, some of them screaming fearfully, lights it all to the level of myth, alludes to the great myths, is somehow related to that great beast in the vision of Mary Lee Settle in *All the Brave Promises*.

What is generalized, however, is most often a pattern of particulars. Here, following the first day of the Seven Days, chapter 31, is a hospital for the wounded in Richmond, collective and general in impression, yet composed of highly sensuous, almost cinematic affective details. In sequence and context this chapter follows the account of a party at President Davis' house and precedes a vivid recounting of the combat around Gaines' Mill.

> The ward was long, low ceiled, with brown walls and rafters. Between the patches of lamplight the shadows lay wide and heavy. The cots, the pallets, the pew cushions sewed together, were placed each close by each. A narrow aisle ran between the rows; by each low bed there was just standing room. The beds were all filled, and the wagons bringing more rumbled on the cobblestones without. All the long place was reekingly hot, with a strong smell of human effluvia, of sweat-dampened clothing,

of blood and powder grime. There was not much crying aloud; only when a man was brought in raving, or when there came a sharp scream from some form under the surgeon's knife. But the place seemed one groan, a sound that swelled or sank, but never ceased. The shadows on the wall, fantastically dancing, mocked this with nods and becks and waving arms,—mocked the groaning, mocked the heat, mocked the smell, mocked the thirst, mocked nausea, agony, delirium, and the rattle in the throat, mocked the helpers and the helped, mocked the night and the world and the dying and the dead. At dawn the cannon began again (444–45).

In both the individual and collective sequences Mary Johnston sticks closely to the things that have mattered to soldiers for all of history—the weather, food and drink, and especially the latter. Thirst in battle is a continuing motif. "*Oh, water, water, water, water! . . .*" she writes.

III

We are so close and yet it all seems so far behind us. It is difficult to un-learn our own century, both the hard lessons and the misinformation, almost impossible to discard our own set of facts and fashions and to ap-preciate fully the stunning achievement of Mary Johnston's story of the Civil War. Some of the language, both literary and vernacular, is inevita-bly dated. It is still too near in time to have faded into the generalized past where the language is no longer a problem. It seems, for the time being, more like a slightly awkward version of our own; whereas, in fact, it is an earlier version of our own. In the language and telling of *The Long Roll* we witness the end of the earlier literary language of the late 19th century and the beginning of our own.

Then there are the problems of what reader expectations and experi-ence demanded of fiction, this pressure being all the more powerful, if not imperative, when affecting a very successful writer. We should re-member that a full decade later the young American moderns—like Hemingway and Faulkner and Fitzgerald—though they were in part inspired by the example of the new poets, were already finding and de-veloping a language and a style to carry the burden of their visions, still had not found the larger secret—how to structure the new novel. I am reliably told that Hemingway's earliest drafts for *The Sun Also Rises,* though splendidly executed in the already established Hemingway *style,* were for a novel structured very differently from the final version he and Maxwell Perkins put together. I am reliably told that his early drafts were arranged in the classic, chronological structure of the late Victorian novel (what novels had he *read,* after all?) replete with many pages of exposition and narration which were eventually cut to pieces. Point is that we have great difficulty escaping our own models and the critical mindset of our times. The problem was all the more acute for Mary Johnston since she herself helped to shape and form the model of the popular novel.

I believe it was the truth—the facts of life, the facts of war—that set her free. We tend to forget the simplest fact of all, that she grew up, among old soldiers, in a defeated society that had lost, killed or permanently disabled, one out of four of its males between the ages of eighteen and sixty-five. A society with one-armed and one-legged men everywhere. Shelby Foote mentions at the end of volume 3 of *The Civil War* that his home state of Mississippi budgeted 25 percent of its expenses for artificial limbs.

Mary Johnston knew the history of it at first hand. Knew also that to tell the truth of it she could not discard the ways and means of factual, historical narrative; but that she must awaken and engage the imagination of the reader and that the ways of fiction could serve this purpose. For all practical purposes she invented a form for our time, the novel which blends fact and fiction in subtle proportions and whose aim is to share the truth of an experience. John Dos Passos would later build an aesthetic and a reputation around just such a blending of real and imaginary history. And Mary Johnston, having finished with that great subject and going off in other directions and in her own way, would live to see that happen. She did not live to see the application of her methods in our own times—by Norman Mailer, in both fiction and nonfiction; by Truman Capote in his celebrated "nonfiction novel"; by E. L. Doctorow with his characteristic use of fictional and "real" historical figures in the same scene, on the same stage; and not least by Shelby Foote, whose magnificent achievement works the other way, telling only a factual history without a fictional character or event, but telling it in the narrative manner and with the narrative selectivity of a novelist.

Our whole idea of what constitutes fiction, the full range of its possibilities, has changed steadily in response to the events and complexities we have faced in this century. Near the beginning of it Mary Johnston, seeking to honor her father's memory and to do justice to the most overwhelming and traumatic experience in American history, was forced to redefine the novel. In so doing, creating first *The Long Roll,* then *Cease Firing,* she served every writer who came after her. We are all deeply beholden to her.

Mary Johnston was born in 1870 in Buchanan, Virginia, and died in 1936 in Warm Springs. Selected publications: *Prisoners of Hope* (1898); *To Have and to Hold* (1900); *The Long Roll* (1911); *Cease Firing* (1912); *Pioneers of the Old South* (1920); *Drury Randall* (1934).

On Evelyn Scott's
The Wave

PEGGY BACH

IN 1929 APPEARED THREE GREAT American novels, two of them southern: Wolfe's *Look Homeward, Angel,* Hemingway's *A Farewell to Arms,* and Faulkner's *The Sound and the Fury.* Also published in 1929 was Evelyn Scott's *The Wave,* which Carl Van Dorn called the "greatest novel on the American Civil War."[1] In "A Literary Calendar: 1911–1930," Malcolm Cowley wrote under the year 1929: "New writers promoted to genius: William Faulkner (*The Sound and the Fury*); Thomas Wolfe (*Look Homeward, Angel*); Evelyn Scott (*The Wave,* her fifth and her only popular novel)."[2]

Evelyn Scott was born Elsie Dunn in 1893 to a socially, economically, and politically prominent aristocratic family in Clarksville, Tennessee, where she spent her first sixteen years. In 1909 her family moved to New Orleans, where Scott, intending to study art, was the youngest student to enroll at Sophie Newcomb College. Three years later, she and Frederick Creighton Wellman, a married professor in the School of Tropical Medi-

cine at Tulane University, changed their names to Evelyn Scott and Cyril
Kay Scott and ran away to Brazil. After much difficulty in securing pass-
ports and passage and making financial arrangements, the Scotts returned to America in 1919 and settled for a time in Greenwich Village.
Escapade, her experimental memoir about the Brazil years, attracted,
along with other major critics, Ludwig Lewisohn.[3]

When Scott published her first novel, *The Narrow House* (1921), in a
trilogy that would include *Narcissus* (1922), and *The Golden Door* (1925),
she was praised by Sinclair Lewis and Ernest Boyd.[4]

Given Scott's penchant for diverging from the usual treatment of subject matter, events, and character through style, technique, and her intellectually individualistic views, it is to be presupposed that when she began her second trilogy in 1927, ranging over American history from 1850
to 1918—*Migrations* (1927), *The Wave* (1929), and *A Calendar of Sin*
(1931)—critics and readers could anticipate a different and challenging
experience.

In *Migrations,* set principally in Mimms, her fictional Clarksville, Scott
produced fragments of her progenitors' lives, melded with fictional elements, as they attempted to resolve identities, search for salvation, and
try unsuccessfully to escape their imperfect condition by migration.

Explaining the title of the second book, *The Wave,* Scott says, "War
itself is the only hero of the book. Whatever the philosophy of an actor in
a war, he must constantly be convinced of his feebleness when attempting to move in an emotional direction contrary to that of the mass. The
propulsion of the individual by a power that is not accountable to reason
is very obviously like the action of a wave."[5]

A Calendar of Sin explores in two volumes the many facets of love as
three generations of a family, caught up in economic and political
change, attempt to use love as a means of escape. The three novels are a
testimony to Scott's belief that love and war are equally perverse and that
neither love nor war is a valid means of escape.

Critics responded favorably to all three novels, but it was *The Wave*
that excited the greatest praise, particularly from Joseph Wood Krutch.[6]
Recognizing that *The Wave* might pose special problems for readers used
to predictable story lines in even the best of Civil War novels, Cape and
Smith secured from Krutch a short essay, similar to the one Scott had
written for *The Sound and the Fury,* to appear with the novel. Krutch

described her conception: "Her effort is to grasp the phenomenon as a whole—to show what it meant in the intimate experience of every sort of person who felt its repercussion—and for this reason her novel can have neither a hero nor, in the ordinary sense of the word, a plot." He alerted the reader to Scott's technique: "Literally hundreds of separate incidents . . . are related only by the fact that each is part of one cataclysm. . . . Nothing could be more different from the conventional historical novel." He tried to provide the reader with some access to her vision: "She has realized that the meaning of such a conflict is to be gotten only by adding together the meanings it had for countless different men and women and she has had the enormous creative energy to vitalize her almost numberless characters."[7]

Evelyn Scott, by applying the method of the cinema, created a plausible variation of the panoramic technique. As late as 1950 in *The American Historical Novel*, Ernest Leisy claimed that Scott's *The Wave* "marked a new advance in the technique of historical fiction"; in 1964, Robert Welker documented fully his claim that this novel became a "standard measure against which novels dealing with the war were tested, and perhaps more than any one book, it is responsible for opening up the materials of the Civil War to fiction. It is unique in American literature."[8]

Out of the Civil War novels written up to about 1950, over a thousand by southerners, Robert Lively, an historian whose literary sensibility has not been seriously faulted, chose to study five hundred by both northern and southern writers. *The Wave* is on his list (a list that satisfies most students of the genre) of the fifteen most effective.[9]

Scott, the southern novelist, focuses neither on a single family nor on a single individual, but on numerous individuals, south and north, both in and isolated from the family structure. She does not attempt to justify either side and there is no hint of the southern apologist, no nostalgia for the South, no sentimentality. She is as objective as a foreign observer (though most took one side or the other). She focuses not on a single battle, but on many separate individuals in the midst of many separate battles, skirmishes, and war-time situations. When *The Wave* does align itself with characteristics of other Civil War novels, it combines them, departs from them, and goes beyond. Scott's novel only faintly resembles any of the others; its complex style and the controlled blending of lyricism, imagism, impressionism, even expressionism, and its severely analytical quality sets it in sharp relief against the other major works.

In her novels, her descriptive proficiency was compared to that of Virginia Woolf, and within that context of commensurability, Scott's technique (both subjective and objective) surpassed Woolf's and exposed the reader—especially in *Escapade*—to both realistic and sensory perceptions. But in *The Wave,* and in the other two books of the trilogy, *Migrations* and *A Calendar of Sin,* Scott's superior descriptive capability for *action* emerges, about which not enough has been said. Within the time frame of the publication of these three novels, criticized by prevailing standards and attitudes surrounding women writers, if it had not been known they were written by a woman, it might have been supposed that they were written by a man. Scott was one of the first tough women writers.

Scott's raw material is the Civil War, but it is how she shapes and molds the mass of clay that places her work, more than any other novel of the war, in an international context.

The point of view that recommends itself as most appropriate is, obviously, the omniscient and it is the one Scott chose. The consequence of the choice of omniscience and its appropriateness and seeming necessity to so broad a subject as war is that it diminishes the immediacy of the events. In *The Wave,* Scott overcame this problem by employing the God-like vision to see the total war without obvious connections among people and events, but she zeroes in on individual encounters, shifting point of view in most cases to third-person, central intelligence which enables the reader to see only into the mind of the principal character in a given episode, and by doing so sharpens the reader's perception of and sensitivity to that character.

Stephen Vincent Benét opened his review of Caroline Gordon's *None Shall Look Back* (1937) by citing Scott's *The Wave* as one of three "excellent" Civil War novels of the past decade and ended with a comparison in use of point of view, concluding that Scott, with her unique kaleidoscopic omniscient point-of-view technique, succeeded where Gordon failed. Scott "gave herself sufficient range and scope so that her many complex threads wove at least into a pattern." [10]

Very few writers attempt, as Scott does, to *cover* the entire war; novelists using the material in the usual way, find this task impossible. In *The Long Roll* (1911) and its sequel *Cease Firing* (1912) Mary Johnston does cover the war chronologically; the work is rich in historical detail, but that sluggish freight of detail impedes the action, in contrast to Scott's more character-centered rendering of history, almost subconsciously absorbed by the reader. Scott follows in loose fashion the chronological order of the war; she begins *The Wave* in Charleston Harbor and ends it in Washington, D. C. But time, place, and even the specifics of this particular war are not of central importance, because in a broader sense Scott is portraying history itself and human conditions within that history.

Lewis Simpson, distinguished in the field of American literary and intellectual history, expresses this theory about Scott's purpose. "I think in a way that the deeper sense of her metaphor of the wave, which is of course the metaphor for the war or the force of war, is of the wave as a metaphor for history, and she is in a sense equating history with war."[11]

As one reads *Background in Tennessee,* Scott's unique autobiographical history of her early years in Tennessee, the range of intellect and the perpetually seeking curiosity of a precocious child and a highly intelligent, opinionated young woman is clear in the relating of personal incidents, the effects of war on her family, and in the cause and effect of historical events—religious, political, social, and regional. Even though she spent two years gathering material for *The Wave* and called on numerous historians for facts, most of Scott's knowledge is firmly rooted in personal history and assimilated in her vision of the South. Historical fact emerges subtly and gives Scott freedom to move from the confines of a strictly historical framework.

Speaking in *Background in Tennessee* of her past, Scott says:

> If the curiosity exhibited has any philosophical character at all, investigation of a personal past may be a gesture of final humility. As the problem, at first stemming from what seems data on things specifically individual, extends itself, spreading circles toward the fringes of all known existence, one returns again, helplessly, to the particular—to a few certainties! It is as if, reaching into the sea, one drew forth, piecemeal, a heterogeneous debris; empty shells, tangles of weed, driftwood, bits of broken bottle—a little assembling of recognized facts and immediate apprehensions, drawn from vast regions unexplored and unexplorable! That people can accept their politics, their conventions, their convenient moralities as ultimate

reports on a cosmos, always amazes me. Fancy taking judgments made in inadequate contexts, not simply as matters for which they themselves will die, but as "principles" which demand and enforce final sacrifices of the lives of others! (125–6).

In 1929, the South—still, in many crucial ways, recovering from the Civil War and Reconstruction—was experiencing changes in life style, socially, politically, and industrially, and, like the rest of America, was about to be cast into the Great Depression. In Tennessee, Robert Penn Warren, Caroline Gordon, Allen Tate, and others were comparing their beliefs and ideas about the direction in which the South appeared to be moving, speaking out about the disruptive intrusion of industry. Recognized by this cohesive literary force, whose members would come to be known as the Agrarians, as an important southern writer and an intellectual, Scott agreed with some of their views. But being well-versed through her family's associations with issues the Agrarians addressed in *I'll Take My Stand* (1930), she disagreed with what she thought was their romantic view of the South, a view over-influenced by either a "before the war" or "after the war" time sense. Scott felt that the Agrarians, like many southerners, spoke not only of a South that had lost through the war, but of a South that had never been. Unlike Caroline Gordon, Ellen Glasgow, Elizabeth Madox Roberts, Kate Chopin, Grace King, and Mary Murfree, who confined their examination of political, economic, religious, and social impact to the South, Scott treated these problems as universal dilemmas.

Physically, *The Wave* is divided into 20 chapters; the chapters are often further divided. There are more than one hundred character analyses. It is interesting to note the disparity in the number of character sketches pointed out by reviewers and critics, indicating that a careful study of the novel is necessary—"some sixty separate narratives," "literally hundreds of characters," "a fluttering chaos of a hundred episodes," "must be almost a thousand in number."

By many critical standards, the success or failure of a novel depends upon whether it fulfills the authors intentions. And if, as a *Boston Transcript* reviewer wrote, "after a while the picture reels before the eye," then Scott has carried out her concept of the ceaselessness of a wave, the ceaselessness of war, the unrelenting agony of both if one is attempting to move against the force. Not only is Scott's conceptualization of *The Wave* important to one's understanding of the novel, but to those decrying the lack of a theme, her philosophical intentions establish a thematic *raison d'etre.*

Scott chose a description by Philip Lake in *Physical Geography* as an epigraph to *The Wave* and the key words in the description are "action of a wave."

> The water of the ocean is never still. It is blown into waves by the wind, it rises and falls with the tides. . . . The waves travel in some definite direction, but a cork thrown into the water does not travel with the waves. It moves up and down, to an fro, but unless it is blown by the wind or carried by a current it returns to the same position with each wave and does not permanently leave its place. . . . In deep water the motion of the particle at the surface [of the wave] is nearly circular. At the crest the movement of the particle is forward, at the middle of the hinder slope it is downward, in the trough backward, and at the middle of the front slope upward . . . waves have very little effect excepting near the surface . . . when a wave approaches a shelving shore it keeps its form as a wave until it is near the land and then the top falls forward and the wave breaks. This is due in part to the fact that the wave travels more slowly as the water becomes shallower. . . . When the water is deep close up to the shore, the waves, if they break at all . . . appear to throw themselves against the cliff . . . and the water dashes . . . some times to a very great height.

In her concept of individuals, caught up in war just as drops of water are caught up in a wave, Scott deliberately places her characters, and her examination of the action of a wave in relation to character situation precludes any helter-skelter, hodge-podge arrangement of episodes. She wrote a novel of individuals in a war and their perseverance. Scott believed in the humanity and the integrity of man, even though in her work, war lives in the heart of each man and is the law of life and recurring history.

In preparation for reading *The Wave,* two things should be avoided— an expectation that a design or pattern of relationships will emerge, and a search beneath the surface for hidden symbolism. It is the expectation that such a pattern will evolve that causes some readers to weary of the novel's length, the seeming repetition, the sense that one thing is merely being added to another, and those readers worry that there are no recurring characters.

There are several clustered incidents. For instance, fourteen surround Gettysburg, seven are devoted to the march of southerners from Charleston to Savannah, three are centered in the Wilderness, and in thirty pages the focus shifts from Grant to Lee and those surrounding them. But except for the fact that the characters in these episodes are in the same place and situation at the same time, they do not interact importantly with one another. They remain, for the most part, isolated in their individual thoughts and actions. Once the reader understands the wave/character concept and the techniques required for its execution—a concept that dictates the structure, but adds to the artistic whole—one can respond to the novel that Scott actually wrote.

The human condition is what Scott was striving to expose, and that goal justifies the technique of the novel. How else might one exhibit so many characters' scrutinization of their emotions, thoughts, and beliefs in over a hundred different situations? She could easily have chosen one or two emotions developed through a small number of characters or she could have emphasized any one of the human conditions that exist in political, social, economic, or religious contexts. Instead she dealt with those conditions as universal and made war "the only hero of the book."

All the religious elements, as in the Kalicz episode (first edition, 312–26), are presented overtly. Kalicz works in a foundry on New York's East River making cannons from molten iron. The illegitimate son of Marja, he thinks that because he has no real father and thus no real name, he is like Jesus. He reflects on the struggle of the angels with evil and compares all things in the foundry to Biblical times and the coming of the Lord. Kalicz fears the draft; he is caught up in the draft rioting and feels he owes some duty to this burning world. He burns a huge grain elevator, and as the mob comes for him, he imagines them yelling: "This is the man! This is he who called himself King of the Jews!"

Robert Welker contends in "Liebestod With a Southern Accent" (197–98), that Scott employed religious symbolism in several episodes. Actually, each episode could be disassembled and one could find whatever symbolism one is looking for, but if this symbolism is read, it perhaps may be the predilection of readers of the 1950s and 1960s to hunt for religious and mystic symbolisms, rather than a deliberate intention of Scott's. One must always return to the place of the individual in the force and disorder of the war, and in that context, symbolism, religious or otherwise, does not function importantly in the novel.

Some characters in *The Wave* "chafe under the inglorious restraint, long for the release of . . . energies, the larger life of a soldier, the opportunity for distinction" like Peyton Farquhar in Ambrose Bierce's "Occurrence at Owl Creek Bridge" to whom war seems to be an escape. Sometimes the longed-for escape is from a mother or other members of a family; Dickie Ross, whose rowboat bobs like a cork in Charleston Harbor, fervently hopes for a rebel attack on Yankee-held Fort Sumter and wishes the world, his mother, and his grandmother would "go clean to hell." Percy, a law clerk in Baltimore, wishes to escape everything connected with the war and nearly the whole human race (17). Will Shuck, after falling asleep at his guard post, is held captive in a tent awaiting execution. His is a mental escape; he recreates his trial in his mind, thinks about running so they will shoot him, and longs for sleep as a simple means of escape (97).

There are those who glory in the differentness of their lives and will be sorry to see the war end. Ginny, who delivers papers that tell of Lee's retreat, would be "sorry when the war was over, but he'd be rich by then" (284); Mary Murdoch, watching a brigade of Zouaves, hates to see these exciting times end (260); a German girl, Elizabeth, thanks God "for the war" (291). Johnny Perkins says philosophically, "And afterward it would come back—this anxiety for 'the worst,' like the hunger of a disease. He simply couldn't live without it . . ." (248).

The individual's search for the "why" of the war is a motif in several episodes. Jerry asks, "What's orders, what's Gettysburg, what's the war to you? . . . Don't care, don't care, I've *got* to rest til I can care about somethin'" (254). At Lynchburg, Jake feels "if he didn't get something in him again by noontime he was going to give up. . . . Here they were, tramping all over the world, and getting nowhere at all. . . . Lookin' for food, they were" (533). Bob, a flag bearer, surrounded by blazing trees in the Wilderness "clung the tighter to the colours which explained his sanity" (377). Jay, who has just killed a rebel soldier and lies mortally wounded himself, "wished, foolishly, that he would get a medal. That seemed to explain something" (260).

Scott's manipulation of Frazer, a soldier in the Confederate Army, illustrates that basic human characteristics, whether under normal circumstances or extreme circumstances, remain the same. Frazer, a poor white, married an older woman when he was eighteen, but he soon left her and became a slave trader in New Orleans. After working at many jobs and quitting each one, he joined the Confederate Army, but because he felt the Confederacy would fall, Frazer deserted. As he lies dying in the snow, Frazer regrets risking his life for all "this Southern quality" (191).

Scott disapproved of Mitchell's portrayal of Scarlett O'Hara as a Nietzchean heroine, an "overwoman" who possessed qualities unusual in the southern woman. Scott felt that southern women had always mustered an inherent courage in times of crises and protected and preserved the home front in the absence of their men. Scott's women have an indomitability of spirit that drives and preserves southern womanhood.

She creates her own starving Scarlett in Carrie, who is from a moneyed family in Vicksburg, but, displaced, has turned to prostitution. Carrying Scarlett's hysteria in the turnip patch to the streets of New Orleans, Scott conceives a situation in which Carrie, who lapses into strange dialogues, stabs a Federal soldier with a bread knife, not because of his motives for befriending her, but because she is maddened by extreme hunger (146).

Fanny May, seriously ill, insists upon being driven to the hills above Richmond in hopes of catching a glimpse of her husband in the battle below (159). Molly witnesses rebel soldiers burning her own and neighbors' houses and hides her silver spoons and her son's rag doll under her skirts (390). Midge quietly guards her misery when her wounded husband, Harry, has an operation and dies. "Her mind wanted her to die," but the body does not give in (612).

Scott uses the occasion of a bread riot to move one woman from the private role of leadership to a public one. Once the belles of Richmond, Miss Araminta and Miss Maude Mary live alone. Miss Araminta, the stronger of the two, goes to look for work so she and her sister will be able to buy food. She is caught up in a mob demanding more food from stores and bakeries, and though she resists the mob, she finds herself ironically at the head of it, having been proclaimed the leader by the other women. A man trying to persuade the women to stop their march draws this sharp response from the normally peaceful Araminta: "You have no right to interfere with these women—with *any* of us" (202).

An illustration of Scott's effective use of shifting point-of-view occurs in a long sub-divided episode in which Mrs. Sutter and her daughter Jemima are in the theater the night John Wilkes Booth shoots the President. Scott moves from Mrs. Sutter to Jemima, to Lincoln and those accompanying him, and to Booth, giving four different approaches to the killing through four accounts (565).

In Civil War novels, children for the most part are undeveloped characters, but Scott includes occasions that emphasize thoughts and problems of children. Henry Clay is torn between religion and the romanticism of war. "He didn't care about the religious part of it—if Mama would only let him go to war and wear a Confederate uniform . . . " (25). Rob and Ophelia Stoner take care of their slightly demented and sick mother in a rebel cabin and try to keep her unaware that they will probably be attacked by Yankees. Mrs. Stoner, after locking the children outside the cabin, hangs herself (401). In a more nearly universal response of children to war, Jamie and Ted run up and down the street behind the depot crying, "Right! Left! Company, *halt!* At-ten-*tion!* . . . Charge those Yankees, blame you, Bill . . ." (460).

In some chapters of *The Wave,* military leaders who must use idealism to reinforce their roles and enable them to lead the men under their command, assume another dimension; in tortured, reflective moments, they recharge their self-image before charging their men to battle. Especially effective are those chapters of meditation by Lincoln and Lee.

Scott uses varied devices to approach the war from many angles: a sermon in defense of slavery; accounts in Cincinnati and Vicksburg papers, showing how sympathies with either North or South affect the reporting of events; differences in war journalism between the *Richmond Appeal* and *The London Guardian;* letters between Lee and Grant. Never is the reader subjected to a mere description of a battle, never is the horror of war laid down in deliberate terms. Scott's war is a war of the senses, an assault on the senses.

In contrast to the assault of water in a wave, Scott uses water in its natural element to extend her title: water for drinking; mud; horses drinking; ships on the water, sinking with men jumping into blazing water; and rain, sometimes too much and sometimes, "Rain, God, if it would only rain" (30). She intentionally sustains water imagery to convey different aspects of the war throughout the novel and her style creates a mixture of sensation and sensory perception. Instead of "The man rode on a horse very fast," she describes his ride—"the landscape flashed in a perpetual torrent." Imagery is a vehicle for implying and enhancing action—"a rainfall of shot"; "fever seemed to run over his body"; "lava flood of cannonading"; "the band was a stream of discordance"; "drifting earth rolled beneath him"; "waves of burning that undulated visibly from the crackling mass"; "subsiding of her mother's footsteps"; and "the mob churned agitatedly."

Often, well-chosen words and phrases call up the image of water even when there is no water relation: "her rent garments flowed behind her"; "in a current of the tint of weak coffee"; "row of billowing figures in cane chairs"; "smoke, like a flood of stained wool"; "waves of reproach flow through his mind"; "a torrent of dark"; "on this watery harp, the flame itself shivering the dulled clouds and making them glorious, ran softly downward." The last word in the book is "water."

The Wave ends with Mrs. Deering and her niece Mildred watching the parade at the end of the war as General Sherman leads the soldiers down Pennsylvania Avenue. Mrs. Deering, who has lost two sons in the war, "feels that until this instant, she had led a mean, crabbed, and uneventful life" (620). She does not understand "how she had lived all these years and never known what it was really, to be a member of the human race, received here and anointed one of them, as by God in a church" (621). "Oh, what a pity we cannot always live on the plane of our finest moments! What she had felt when the salute had sounded and General Sherman appeared must be the real truth of things. And now—as with her boys—she could only feed on memory" (625). With this last line, Scott sums up the post-bellum heritage of the South.

In "The Evolution of Evelyn Scott," Robert Morss Lovett regarded Scott as an "unusual" and "unexpected" American writer because her purpose was "purely aesthetic." And he saw all her work as "preparation for the writing of *The Wave*, clearly an effort to do in a series of narrative episodes what Thomas Hardy has done in his epic-drama, *The Dynasts*. If Mrs. Scott's success is less impressive it is because the dramatic form compels a sense of unity which may be lost in short flights of narrative. It will be the failure of Mrs. Scott's readers if they take *The Wave* as a collection of short stories of the war."[12]

Scott's style is elaborate, her sentence structure is complex and often convoluted. Her characters, even when they are the great men about whom much Civil War fiction is written, exhibit particular human behavior in a particular situation. Upon the firm foundation of her intellect, her interests in various groups of people—Negroes, Jews, poor whites, politicians, military leaders—her strong compassion for and identification with the plight of women in the South, and her knowledge of history, Scott conceptualized and composed a novel unusual in content, character, tone, and structure. The book is long (625 pages) and may be considered, as Mark Van Doren said of *A Calendar of Sin,* "arduous reading." But he concluded, "It will repay the effort."

In the Preface to *Bread and a Sword,* the last book in which she addressed the plight of the artist in an alien society, Scott says:

> But the artist who feels a genuine need to revise an established form in a fashion which will represent accents in his experience which mark the divergence of his personal vision from the established, when he asks for a critical elucidation of his works, begs for a dedication of effort to comprehending him which is, usually, the world's gift to a few dead men only.

1. *The Saturday Review of Literature* V (July 6, 1929), 1163.

2. Malcolm Cowley, *After the Genteel Tradition* (New York: W. W. Norton, 1937), 248.

3. Ludwig Lewisohn, "Defiance," *The Nation* CXVII (August 8, 1923), 7a. *Expression in America* (New York: Harper & Brothers, 1932), 408–9.

4. Sinclair Lewis, review of *The Narrow House, The New York Times Book Review* (March 12, 1921), 18. Ernest Boyd, review of *The Narrow House, The Freeman* III (July 20, 1921), 425.

5. "Evelyn Scott," *Living Authors* (New York: H. W. Wilson, 1935), 366–7.

6. Joseph Wood Krutch, review of *The Wave* in *Wings* III (July 1929), 1. Bulletin of the Literary Guild.

7. This essay by Joseph Wood Krutch appeared also on the jacket cover of *The Wave.*

8. Ernest E. Leisy, *The American Historical Novel* (Norman: University of Oklahoma Press, 1950), 167. Robert Welker, "Liebstod With a Southern Accent," *Reality and Myth: Essays in American Literature,* ed. William E. Walker and Robert Welker (Nashville: Vanderbilt University Press, 1964), 76.

9. Robert A. Lively, *Fiction Fights the Civil War: An Unfinished Chapter in the Literary History of the American People* (Chapel Hill: University of North Carolina Press, 1957), 76.

10. Stephen Vincent Benét, "The Long Shadow of Bedford Forrest," The New York *Herald Tribune Books* XIII (February 21, 1937), 3.

11. *Louisiana Literature*, Vol. 1, No. 2 (March 1985). Transcript of a Public Radio Program, "Evelyn Scott: A Rediscovery," in which the focus was *The Wave*, with Lewis Simpson and Peggy Bach.

12. Robert Morss Lovett, *The Bookman* (October 1929), 153–5.

Evelyn Scott was born in 1893 in Clarksville, Tennessee, and died in 1963 in New York City. Selected publications: *Precipitations* (1920); *The Narrow House* (1921); *Narcissus* (1922); *Escapade* (1923); *The Golden Door* (1925); *In the Endless Sands* (1925); *Ideals* (1927); *Migrations* (1927); *The Wave* (1929); *Witch Perkins* (1929); *The Winter Alone* (1930); *Blue Rum* (under the pseudonym Ernest Souza), 1930; *A Calendar of Sin* (1931); *Eva Gay* (1933); *Breathe Upon These Slain* (1934); *Billy the Maverick* (1934); *Background in Tennessee* (1937); *Bread and A Sword* (1937); *The Shadow of the Hawk* (1941). Elizabeth Hardwick included *The Narrow House* and *Narcissus* in her series, *Recovered Fiction by American Women* (New York: Arno Press, 1977). The University of Tennessee Press reprinted *Background in Tennessee* (with an introduction by Robert Welker) in 1980. *The Wave* in 1985 and *Escapade* in 1987 (with an introduction by Peggy Bach) have been reprinted by Carroll & Graf.

On John Peale Bishop's
Many Thousands Gone

Mary Lee Settle

Many Thousands Gone IS A CONNECTED SERIES of stories about the
Civil War by John Peale Bishop. They happen in one small town on the
north-western border of Virginia, Charlestown, his childhood home,
which he called Mordington. It is near where one of the bloodiest and
most stupid battles of the war was fought—Antietam, or Sharpsburg.

I had the book recommended to me just after the Second World War
by an English writer who was the most perceptive reader I have ever
known. They were a revelation to me. Here was war as I knew it—life-
draining war as a way of living day after day after day.

Bishop's stories are of no great matters, no battles, no heroes, or only
one and a subtle one at that. Instead of the easier events, the battle cries,
the burnings, the heroic deaths, there is the silent, grey dying fall of years
of war. Dust gathers in the genteel houses; soldiers stand around in the
streets. The scenes are so memorable that when I go now to the towns

that are reflected in them, I seem to see the front stoops that look much as they did then, haunted by the shadows of bored, scared, sad young men.

They have faces instead of ranks and numbers. One darts out on a dare, a young young boy, teased, and kisses a Confederate woman, a woman we already know, middle-aged and pretentious, who has made her bonnet out of corn shucks and who has never been kissed by any man but her father, now dead, a general in the United States Army, whose uniform is kept under the mattress where her bed-ridden cousin lies, to protect it from being looted.

And yet was there anything in her appearance she would have changed? A little flush became her, and did not her whole air and bearing conspire to show, even to the casual observer, just what she was, the very type of young Southern womanhood, and one who gloried in the honor. She wore a pretty but plain debeige dress, trimmed with Confederate buttons and corresponding ribbons. And her bonnet, though she had plaited it with her own hands from the inside corn husks of last summer, might have rivalled the finest Milan straw, especially after she had added the ribbons and the rosettes of the same dye. Hers was not Vanity, but Pride. The race whose women could achieve such elegance under circumstances so poor must be indomitable. Even the Yankees should see that, though as a matter of fact the first soldiers she had encountered had refused to get off the sidewalk for her and had just stood and let her pass as best she could.

. . . .

"Wait a minute," said Danny. Down the street he saw coming toward them a mincing figure of a woman faded as an old piece of calico that's been left in the sun, a funny little bonnet on her head that was the only still thing about her. She held her head very stiff, but her skirts were gathered up in a pair of black gloves, and every time she passed a soldier, which was about every second, she lifted up her skirts as though she thought he was a mud puddle or something.

"She must be afraid of touching somebody," said Gallop.

Danny had slid down from the wall and was standing squarely in the middle of the sidewalk.

"Watch me!" he said.

As she came up to Danny, she drew her skirts in and made as if to pass between him and the mule wagon at the curb. With a step Danny was again in front of her, smiling. She stopped and her hoops swung against his legs. He reached out quickly, caught her with one arm round the waist, with the other drew her head toward him and kissed her unevenly, on the mouth. He held her, struggling, and kissed her again. Then his arms fell, he stood aside and stared at her with a grin.

A shrill whistle went up from the wall.

"Why, Danny," called the corporal, "why, Danny! You mustn't do that. It's not decent. She's old enough to be your mother" (first edition, 155–56, 164–65).

Grey dawn falls on the scars and dirt of a once highly polished table. A grease candle gutters where there has been beeswax. Nights stretch deeper and deeper into darkness, slow death, and passion as an act of survival.

Nowhere is energy's loss better shown than in these stories. It is the attrition of that illness without a name that is caused by war. Bishop drew his metaphors from his childhood, listening to the women who remembered—and remembered and remembered as if nothing had happened since that time when, as in Bertolucci's film, *Before the Revolution,* life ended and survival began.

It was true in Bishop's own life. It is as if he were like the border states, split in loyalties, never quite recovered, too civilized among the losses of lovely things and people, both grown rarer in memory, more gleaming, lovelier, in the long tired years of his memory and his mother's and his grandfather's, whose stories he listened to on the porches of Charlestown in the huge summer evenings.

His own family, like the part of the south where he lived, was split. Behind the Chippendale, shadowed under the politeness, he caught the echoes. His own grandfather had come south from Connecticut to make a life for himself before the Civil War, and his father had been stoned in the street as a "Yankee" by other children when he was a little boy. All of that is reflected in the longest story in the book, which gave the book its title, *Many Thousands Gone.* A Union colonel comes back to his home and takes revenge on his unfeeling Presbyterian family by burning down the house he has visited, the house he slept in as a child.

Colonel Strother flung himself down in the great flowered and flounced arm-chair by the dark fireplace and stretched his legs out, propping his rowelled heels over the brass fender. Yes, this would be the place—this was the room his father and mother had always occupied when they came visiting. Nothing was changed: the blue of the paper on the wall was a little more faded, there was a broken pane in the window. But the smell was the same, the remembered smell of Virginia bedrooms, like wet straw. And the sash, he saw, was still sustained by a stick; the window weights had not yet been mended. . . .

. . . .

Nothing ever changed in Virginia, nothing but the seasons. It had been winter then, and winter when he was born. It must have been here in this room.

"By God!" He started like a man surprised, pulling in his long legs. "I never thought of it before. . . ."

. . . .

"I always knew she [his aunt] had something on my mother. It's funny how little gets by a child. But just the same, it's not that. I just don't like them. I don't like their manners, I don't like their ways." And he said again, "I despise the ground they walk on." He snatched the slat that held the window and let it fall with a thud and a sudden splintering of glass. "They are all alike—shiftless and pretentious. Virginians!" He turned toward the door. "And to think, by God, I was born one—" (175, 176, 178).

Bishop found a voice in the fatigues of memory instead of the false past that was more strident, falser, more dangerously self-deceptive in the South. He caught the self-questioning of soldiers, "You have to fight, whether you want to or not. If you don't, you're never quite sure you're a man" (123). And there is the definition of a soldier, told by a veteran of the war, "What is a soldier, but a man you can count on?" (30)

He defined in these stories what made the Civil War different from the wars that came before and those (he was an officer in France in the First World War) that came after it. "It never, in its worst suffering, surpassed the human scale."

For me, finding them, there was another dimension. They were about my own part of the world, the highlands and beautiful valleys of the Alleghenies that became West Virginia as an act of war. The stories broke through and shattered for me some of the holiest misconceptions of my own childhood learning. They quietly and finally overturned the icons, one after another.

So it was no surprise to find out that not only was John Peale Bishop from my own part of the world but that he was a stylist who reflected the kind of European writing that I most admired. There was the honest vision of the scenes of Fabrizio at Waterloo in Stendhal's *Charterhouse of Parma*. There was, too, an echo for me of the work of Turgenev, its quiet insistence on reality, its subtle burning truths.

It was, for me, an admiration that had come out of profound experience. I had been in World War II not long before reading *Many Thousands Gone*. The slow and inexorable disintegration of domestic life in the attrition of war rang truer than anything I had ever read about the Civil War. Only Ambrose Bierce's stories had touched on this. The whole of Civil War literature, up to that time, seemed to have been stories of heroics, tragedies, earth-moving, dramatic events instead of the slow, deadening waste of time that I had just witnessed and been a part of.

In 1931, Bishop wrote to Allen Tate about these stories: "They are, as you know, conceived with the intent of providing a criticism, long in time, of the civilization from which we both derive. I could not present heroism in terms of the gallant Pelham." Pelham, dead at twenty-three, a handsome, brave flirt, was for the South the epitome of dashing Confederate glory. "My hero who defends the earth from which he sprung is Charlie Ambler." Charlie, by the way, had the toughest Southern mother in literature since Mrs. Blount in Conrad's *Arrow of Gold*. "My Southern belle is the faded and affected Celie Cary, my evaluation of the ancient courtesy is the tipsy and bewildered Dr. Burwell."

Bishop was his own critic. Thank God he did it after, instead of before, the fact. "Facing our own past is a way of facing the present," he said, and he remembered that a child is closer to women than to men, and that reminiscences of women are "more fluent" than those of men. "In all wars," he said, in an uncustomary general indictment for so meticulous a thinker and writer, "men are silent or liars."

This was what he thought he recorded. What he had done for me was to write stories so compassionate and so true that I remembered them for years as if I had experienced them instead of finding the images in prose.

"The sun was sudden on the river," became a recall of sun and not of words. The soldiers who had come from battle with their feet bound in white satin, the hidden silver, the broken wine glasses, and the haunting refrains were the undercurrents of defeat, still, when I was a child. He was a generation before me, but things don't change that fast in the South, or didn't, not then. That echo of the lives of disappointment that are mankind's and womankind's inheritance was blamed on THE WAR in our part of the South. "You think life is going to be so wonderful, and then you find out that it has been wonderful," Celie Cary thinks in the story, "Many Thousands Gone" (214).

Bishop was a man of wit. Humor was too bald for him, optimism too easy an assumption. At Princeton, where he graduated in 1917, he was thought of already as a stylist and a dandy, older than his friends Scott Fitzgerald and Edmund Wilson. He was a published poet long before the others.

He is remembered—alas, our loss—as a friend of the great of his time, and not as a literary personality in his own right, a position that, with the streak of pride that accompanies the genteel shyness of the mountain kingdom, he would have thought demeaning. The new offended him; his attitudes were older than he was. He joined no new movement, used no tangled modern language, can be accused of prejudices through some of his words that all of his contemporaries held as well.

He retreated, instead, into being a man of letters. It is a loss to us all, that drain of energy, that falling into what Yeats called "the gentle sensitive mind."

But he left work that should never be buried in academia's arid precincts. It is some of the finest writing, principally poetry, of his time. He was not an "Agrarian," but he knew them and, for the most part, was— or should have been—their model.

As a novelist he made the mistakes that poets tend to make—masked autobiography without the intuitive jump he made in these short stories—but his one novel, *Act of Darkness,* fragmented as it is, is remarkable as these stories are, in scene after scene. Bishop seems to have been, always, an elegiac man, a man "acquainted with grief." Nowhere is this better seen than in his elegy on the death of Scott Fitzgerald, "The Hours," and in *Many Thousands Gone.*

He died in 1944. He had dictated his own epitaph to his wife.

Long did I live
Consistent, lonely, proud.
Not death, but fear of death,
Restores us to the crowd.

John Peale Bishop was born in 1892 in Charles Town, West Virginia, and died in 1944 in Cape Cod, Massachusetts. Selected publications: *Green Fruit* (1917, poems); *Many Thousands Gone* (1931, out of print); *Act of Darkness* (1935); *Collected Essays* (1948); *Collected Poems* (1948).

On DuBose Heyward's *Peter Ashley*

Rosellen Brown

THE "OLD SOUTH," LIKE ANY AREA that possesses distinctive characteristics and a complex and tragic history, has served many purposes
in the world's imagination. Henry James, for one, fell in love with
Charleston, whose fabled houses recalled "the fallen pride of provincial
palazzini," whose walled and secret gardens called to mind some "little
old-world quarter of quiet convents."

No surprise that a writer who made his meanings out of vivid
oppositions—American youth and innocence vs. European age and
experience—should have appropriated Charleston as an emblem of the
lost beauty of a more genteel age. Whatever corruption or oppressiveness
might have existed there he conveniently overlooked in the search for
a memory of near-sacred traditions, physical loveliness with perhaps a
touch of wistful sadness overlaid, and the "simpler" charm of a rigidly
stratified society. "One sacrificed the North on the spot," James admitted,
whether with reluctance or relief we can only guess.

DuBose Heyward had not yet cast his backward glance at Charleston when James took his brief tour through the Carolinas. Nor did Heyward have to be an avid reader of the expatriate James to share the same propensity for making fable of reality and casting antebellum Charleston in a kind memorializing light. Heyward did and did not stop there. With the advantage of lifelong familiarity, the Charleston-born Heyward, in *Peter Ashley,* was far more critical of his home than any visitor like James could have been. On the other hand, given the possibilities for the kind of candor that a great novelist like James arrived at, Heyward pulled back at the brink and abandoned, or at least fumbled, the critical project he seemed to have begun.

In the end, having prepared him for truth, Heyward sacrificed his Peter Ashley to the picturesque fogs of romantic fiction. His own ambivalence about what mattered most to a man, his independence of mind or the mindless demands of his "heritage," coupled with an outmoded conception of plot, confuse the picture and make *Peter Ashley*, an interesting book, far less interesting than it could have been.

Edwin DuBose Heyward was born in Charleston in 1885, the son of an old, comfortable family that had fallen on hard times. He was descended from Kings' officers, Lord Proprietors, a Signer of the Declaration of Independence and a host of confederate officers; his ancestors had had large land and slave holdings and had lost their fortunes through a variety of inopportune dealings (some say over those slaves; others insist it was cotton). In either event, by the time DuBose was born his father worked in a mill.

When he was two, his father was killed in a work-accident, cruelly reducing the already modest circumstances of his family but providing the boy with what, in hindsight, seems almost a textbook model for a literary southern childhood. As Julian's mother says in Flannery O'Connor's "Everything That Rises Must Converge," her life a mirror of the South's helpless fall from grace, people could be in reduced circumstances but "never forget who they were." When it came to Charleston, Heyward was indeed like Julian, though a more polite version: remembering the family mansion which Julian had never seen, "he never spoke of it without contempt or thought of it without longing."

DuBose's own mother played out the once-grand region's humbling and proud refusal to be pitied. She struggled to maintain status by refusing to work at any job, clerking or office work, in which she would be seen in public; instead she did sewing, took in guests and, according to one source, even tried to sell poems to magazines ("often about Negroes"—these from the mother of the man who was to write *Porgy*).

DuBose was kept in private school despite the family's penury but quit early to go to work; eventually he found his way into the insurance business. He was sick often and it was during a mountain retreat to which he'd gone during one of these illnesses that he seems first to have begun to paint and then to have turned seriously to writing (though a one-act play had been produced much earlier, in 1913). H. L. Mencken in a famous essay writes of the South around this time as "the Sahara of the Bozarts," and in *Peter Ashley* Heyward was to acknowledge the undeniable Philistinism of his beloved Charleston. But the desire to write had somehow taken hold, and, though he was not, as glimpsed in several biographical studies, overtaken by anything like a fierce or willful passion for self-expression, he did devote himself emphatically from around 1917 until his death in 1940 to poetry, fiction and the stage. His most famous work, of course, is the *Porgy* that began as a short novel, became a play in 1927, and in 1935 was transformed into the classic Gershwin musical through which many of us were first introduced to Charleston via the wild and fateful entanglements of a local alley Heyward renamed Catfish Row.

Heyward was attracted to the lives of black Carolinians—his novel *Mamba's Daughters*, a book of poems called *Jasbo Brown,* and the play *Brass Ankle* are attempts to write from within "Negro" life. He also published one novel, *Lost Morning,* about the bitterness of an artist's compromise with local mores—the Sahara Mencken spoke of. But *Peter Ashley* (1932) is the single work in which his preoccupation with class, family rank and tradition, as well as the pressing history of the start of Civil War, come into play. The novel he made of all those is more confused than clarifying but it delivers some pictures of pre-Civil War Charleston worth studying.

Bear in mind as you read about it, though, that *The Sound and the Fury* as well as *Sartoris, As I Lay Dying, Sanctuary* and *Light in August* all emerged in the three years prior to *Peter Ashley.* Given such new standards of daring and difficulty—of both conception and execution—Heyward's style and structure hark back even more obviously to the conventional popular novels of the 19th century, still very much alive and accessible to the ordinary reader. More significantly, although he raises the kinds of questions only an ambitious author would try to deal with—Heyward had written to a friend about his idea for "an epic novel" to deal with the period just before and during the Civil War—he answers them with infuriating laxness and a lack of clarity that demonstrates that, as someone said about the Charleston compatriots he helped organize into a Poetry Society, a little oasis in a cultural wasteland, "although serious, they were not serious enough."

Peter Ashley begins in 1860 on Meeting Street in Charleston. (For anyone who has been in Charleston, there is an indelibility to the names of streets and buildings, partly because the town is so small and partly because it wears its history so palpably and, taking it seriously, invites—even commands—the visitor to do the same.) Pierre Chardon, of French-Huguenot lineage, an educated aristocratic pro-Union man, watches the completion of the signing of the Ordinance of Secession and hears South Carolina pronounced an independent commonwealth. It is an exciting beginning for a story about the pre-war South, this scene in which "a horde of jubilant Secessionists" surges forth from the hall and surrounds the alienated Chardon with their enthusiasm for a cause he thinks both morally repugnant and futile.

Having fought his own battles as a volunteer in the Mexican War from which he returned in 1846 to find his wife and children dead in a yellow fever epidemic, Chardon has informally been "given"—loaned may be the word—his nephew Peter Ashley to raise. Peter's mother has recognized that her lonely and grief-stricken brother would not only be comforted but might make a more congenial guardian than her own bluff and hearty family for the very sensitive Peter.

And it is true: Pierre raises the young man to go off to Harvard and Oxford, which hardly surprises his real father, who had recognized from the start that he'd never make a planter. But his father's reaction to the news that Peter wants to be a poet is classic (and all too current even in greener places than that Sahara): ". . . even for a bookworm there were dignified alternatives—medicine, the law, statecraft. 'But great God, Pierre, not a poet! I have done nothing to deserve that!'" (first edition, 31).

Peter, worse yet, sails home from Oxford into the rising gale of war, and here is where he shows himself still more out of step with his real family and his compatriots. Ironically, though he is greeted when he steps off the ship as "one of the first who has come home to fight," in fact he shares his uncle's lack of enthusiasm for the spirit of war. He has, in fact, come home not to fight but to write, and instead finds "like that— my world (is) gone." His uncle freely and proudly takes responsibility: "I have taught you to think, and that is fatal in time of war." Uncle Pierre warns him that his position as skeptic will "not be altogether pleasant . . . If you do not enlist at once (your father) will probably suspect me of practicing Unionist black magic upon you" (62). He promises "for the nonconformist . . . only the approval of a small, stubborn, inner voice that will not be silenced. And for food, the bread of that utter loneliness that is possible only in the press of a crowd" (103).

But for Peter there is more separating him from Charleston than ideological views of slavery and secession. He is the quintessential outsider, an artist and an isolate, especially in this city of unintrospective joiners. "Ever since I returned," he confides to his uncle, "I have felt that I was looking on from another star. Yesterday when the crowd cheered, for a moment I seemed one of them. Then something perverse took possession of me and I was back outside of it all again. I've got to be a part of it. I've got to feel it here inside of me. It isn't a question of the Union. I haven't even that excuse. It is just that if I went in now, feeling as I do, I'd be an alien in either army. I'd be breaking faith with myself" (62).

Peter walks through a parade of pro-war demonstrators—instead of "a preface to the grim business of civil war," he finds the crowd engaged in "some new and thrilling game. The atmosphere was more comparable to that of Race Week than to the prospect of imminent death" (64). The city which he'd always seen as "predominantly English in temperament" suddenly seems Latin to him in its excitability. Again he wavers, almost one of them, then flung to the margins by his inability blindly to join the mass in its enthusiasm, uncertain whether it is forced gaiety to hide "the hideous premonition of war" or "the voice of a people" marching in a congruence of ideals. He extricates himself from the pageant and enters the newspaper office where he will presumably pursue his own dream of writing, serving the exhortations of his own voice.

These are the basic tensions Heyward sets out to explore in *Peter Ashley* and they are compelling. We are given a young man with his own unique personality, demanding of himself and others, who marches to his own drummer, but the story also promises a conflict between individual and collective action. When reason dictates resistance to a call to arms, how can one refuse to join the majority without becoming an outcast? As forces mustered for the Civil War, that most intimate of conflicts, what were the limits of debate? What kinds of dissent were possible, and on whose part, and how were they received by a population desperate to assure unanimity in its ranks? How common was dissent in 1860 and what became of it? It's a pity we never really hear Peter and his (would-be) friends discuss their doubts and fears in any depth. There is a single scene in which Peter enters into something like debate (though it's more like monologue) but it is Heyward's presentation of a block of information, not a believable speech by a real character. His dissent and that of his uncle are alluded to more than demonstrated; even, as we'll see, the action that emerges in response to Peter's reluctance to join the majority is muddied by appearing (in spite of protestations to the contrary) to stem from romantic, not ideological, rivalry.

These are classic moral dilemmas that will always be with us—every war tests the elasticity of the population that is asked to support it. But this was not the Vietnam War, or the Persian Gulf: the specifics of the Civil War, fought in the very yards and meadows and sometimes even the parlors of one set of antagonists, a challenge to the economic and social foundations of their own lives, give an author a great many opportunities to nurture the painful conflict at home. But Heyward seems to do everything he can to deflect his story from the highly significant questions it suggests.

Early on, for example, he shows Peter as a boy of sixteen disturbed by an advertisement he sees for a slave girl whose sale is being engineered, with conspicuous care, by the man who is clearly her father. His Uncle Pierre is fascinated by what seems to him an act of defiance on the part of the slave owner, who ("a wastrel and a gambler") is being sold out but who is taking his revenge as he goes under. "Read this advertisement seriously in all of its implications, and suddenly this mulatto ceases to be an act of God performed miraculously without the assistance of the Caucasian race, and if she ceases to be a miraculous creation, why, so probably do thousands of others." He muses about the perpetrator, Archie Holcombe, who "has taken our virtues and by his excesses has made them vices . . . has caricatured us and made us seem ignoble . . . He emerges as a revolutionary, and a revolutionary may be an even more vital factor in life than a gentleman" (34).

But when he suggests that he and Peter have Holcombe to dinner some day "to get his side of the question," presumably of slavery, responsibility, obligation—of power—Peter is not much impressed by the man's honesty and fearlessness, nor by what his uncle sees as his "diabolical sense of humor." Instead he announces with rather uncharacteristic snobbery, "I don't want to have him here. . . . He's not our kind."

Uncle Pierre insists that if Peter is going to write he must see life impartially, must be "more than a spokesman for your class." Is Peter, as even the most sensitive adolescent can believably be, caught in a stage of narrow class chauvinism and self-protection? Will this be the beginning of his instruction in human dealings with difference? Does he now or later give much thought to the substance of his uncle's critique of a way of life built on hypocrisy and the oppressive wielding of power? Or does he, early, have the makings of an apologist for the inhumanity of slaveholding?

A little bit of both, as it happens. Repelled by some of the excesses (such as whipping) attendant upon the ownership of human beings, he discovers what separates the tolerable from the intolerable: "good form," like that which "surrounded the institution of dueling or behavior upon the ballroom floor." There were "decencies to be observed," there was a gentleman's unwritten code. "That the conventions of his particular locality and class had crystallized from the attitude of individuals of high moral character was a matter for gratitude, Peter thought. It made it easier in the present crisis to reconcile conscience and necessity. It buttressed the threatened edifice with certain Christian virtues and endowed the impending conflict with the indispensable elements of a crusade" (71).

In one scene a particularly harsh slave-trader repels him because, by the physical cruelty he inflicts in his inspection of potential property, and because he is known for casually, even purposely, splitting up slave families, he is a more dangerous enemy to the complacency of the others "than an abolitionist, for he held their peace of mind in daily jeopardy. His existence in the flesh before them imperiled the beliefs by which they lived, in the support of which they were prepared to die. . . . But they

were gentlemen. All that they could give him was . . . silence." In order
to foil the trader's interest in buying at auction a particularly fine and
independent-looking young man (whose gaze carries "the sullen lumi-
nousness of molten ore") Peter joins two friends in outbidding him. "I
thought you were a Unionist," one of the friends says, "and it's rumored
you are even for emancipation. But I am glad to see that you are still one
of us" (82).

Peter does not reflect on this scene beyond his momentary surprise and
disappointment that the slave shows no particular gratitude at his salvation. (True salvation being absolute, not relative, he is not particularly
impressed at his slightly ameliorated fate. Having been called a "damned
worthless rascal" by one of his new owners—affectionately, we are
to understand—"the negro grinned under the familiar and reassuring
words of abuse.")

Whatever the rumors that he is unsympathetic to slavery, the scene
at the auction only serves to remind Peter what a superior lot these
Charlestonians are: "They looked remarkably alike, bearing as they did
the marks of their class. Clean cut, high bred, erect. Movements free,
easy, assured. Eyes direct and candid. Not the eyes of analysts, but of a
people with an enormous capacity for faith in its accepted beliefs. Faces
singularly free from the marks of mental conflict, hale and ruddy from
good whisky, offset by hard riding under a semi-tropical sun" (80). An
uncle of his sums it up finally. Travel though he may have, trying to "find
out" for himself, in the end he has decided that the United States has
proved "preeminently the most desirable; of all the states South Carolina
stood far in the lead; and of all sections of South Carolina the Parish of
St. John's is infinitely the most superior" (251). Is this complacency or the
abiding love of home that justifies defense to the death? Is it possible to
see it as both and survive the conflict?

The auction at which Peter discovers himself once again attracted and
repelled by his fellows takes place quite early in the novel. If Peter is
pulled this way and that, morally and aesthetically speaking, we feel he
has plenty of time to clarify his commitments. But what preoccupies him
(and alas Heyward as well) for the center of his story does not turn out to
be the question of how to live honestly in a flawed community but rather
how to win the love of a coy charmer named Damaris Gordon.

Every cliché of the High Romantic style is piled on Damaris's beautiful white shoulders, and in pursuit Peter is driven far beyond platitude into actual physical danger on her behalf: he is challenged and must rise to a duel by his crude and ungentlemanly rival Archie Holcombe, the "revolutionary" who so fascinated Uncle Pierre by his lack of hypocrisy over the issue of claiming one's bastard slave-children. Holcombe is so reprehensible (and so much the foul breath of the future that waits to overpower the high-toned life of the South) that, not only the father of slave-children, he also seems the spiritual grandfather to Fay, the "common" second wife of the judge in Eudora Welty's *The Optimist's Daughter*—Snopes or fallen Sartoris, Archie and Fay are what happens to good form when gentlemen blink.

So: there is a love story complete with jealousy, misunderstanding, and a joyous denouement; there is a horse race, just as hotly contested; there is also, tangentially, Peter's disillusionment with journalism (or is it art?)—the issue is left inconclusive—when a heartfelt story, his own version of the horse race, is pitilessly mangled by his editor, Who Does Not Understand. Then, goaded into a preposterously well-informed and eloquent public discussion of what he saw while he was abroad of England's negative opinion about secession and slavery, Peter is condemned by Holcombe as a "damned abolitionist"—fighting words when they're uttered by a rival in love—and, terrified that he has broken faith with "his own" (though Holcombe is the very man he pronounced years earlier "not our kind"), Peter regrets his treason. "If being an abolitionist meant that he was opposed to the principle of slavery, very well, he was one. But it meant more. This had nothing to do with literal definitions. Into the single word was packed the poison of a hundred insults. It meant that he was a traitor to his clan, to his past. That here on his own soil he was being disinherited, flung out, a man without a country" (207). Somewhere in the previous few hundred pages Peter seems to have gone from a tormented outcast proud of his integrity to a man willing to compromise because of the "incomparable beauty . . . (of) his town, his state. And these men about him, waiting, headstrong, blind perhaps, but generous, impulsive, passionate, surrounding him, pressing in upon him with the weight of a single unalterable idea. . . . The rhythm of the crowd pounded in his blood" (207–08). From there it is a short step to the absurdity of the duel, for which Peter prepares as if he were going to war. (There is some fine prose here, as he hones his responses and readies himself for the first physical combat of his life.)

Injured in this questionable but not deeply questioned execution of the duty of his class, Peter spends a long time recuperating, claimed finally by Damaris (who, it turns out, not to our surprise, loved him all the time) and sinking—one critic calls this his "self-inflicted lobotomy"—into "a life that was completely satisfactory, that had beauty, harmony, dignity, continuity." The last portion of *Peter Ashley* is a fairly gratuitous narration of the attack on Fort Sumter which Peter presumably assists in by carrying messages for what is now unquestioningly "his side." It is an odd and infuriatingly ill-digested hunk of writing (so little a piece of the whole that Heyward ultimately published it separately as a short collaborative book called *Fort Sumter* alongside a portion of a novel called *Look Back to Glory* by Herbert Ravenel Sass).

The real moral summary of *Peter Ashley* is more properly found around three-fifths of the way through when the fondly admiring Uncle Pierre says to Damaris, soon to become his niece-in-law, that "Man is a strange creature . . . strange, yet simple. And still as primitive as Adam. You may lash him to war with a patriotic ideal. But in battle he forgets all of that. He must have a symbol to fight for. Something that he can compass with his imagination . . ." (242–43). Later, after Peter has yielded up the last of his independence and recalcitrance, Pierre thinks about his nephew "how unaffectedly emotional he had become, how unquestionably he accepted what he was told, how complete had been his escape from the tyranny of reality." Was "the comfort of a present illusion . . . worth the terror of the ultimate tragic awakening"? (302)

In the latter case it is the possibility of winning the war that Pierre sees for the illusion it is; at best, even if Peter comes back alive, he will never again be "this boy . . . with the glory of youth upon him, and his faith like a bright, unfleshed blade in his hands" (304). Peter, Hamlet-like, has hardly been presented as this golden boy but that is the way his uncle chooses to remember and mourn him: he has somehow metamorphosed into a Norman Rockwell figure of innocence, his light about to be dimmed. Uncle Henry James might have approved, though surely he'd have done a subtler job of it.

Uncle Pierre, so prescient now about boys at war, has earlier shown himself less than a revolutionary (to annex his word for the odious Archie) when he delivers himself of his heroic view of womanhood: "We demand that they satisfy the hunger of our bodies, and still remain divine; that they conceive our children, and continue immaculate. . . . We have created a deity of our womanhood, and we can forgive it anything short of disillusioning us." But he goes on to say about his long-dead wife, when asked about "mental congeniality," "That . . . is not in the curriculum. So few of us demand it . . . besides a superficial brilliance, we ask nothing. I never explored her mind. . . . She satisfied my need for beauty" (192–93). He sounds only partially regretful. It is the same mixed message—in fact, clearly, it is the author's unmediated message— that Pierre gives every time: weary disillusion, a fatalist's sense that things will always stay the way they are, a distant comprehension of all he seems to have learned too late and can describe but cannot seem to teach Peter with enough force to protect him from the same mistakes. And Peter, raised to claim for himself the kind of superior critical judgment taught in his uncle's house but no capacity to act on it, is ultimately just as weightless in the scales of behavior.

All the tension of his earlier resistance to the happy mob has been obliterated by the opportunity to be a homesteader alongside this lovely woman, to be a husband and father, a link in the endless chain of uncomplaining citizens propagating everywhere. He marches off to war, perhaps to return, perhaps to yield up his life for a myth. The book closes on an elegiac poem (Uncle Pierre's, as one might expect) about harvest in the autumn fields.

Nowhere is it written that the protagonist of a novel must discover in himself heroic depths of resistance. What makes characters memorable, in fact, is their refusal or inability to simplify their choices and give us perfect models of behavior or belief. Why, then, is *Peter Ashley* at the same time so engaging a book and yet so irritating? And why does Heyward seem not so much the orchestrator of hard questions as the author slightly out of control?

For one thing, he has not made a believable character out of his hero. Peter exemplifies any number of nobel aspirations—political thinker, poet, lover, youthful idealist and dreamer, all of them attractive—but Heyward has shown them to us in succession; he seems a series of desires and frustrations hung out like banners for us to view. There is little organic growth in Peter from reluctant outcast to complacent team player—the contemporary term would be *co-opted*. Heyward has wanted to show the power of the collective to work corrosively on the spirit of a single man, but the irony of Peter's decline is muffled by its forced quality. Where do the old arguments against the gentleman's game of good form disappear to? In jerky alternation they advance and recede and finally, with far too little convincing outcry either from character or author, Peter becomes the man who listens to Balaam's ass and believes him when he says the South can be victorious and its least supportable institutions justified.

Certainly it's true that most of the rebels of any generation end up becoming its pillars, stiffened and immoveable. The "conservatizing" influence of wife- and land-owning do, more often than not, prevail. But Peter's fall from rebelliousness seems contrived, willed, his inner life felled at a blow and we no longer privy to it. He reflects not a bit, neither nostalgically nor guiltily, on his early criticism of Charleston's unthinking solidarity. The psychological, not to mention the ideological and tactical, underpinnings of his allegiances are slighted, and what we get by the close of the novel is a wooden man, a victim of Forces, rather than a true sufferer of conflict and, perhaps, of an excessive zeal to resolve it.

Nor does it help that so much of the book is devoted to the pursuit of the perfect woman, a smart, possibly superficial coquette whose wiles are stylishly false (unlike, say, Jane Austen's head-clearing women whose every word, gesture, even choice of dress, enacts a moral challenge). If the irony of *Peter Ashley* is in part meant to be that the hero gets the heroine and thereby unwittingly forecloses on his kingdom (which is actually autonomy of spirit, not a plantation with a nursery), Heyward cannot spend so many pages leading us in routine romantic pursuit. "Happily ever after," in this book, is a dupe; it is the very worst thing that can happen to Peter. (Damaris is an ambiguous figure at first—the kind "who breaks down resistance, disarms at a glance, and endows the process of surrender with a strange sensual delight"—but she becomes all cliché thereafter.) We are meant to root for the lovers during their courtship, and then, too late, remember that women like Damaris weave dangerous webs that stifle spiritual independence. It is the convention of the love story that's to blame—a pity Heyward did not resist or transcend it.

Finally, I have the sense that DuBose Heyward is closer to Pierre Chardon than to his nephew: he is, that is, a canny diagnostician whose own wishes are never quite clear. When it comes to describing the symptoms of mindlessness and conformity, his eye is remarkably acute. But is he appalled or, on a level just beneath the surface, satisfied in some unacknowledged way by the status quo just as he was satisfied to worship dumbly at his wife's beauty? Is the "gentleman's code" that equates slavery and ballroom dancing truly as much an affront to him as he seems to suggest?

One critic, William Slavick, puts it well: "Heyward seems to be saying, if with some irony, that to live with one's fellows, one must accept and share society's values, whatever they are, so that social conformity becomes the ironic hero of the novel, with power over the heart and will" (*DuBose Heyward,* 132). Although we are meant to see Peter deteriorate into complacency, I am less convinced than I ought to be that the warmth and comfort of the life he's chosen (or allowed himself to be chosen by) isn't, in Heyward's mind, worth the suppression of dissent. Peter is a man bought out, lock, stock and barrel, by the idea of Home; in spite of all, the deal has something to be said for it. The facts and the tone do not quite correspond.

The ambiguity is unsettling and, I think, unintentional and I would guess that the narrator's failure of distance, his willingness to compromise in the hard parts, typifies Heyward's own: Edna Ferber, snobbish, of course, in her own way, said about DuBose Heyward, "He is incurably a Southern gentleman, and he doesn't know it's not done."

Nonetheless, *Peter Ashley* has some extremely lucid writing to recommend it. If it were possible to loosen it from the armature of its conventional story and simply enjoy its descriptions of Charleston at the brink of war and of irremediable change; if it were possible to detach some of its characterizations from their integration in the whole—in short, if Heyward had not weighed down the parts with their obligation to pull the awkward vehicle of plot, *Peter Ashley* would be a superb evocation of the burden of choice in a difficult time. Only one class is represented, and for the most part one sex; but Heyward writes beautifully about the abstract questions that must present themselves to both public and private speculation at their meeting point. There are individual speeches— hardly conversational encounters—that are wholly absorbing, grave and satisfying meditations on the highly charged situation. That his own voice tends to prevail as if he were an essayist, so that the speakers have little idiosyncracy or naturalness, is the fault in part of the outdated models he took for his novel. Combine this with his own confusions as a born Charlestonian bred to art and alienation and it is no wonder that *Peter Ashley* is at the same time well worth reading yet far from satisfying.

Heyward knew his own weaknesses: He wrote about his work in a 1920 letter, "I cannot quite find the middleground between the melodramatic and the strong, the realistic and the romantic, but some day, who knows." One can't help feeling that, in the end, the debt he owed his background accounts for the too-frequent triumph of sentimentality over realism in his books. Sheer socially-dictated politesse—at least a gratitude for belonging that blows gently on the heat of criticism—cooled his irony down to a slow burn. Is there a more familiar frailty of the Southerner than his allowing manners to overwhelm morals? *Peter Ashley* is a perfect exemplar of the conflict wrought in its author right before our eyes.

DuBose Heyward was born in 1885 in Charleston, South Carolina, and died in 1940 in Tryon, North Carolina. Selected publications: *Carolina Chansons: Legends of the Low Country,* with Hervey Allen (1922, poems); *Porgy* (1925; play version, with Dorothy Heyward, 1927; musical libretto for *Porgy and Bess* 1935); *Mamba's Daughters* (1929); *Peter Ashley* (1932; out of print).

On MacKinlay Kantor's
Long Remember

ROBIE MACAULEY

A LITTLE PENNSYLVANIA COUNTRY TOWN drowses under the July sun. There is a "placid opulence" about the morning—and "you could smell the honey and the hot, drying grain." Many of the fields just beyond the end of the streets have a froth of white daisies or bright green clover. At Codori farm, somebody sharpens a scythe and the "juicy *weet, weet* of a cold whetstone keens against the solid blade."

Dr. Duffey, the town medico, has burned his hands making a tonic over a spirit lamp and Elijah Huddlestone has to drive the buggy as the doctor makes his rounds. Tyler Fanning is on sick leave from the army because he has chronic indigestion. Irene, his beautiful young wife from Philadelphia, lives with his mother and father in a big house just outside of town. A fat man named Elmer Quagger has been fired from his job at the factory because he's considered a subversive. Pentland Bale, a respected man in the community, has just died and his grandson Dan has come back from out west in Minnesota. Thus, at the beginning of Mac-

Kinlay Kantor's novel, *Long Remember,* the small town cycle of life and death is going on much as always.

But this is not another American regional novel—the town is a very particular small town called Gettysburg and the very particular time in history is early June, 1863. Although no one there quite realizes what is happening, two great armies are slowly converging on this place. That sunny morning holds small hint that the dusty streets, the wheat fields, and the little cemetery on the hill are fated to be the stage for three days of the greatest military butchery since Waterloo.

For my generation, those three days in July 1863 were still close and the local place names full of ominous meaning. For us, Round Top, Cemetery Hill, Peach Orchard, Devil's Den, Culp's Hill, and the Angle all held both a shudder and a sense of mournful pride. When I was fourteen, I was taken to Gettysburg and my mother, my brother, and I spent a solemn day at the field where died two Cameron boys, my grandmother's older brothers. On my bookshelf, I still have a minié ball and a musket ball I found at Gettysburg.

Back home in Grand Rapids, I used to ride my bike to visit Captain Hoag—a relative by marriage—in the Old Soldier's Home on the hill. He would tell, as he sat in his wheelchair under a tree, about how he and the rest of the Twenty-Fourth Michigan, part of the Iron Brigade, had stopped the Rebs on McPherson's Ridge during the first day of the battle, losing eighty percent of the regiment while doing it.

Then, when the Grand Army of the Republic came to Grand Rapids for one of its last reunions—together for the first time with the surviving Confederates—I did my Boy Scout duty. I met the trains from the south, carried luggage, pushed wheelchairs, smuggled small bottles of whiskey, hailed taxis, and stood around in the lobby of the Pantlind Hotel until after midnight listening to those old beaks and grizzled chins swap their tales of Shiloh, Gettysburg, or Lookout Mountain long after my mother's deadline for getting home. In the grand finale, I carried my troop's flag in the Fourth of July parade, dizzy with the thought that I was marching with men who marched with Grant or Stonewall Jackson or rode with Stuart or Custer. (Most of them, to be truthful, sat in cars or were pushed in wheelchairs.)

Later on, I went to a small Ohio college where there were two literary societies—Nu Pi Kappa and Philomathesian. In 1861, one was made up of northern boys and one of southern. As Kenyon legend has it, the southerners departed in a body to join the Confederate army and the northerners to the Union flag.

I say all this to note how close to us that war and that bloody field in Pennsylvania still were. In some ways, it seemed only yesterday, and yet in others a thousand years away from the twentieth century America in which we were growing up, vividly remembered and yet remote and legendary.

In one of his essays, Gore Vidal says the the Civil War was for Americans what the Trojan War was for the Greeks. It is a fine perception and almost true. For Agamemnon take Lincoln, for Priam, Davis; for Hector substitute Jackson, for Odysseus (translated into Latin), Ulysses Grant—figures from legend all of them. Furthermore, it was probably the last American war in which the gods took a part—the goddess Dixie, Stonewall Jackson's God of Battles, and the Lord who tramped out the vintage from the grapes of wrath after the death of John Brown, His mad prophet. It was our last war of gaudy uniforms (zouaves or hussars), of swords and cavalry charges, of infantry columns moving into battle behind their flags, of oratory, grand gestures, and fevered chauvinism.

The epic version of history has survived in such places as early Faulkner fiction and Hollywood films, but the realistic one, created by the telegraph, reportage, Brady's camera, and personal accounts such as John Ransom's diary are what we believe. *Long Remember*'s realism is rooted in eyewitness accounts and recorded memories and it is less about a battle then about people—both soldiers and civilians—who found themselves swallowed up by a battle.

On that bright June morning, Daniel Bale, who is the protagonist of the book, is under some pressure and suspicion from his friends because he refuses to join the army. He is not afraid, he explains, but he simply doesn't believe in war or killing. (Bale has fought Indians in the west and, against his principles, has killed some.) He is also about to fall guiltily in love with Irene Fanning, the wife of Captain Tyler Fanning, his boyhood friend.

Elmer Quagger, a Southern sympathizer—or Copperhead—is about to approach Bale under the impression that Bale shares his attitude. When Bale rejects him, he will write a letter to Fanning (by then departed to join his regiment) accusing Bale of having an affair with Irene.

On the climactic third night and day of the battle, Bale, goaded by Irene, will set out to make his way through the front lines in order to find Fanning and deny the accusation. Irene simply does not want her husband to die knowing the truth.

This is the simple, ironic plot of the novel—an involvement of personal lives that—with one strange exception—has little to do with the thunder of history around them. This exception is when Dan Bale stumbles into the middle of an episode that seems to him little more than a hand-to-hand muddle, but which, as the reader knows, in the hindsight of history, will become the crisis point of the battle, the climax of the war, the "high-water mark of the Confederacy."

Looking around at the chaos of battle from the viewpoint of a lone, confused man was hardly a new idea in fiction. Stendhal had done it with Fabrizio in *The Charterhouse of Parma* and, even more notably, Tolstoy had seen Borodino through Pierre's eyes. One might think that Daniel Bale was a kind of American counterpart of Pierre Bezvhov in that their roles are so similar—both of them idealists and uninvolved bystanders who are flung, willy-nilly, into the action. That would make a neat literary derivation if it were true—but it isn't. *Long Remember* was published in 1934 but, according to MacKinlay Kantor's son Tim, his father didn't read *War and Peace* until sometime after 1938—and then only at the urging of Peggy Pulitzer, his lover. It is a curious question—why did the man who had read eighty-four source books about the battle of Gettysburg have to be talked into reading his novel's great prototype? Unfortunately, the question goes without an answer in Tim Kantor's memoir, *My Father's Voice,* nor is there any mention of Kantor's reaction when he finally did read Tolstoy's book.

In any case, the predestinarian theme is an old one in story: sudden death in the midst of daily life, the unexpectedness of our appointment in Samarra. Kantor is obsessed to show how real and ordinary people pass, in a moment of impact, from living and breathing to broken and dying flesh. He has no interest in such hero figures as Lee and Longstreet—like Agamemnon and Achilles—in dissention at the command tent while masses of nameless men rush to death. His story lights with exquisite, cruel clarity on the individual's moment between the saddle and the ground.

Irene Fanning watches as a wounded artilleryman—a boy of about eighteen—is brought onto her porch. She notices that his hands, "slender as a flute-player's," are raw and blistered from handling harness and cannon. They carry him into the kitchen to die. His eyes roll and the blood rises up in his throat, then courses onto the clean-scrubbed kitchen floor. He makes a trilling sound and, finally the most telling detail: he reaches for Irene's skirt and wads it in his hand as he dies.

Running wildly across the yard comes a fleeing soldier. The family dog goes after him, snapping at his heels; the soldier shoots the dog with his revolver and stumbles on. Irene cradles the dog in her arms as it dies.

One minute, General Reynolds, a capable and respected commander, a man with "a close-clipped, scrubby beard, and a way of appearing neat and on parade even when the hollows of his cheeks were larded with grime," is sitting erect on his horse. The next moment, he is lying on the ground, his hat fallen off, straws caught in his beard, a blue hole in the skin where his neck joined the head, squarely behind his right ear. His staff officers bend over him "mumbling dazedly" and young Lieutenant Steele has tears in his eyes.

Lying under fire in a bean patch, a Gettysburg parson argues in scriptual quotations with a Southern soldier:

"'But these have altogether broken the yoke and burst the bonds'" (said the preacher).

The soldier swore. With his unwounded arm he hitched himself forward, and propped the rifle barrel higher. "That's Old Testament, and you're talking about the Right of Secession. Oh yes, you are—"

"'Wherefore,'" quoted Simon Solt, earnestly, "'a line out of the forest shall slay them, and a wolf of the evenings shall spoil them, and a leopard shall watch over their cities.'"

". . . . Seems like this is somewhere thereabouts: 'Go ye up on her walls, and destroy, for the houses of Israel and Judah have dealt mighty mean to me, saith the Lord.'" . . .

Something went *put*. He said hoarsely, Nuhh, and the burned hands slid down from his gun . . . his head cocked forward. The other soldier rose suddenly on his knees. "Lane!" he cried. "Hi thar, *Lane!*' The limp head tumbled against the bottom runner of the fence, and the rifle clattered loose.

They dragged him into the shelter of the woodshed, his boots making furrows through the green garden. His face had a little velvet hole close beside the left eye, and a drop of red wax slid from it. "Sealed," Reverend Solt whispered.

The dusty-bearded survivor raised up on his haunches. "I reckon yore glad, you Yankee Palm-shouter! Lane had two little gals to home."

"Glad?" cried Solt. "Man, man—listen to me—" He looked at the long body . . . a thin, a giant height pressed flat among old ashes and chick-weed. He began to cry. "Oh, Lord," he sobbed, "our Father, our Heavenly Guardian . . . we come to Thee in a—midnight of sorrow and lone-liness. . . ."

The climactic sequence of the story begins on the evening of July 2nd, the battle's second day when Dan Bale sets out to cross the lines to find the 72nd Pennsylvania Volunteers and Captain Tyler Fanning among the some 98,000 Federal soldiers defending the ridge. He goes into the streets of the town, finds a Federal corpse, strips off its trousers and makes himself put them on—in order that the Union sentries won't fire on him. In the dusk, he holds an imaginary dialogue with the body:

Bale says, "I would have spared you this if I could. . . ." The ghost says, "Why should I have such indignity? I was a virgin, a German, a good wrestler, twenty years old: my name was Emil, my uncle said I was a reliable boy and cried when I went into the army, and now you leave me naked in the sight of a relentless world."

Bale finds himself caught up in a shadowy gray column whose soldiers speak a language he doesn't understand. "Oui. . . . Le too onsommell," he hears one say. They are Louisiana Cajuns. The column is on the march south and west of the town. In time, it reaches a valley and, in the dark, begins to advance up the hillside ahead. Soon it is under fire.

Nearly crushed under a fallen body, blinded and deafened, struck in the head by a rock splinter, Bale lies thinking, "Cannot stay here, cannot stay—She insists that I tell my lie." The Confederates retreat and the firing dies down. The moon comes out. Then, in the new silence, he can hear wounded men all around him on the rocky hillside muttering in French. Their voices sound like the soft hooting of owls.

In the morning, he makes his way up into the Union position and spends half the day working his way along the ridge line looking for Fanning. Again, there are those sharply-detailed moments that give Kantor's war such a ring of truth: when the huge Confederate cannonade begins, some men are playing cards near a stone wall and when the wall is hit, the air is full of fragments. "One of the card players stood up and screamed. He beat his chest with his open hands, shaking his head and rolling his eyes until the whites puffed out and glistened."

At last, the Confederate advance begins to move across the half-mile-wide valley into the teeth of the Union artillery and infantry on the ridge. Though that attack was nameless at the time, it later became known as "Pickett's Charge" because General George Pickett's division of Virginians almost penetrated the Union defense and, in the course of things, suffered two-thirds casualties, the worst of any unit engaged.

In the bloody melee in the very center of the Union line, there occurred a notable incident that Kantor takes the liberty of appropriating for the purposes of his story. Just as Bale finds Fanning in the midst of the fight, he sees "a bald man in a gray jacket—he was middle-aged, he held a sword high above his head and he was crying aloud." The man raises his sword to strike Fanning and Bale, who has had a rifle thrust into his hands, does what he has always denied that he would do—he aims, fires, and drops the man with the sword.

That man was General Lewis Armistead, one of Pickett's brigade commanders and, at the moment of his death, he and about three hundred of his men were within a few yards of breaking through the Federal line. In Kantor's story, a surgeon casually identifies the dead general a little later. There, but unspoken, is the thought expressed in the old rhyme, "For want of a nail, the shoe was lost. . . ." And how gratifying it is that Kantor held back his pen. He loved accuracy and he has been meticulous until now to avoid taking fictional liberties with history. This, as far as I can tell, is his only dereliction.

He does it in order to double the burden of Bale's guilt. Bale says, "That letter, Ty, it's not true, not a word of it. . . . I was here and killed somebody—he was middle-aged—I shot a man, just to tell you." Thus, it seems that the story is saying that Bale might have unwittingly changed the course of history in order to tell his lie to Fanning. Such things do happen in real life and yet they always strike us as too contrived for fiction. To his credit, Kantor prudently avoids any implication so outside the purview of his characters and so grandly consequential. His only comment on Bale's momentous single shot at Gettysburg comes in terms of Bale's personal sense of guilt. "I shot a man just to tell you [a lie]" is the devastating truth Bale will have to live with the rest of his life.

This is a good example of the restraint in Kantor's conduct of the novel. And, again, everything could have gone wrong in the aftermath. After a battle fought in the cemetery, all the fields around the town were full of unburied dead. Churches, schools, houses, the seminary, and tents in the woods groaned with an army of the dying. An overambitious writer might have tried to encompass the whole terrible vision with all its obvious symbolism. But, true to his method, Kantor touches on it more effectively in moments, details, quick glances.

As night falls, there is a rainstorm and Bale founders around among Hieronymus Bosch horrors by lantern light on Cemetery Hill.

To try to calm herself, Irene Fanning plays the piano in the twilit library and something falls on the floor. "It was a round, gold-rimmed wafer of ambrotype which had been set in someone's watch case." In it is a picture of a young woman and on the back is written "Triggie Richmond August 1861." Irene thinks, "Triggie, he is dead and you do not know it." Irene realizes that the owner must have been the man who died under the surgeon's knife on the library table a few hours before.

A team of men—Bale among them—labor up the stairs of the Fanning house to carry Tyler Fanning to a bedroom and all around them is horrifying odor from his wound.

In a strange incident, Bale looks for and finds the body of his friend Elijah Huddlestone among the shambles of the wheat field and carries it off to the ruined cemetery to bury it in the Huddlestone family plot.

The novel ends with Irene choosing to stay with her crippled husband rather than going off with Dan Bale and then Bale's setting out to walk four miles to the railhead. He has decided—suddenly and without explanation—to join the Union army.

MacKinlay Kantor's three memorable novels about the Civil War are this one, *Arouse and Beware,* and—his greatest success—*Andersonville*. The latter is an enormous 726-page vehicle for many individual stories, hundreds of characters, drama and melodrama, and several modes of fiction. The subject and setting were, of course, the infamous Southern prison camp in Georgia and, in 1955, when the book was published, the unspoken parallel between Andersonville and Nazi concentration camps was evident and powerful. Bruce Catton called it "the best Civil War novel I have ever read;" it became a bestseller and it won the Pulitzer Prize for fiction. Overwhelming and full of *bravura* as *Andersonville* is, I prefer the simpler virtues of *Long Remember*.

As for the reception given *Long Remember* itself, the highest praise came from Allen Tate in the *New York Times Book Review,* where he said that "There is no book ever written which creates so well as this the look and smell of battle. . . . As a spectacle of war, the novel has no equal. . . . [A]nd still it is above and beyond war with the saving humanity that survives slaughter. . . ." Tate—author of *The Fathers* and "Ode to the Confederate Dead" and a first-rate critic—did not carelessly praise fiction—especially fiction by Yankees—about the Civil War.

Since 1934 there have been many good novels that create the look and smell of battle powerfully—so why then am I making a special plea for recalling *Long Remember?* One reason is that its Battle of Gettysburg happens right in the midst of American life. Although the early battlefields of that war were—in the tradition of wars—fought in open fields, woods, on hillsides somewhere, the Civil War was, essentially, a war within a family fought in the family house, as Lincoln suggested in that famous phrase. Eventually, it had to come into the farmyards, towns, and cities and eventually it had to alter the lives of everybody. Kantor is always mindful of the sense of sudden unnatural death in the midst of common, daily life—or of brothers lunging at each other with knives across the family dinner table.

In one place, Dan Bale is making his way along the Federal lines on Cemetery Ridge and, as the morning sun climbs, he sees a sparkle like quartz on the ridge opposite and he knows that it comes from Confederate troops moving into position. He thinks back to the morning before when he sat in his own kitchen eating breakfast with some Confederate officers and someone on the porch outside began to sing an English love song, "*Oh let not my own love. . . .*" He reflects that the men who talked and joked with him and the unknown one who sang a song are now—seen from the lines on Cemetery Ridge—no more than a menacing shine of metal in the distance. Like the incident of the Yankee preacher and the Confederate soldier arguing by scripture in the bean patch, it is an unstressed reminder of common feelings and common heritage in terrible division.

This, for me, is the special force and virtue of *Long Remember*.

MacKinlay Kantor was born in 1904 in Webster City, Iowa, and died in 1977 in Sarasota, Florida. Selected publications: *Diversey* (1928); *Long Remember* (1934, out of print); *The Voice of Bugle Ann* (1935); *Arouse and Beware* (1936), Civil War novel; *Author's Choice* (1944, stories); *Glory for Me* (1945, a novel in verse); *But Look, the Morn* (1947, memoir of childhood); *Lee and Grant at Appomattox* (1950, juvenile); *Gettysburg* (1953, juvenile); *Andersonville* (1955), Civil War novel.

On Andrew Lytle's *The Long Night*

Robert Penn Warren

ONE EVENING, BACK IN THE 1930's, in a camp on a bluff over-look-
ing the Cumberland River, my old friend, the historian Frank Owsley,
launched into a story of his youth—or rather, into a story that he had
learned in his youth, back about 1910, as well as I can now calculate it.
Away from home, at college, he received a letter from a kinsman whom
he had never seen, a great-uncle, an eccentric who had long since withdrawn from the world and was remembered in the family as only a dim
legend. The letter commanded—and it was a command uttered with,
apparently, perfect certainty of obedience—that the young Frank come
to the kinsman's house on a certain day, and gave careful directions. The
matter, the letter declared, was one of the greatest urgency.

Frank, impelled by curiosity and family loyalty, obeyed, and found his
way to the remote spot in Alabama where the old man lived in a solid
old-fashioned prosperity, in a sealed-off valley that in all particulars
seemed to belong to the middle of the preceding century. The uncle, a

powerful and handsome old man (the power and handsomeness easily believed, for Frank had those qualities), received the guest with affection but, also, with antique formality, and after dinner began a nightlong tale that left the auditor shaken and sweating, in the first cold dawn light.

The tale went back to the late 1850s, when the father of the old man, the great-grandfather of Frank, who had lately come to Alabama from Georgia, was shot to death in his bed, while his wife and youngest son looked on, by a gang of men who had burst into the house. The victim had fallen foul of a gang somewhat like the organization of Murrell, the great outlaw who earlier had terrorized the old Natchez Trace, and who, in his bloodlust and ambition, was reported to have dreamed an empire. This gang, as that of the prototype Murrell was reputed to do, operated in the guise of decent and respectable men, men who had, over some years, been corrupted and blackmailed or gradually sucked into the power of the mastermind, and the murdered man had had the ill fortune to stumble upon the fatal secret. The gang had framed the victim as a slave-stealer (and, I think, an abolitionist), and had made the murder appear as the act of outraged citizenry; and since the gang's tentacles reached into places of influence and power, any real legal investigation was blocked.

The murderers, however, had reckoned without the young boy who had watched the deed and who was able to penetrate beneath some of the perfunctory masks and disguises. The boy became obsessed with vengeance. His life was one long act of execution. So the young Frank, sitting by the dying fire of that remote farmhouse, heard the avenger, now an old man, tell how over the years, he had sought out, one by one, the members of the gang. He had lived his strange, withdrawn life, and even in his later years had raised a family, but in his isolation and eccentricity, his goings and comings had long since ceased to arouse comment. He might be gone for a year or two on the trail of some victim concerning whom he had gleaned word in his indefatigable search; and when he had his satisfaction he would come home to his valley. His family knew nothing of his mission and mania. They knew only that "Poppa" had "business."

The old man had not summoned Frank because, at last, he had to tell somebody, had to confess to clear his soul or to make his boast. Far from it. He was getting old. He could no longer thrust his thews or his cunning, and two or three of the murderers yet remained alive. He had

traced them—one to some town in Kansas, one to San Francisco. Frank
was the male kin next in line for the mission of vengeance. As dawn came
on in the room where the ashes had long since gone gray on the hearth,
the great-uncle declared the obligation. He had all necessary data about
the intended victims—very old men now forgetting or perhaps not even
believing their own old deed of blood that cried out for vengeance.

Needless to say, Frank did not accept the mission offered by the bloodthirsty old loon, went on with college (punctuated, I think, with some
stints of school teaching), and on to a Ph.D. at the University of Chicago.
As for the story told so long after, it delighted me, but it was only one in a
long line of stories from the old times that not infrequently were strange
and bloody, this one different from others only in being somewhat
stranger and bloodier. But a littler later—or perhaps a little before Frank
told the tale to me—he told it, sitting on the porch of a plantation in
Alabama, to the perfect listener—to Andrew Lytle.

Andrew was always the perfect listener to tales, for the simple reason
that he himself was the perfect teller of tales. I have heard a few great
tale-tellers—Stark Young, Katherine Anne Porter, Brooks Hays, Lyle
Saxon, and Roark Bradford; and Andrew was second to none—unless
his own father. But if he was capable of listening in appreciation, he was
also capable, on occasion, of listening for appropriation. This act, too,
might be peculiarly selfless. The ill-formed tale needed to be set right, the
ill-telling of the tale needed to be set right, to have pace, tone, or gesture
amended. But out of a deeper reason yet, Andrew might appropriate a
tale—because it touched something in his nature, in the way a subject
"chooses" the writer. And the tale that Frank told him touched, I have
always believed, that kind of "something" in the listener's nature.

The tale also sprang from the world that always most stirred Andrew's imagination and humor. He knew the world of the plantation and
of the deeper backcountry in the hills beyond the plantations. He knew
the language, every shade of it by tone and phrase, every inflection, every
hint of pain or poetry, the humor, the bawdiness, every expression of face.
He knew the objects and practices of the old times, and of the backcountry, how meat was dressed, how food was cooked, how meal was ground
or hominy made, what people—men or women or children—wore,
how wool was carded, how shakes were split and whiskey run. He knew
such things because he had the keenest of eyes, the shrewdest of ears,

insatiable curiosity, and an elephatine memory; but most of all because he had a natural generosity and simplicity of heart and could stop a stranger on the road or lounge on the steps at the most desolate crossroads store and in ten minutes be swapping crop-talk or tales with the local whittlers, in perfect ease and pleasure and with devoted attention. He was soaked in history, as a youth had lived in France and loved French literature, and was not only a natural-born actor but a trained one who had done a little stint on Broadway. But such things as travel and education had merely sharpened his appetite for, and appreciation of, the world from which he had sprung.

In any case, Andrew was the perfect listener to the tale, and Frank, sensing this, finally "gave" it to him, lock, stock, and barrel. It became a novel, *The Long Night,* published in 1936.

"His voice stopped suddenly, as a clock might stop"—that is the first sentence of *The Long Night.* Dawn has come, the voice of the bloodthirsty old loon stops, the tale is over, and the "I"—who corresponds to the young Frank Owsley—says, in the next sentence: "I remember the room for a moment seemed to hang in a hiatus of time, in such a hiatus as only the body can know when the heart's last stroke sounds down the blood stream." We know that we are in good hands. This teller knows the craft of telling, and we are ready to turn back in years to the moment when all had begun.

The tale unfolds, uncoils, thrusts forward, hesitates, lingers luxuriously in a sunlit moment, lifts, again thrusts forward. Like all good tales, it has its own life and will, and works its will on us. We forget the teller of the tale—the tellers in fact, for there is the old man, now Pleasant McIvor by name, and the young man who, there in the firelit room, had been "spitted" by the obsessed glare of the old man's gaze, held hour on hour while the fire dies, and whose voice now interfuses with that of old Pleasant McIvor: "From what he told me that night and from what I was able to learn from other sources, I was able to piece the story together, and of course you must understand that, at this late date, I cannot tell which words are his and which are mine . . ." (Avon paperback, 18). But there is another voice behind these voices. It is the voice that, in the art of the telling, we forget—except in those few moments when the artistry flags. It is the voice of Andrew Lytle.

The tale had already been told twice—really "told"—once in the camp on the Cumberland bluff and once on Cornsilk Plantation. But, inevitably, the shape, pace, and "feel" of an oral tale is never twice the same. The hour of the day, the state of the weather or of the teller's digestion, the season, the attitude of the auditors, the kind of drink in the hand—a thousand things modify the tale. But when, in the cold light of morning, the teller faces the blank, white page, alone, with no friend present and no glass in the hand, all is different. The greatest difference is that now he is to freeze the tale in the act of telling. That is the terrible fact.

What does Andrew Lytle do *to, for, with,* the tale that had lived in voices? What, that is, beyond his own special narrative élan?

First, he gives it a world. In the other tellings the tale had not needed a world. The world had been solidly there in the consciousness, in the blood, even, of the listeners. But once a tale gets frozen on paper, what the reader knows or does not know about the world of the tale, in consciousness or blood-stream, is no longer relevant. In a sense, the reader is now an abstraction. He is not there when the telling—i.e., the writing—takes place. The tale must now "be" its own world as well as what happens in that world, and the "being" of this world is not mere information about geography, sociology, and history, but, ultimately, an aspect of form. Form is merely a complex of dynamic relations, and the relations between scene (world) on one hand and action and character on the other, are fundamental and germinal.

Effortlessly, as naturally as breath is drawn, as secretly as Pleasant McIvor ever stalked the appointed victim, the author of *The Long Night* creates his world. He never "describes" the world, he is merely aware of it. This is not to say that description does not appear. It does. At a summer dawn the sky "snapped open like a colored fan." At a moment of tension, when the outlaw chief instinctively asserts his authority over his gang, he let his gaze "slide across their faces like a plane." The avenger watches the "first bodiless flame" lick the wood of a house he has fired to burn the body of a victim. Or when a deputy reports the finding of the body of Judge Wilton, another victim, who had presumably died of an accidental fall from the balcony of an inn to the stones of the riverbank and has lain there all night, with one hand in the water, the deputy says: "The water had washed it plumb white. It was wrinkled like a old woman's hand" (99).

Ordinarily, however, description appears in terms special to that world, opening some fuller or deeper glimpse into the world. On the first page, as the simplest kind of example, dawn light lies upon the "puncheon floor"—because the floor is of puncheons. In the next sentence, the fire curls over the "back stick into the dark suck of the chimney's mouth." True, the "dark suck of the chimney's mouth" is description, vivid with the word "suck," but the key to the world is in the innocent phrase "back stick"—instead of "back log." Or take the picture of exhausted hounds that "let their tongues hang dripping in the dust and trash." This is nothing, worse than nothing, until the word "trash," the only word the speaker of that world could have used. Or take the biscuits on Sheriff Botterall's table, "large as saucers and puffed out on top like feather pillows"—the kind of biscuits to be found on a Botterall table but not on that of the gentry like the Harrisons, however come down. Or take the remark about the close friendship from girlhood of two women now old: they "had set up housekeeping at the same time and had boiled water for each other when the children came." Or the remark of one of these old women to a young girl who can preen herself that her husband has not changed since the birth of their child: but "you're eaten yore white bread now"—not the bread of bran and tailings near the bottom of the barrel. Here is the glimpse of a world—the hard world for women in that country just two jumps and a spit this side of the frontier.

It is such glimpses, casual but profound, that give the texture of the world in which the action occurs, but the author has used more radical measures to create a human context for the action. Bit by bit, the reader's attention is shifted from the story of the avenger, Pleasant McIvor, to the common, daylight life of the community, the life that the secret members of the gang must live with their families and friends. Again and again, we enter that common life. It is a life of affection, pathos, and humor intertwined with the secret evil, but rendered with full fidelity to those normal interests and values.

For example, take the sequence of the shrouding of Brother Macon, the lone Campbellite in the region, slain as a member of the posse chasing Pleasant. In the kitchen the neighbor women preparing food for the wake discuss the recipe for jugged pigeons, or discuss, as we have already remarked, the woman's world. Outside, in the dark, two lovers meet. In the "laying-out room," the men, under the command of Brother Abner Buchanan, pass the jug and brace themselves for the doleful duty:

"All right, men," he said, wiping his chin and setting the empty jug by his chair, "I'm ready for Brother Macon."

Beatty and Simmons drew back the sheet.

"Where do you want him, Ab?"

Abner stepped back unsteadily and looked at the body.

"Well, now, you've got me stumped. I'm new to this kind of a trade."

"Somebody git the wash tub," growled Botterall.

"You ain't figgering for me to set him in the tub, Lem?"

"Hell, no. But what's to keep you from standen him up in it?"

"That's an idey. I deputize you to hold, sheriff."

"You can't deshutize the sheriff."

"That's a fact. Well, Joe, you hold him."

Joe looked at the corpse.

"He'll lean ag'in the wall," he said.

The tub was brought, and the corpse of Brother Macon, after the clothes had been clumsily stripped, was lifted in. At this moment Damon returned with another bucket of water. He saw the grayish-brown figure leaning grotesquely against the mantelpiece. The body was thin and drawn, and it had the cold shine of death. The icy eyes stared into the room, and the beard hung softly down. From the hole in the stomach a black stream of dried blood had spread down the inside of a thigh, streaking the calf, to the twisted toes. The hands were clenched, and at the corner of the mouth dark stains turned down like tusks. A look of fear and horror spread over Damon's smooth features. He felt his scalp tingle, and when he spoke, there was hatred and disgust in his voice.

"Here's the other bucket of water. Be enough?"

"A bucket of water? Dump it in the tub, my boy," Abner said gaily, rolling up his sleeves.

Damon's face lost its color and he hesitated; but, looking down, he did as he was told. He could not help but see the water splash around the still, ashen legs. As soon as he had emptied the pail, he picked up the other one and left the room.

"The boy's got weak guts," said Beatty pleasantly.

"That's a sight to turn stronger guts to jelly," answered Botterall.

The assistants began to look a little grim.

"You boys ain't white-eyed on me?" Abner asked cheerfully.

"Hell, no," said Beatty. "He won't bite."

"Pitch the soap in that ar bucket and swing out the pot."

It was done in silence, and Buchanan picked up the broom. He dipped it in the kettle and swung the scalding water on the corpse.

"Ain't you a-goen to mix the water?"

"If it's too hot fer'm, he'll holler."

He ran the broom into the water, over the soap, then over the legs of the corpse.

"'Y God," he said, "but I believe the dirt's set on him" (149–50).

In the world of common life, the members of the gang wait for the moment when the avenger will again emerge from his shadows. And our knowledge and suspense give an image of, and empathy for, the growing dread of the guilty as they realize, death by death, the doom hanging over them. In a sense, they are not, after all, villains. They are merely men, certainly no better than they should be, but trapped somehow in their destiny. Whose side are we on? This doubleness of view, and the irony it entails, is a fundamental fact of the story as it appears in the novel.

If the novelist has undertaken to create a world and a human context for the deeds of vengeance, the main change from the original tale is in the nature of the avenger. In the tale, once he is in the grip of his obsession, he becomes, simply, his "role." This is all the tale demands, and from the avenger's side of the action, the only variety possible will lie in the method and circumstances of the killing. If, in the tale, he ceases his pursuit of the guilty, it is only because he has grown old. The novelist, however, cannot settle for this. He wants a deeper drama. So he lets the Civil War fall across the action.

It is the outlaw chief, Lovell, who gives Pleasant the news of the coming of war—this in a dark room where Pleasant has surprised him and is ready to exact the penalty. But Lovell doesn't care now. His life is over, for his maniacal ambition to found an empire is cut off. His own scheme dwindles to nothing in the great convulsion of history. So Pleasant, to compound his vengeance, spares Lovell to let him taste the frustration of his dream and await, over years if necessary, the death stroke.

Meanwhile, for Pleasant the war provides the perfect cover for his operations, for as a soldier in the vast namelessness of the army, he can stalk his prey with impunity. But bit by bit, the great public bloodletting

drains him of his private thirst for blood, the great public mania under-
mines his private mania. He finds that he can no longer sink himself in
his role, even if he conceives of himself as merely God's hand exacting
justice. He finds that he is human, after all. He is capable of friendship,
and in the end he finds that friendship is a trap; in pursuing his private
war he causes the death of his friend in the public war. He is caught up in
human loyalties—to his friend and to the men with whom he marches.
He has, however, discovered his humanity too late. The long night will
never end.

> Then suddenly he knew what he had done, what no man in this world
> may do. Twice he had loved—once the dead, once the living, and each by
> each was consumed and he was doomed. In the partial darkness he raised
> his eyes to the river. Stone's River, icy-cold and black, turned between the
> town and the cedar thickets across the Nashville pike, broke over the shal-
> low rocks at McFadden's Ford, fell again into deep chasms, flowing north,
> silently flowing through the long night.
>
> Pleasant straightened his body, looked once about him. The camps
> were still asleep, only the sentries walked their posts, frozen shadows in
> the darkening world. He looked to the south. Far to the south the hills of
> Winston rose close and stubborn out of the lowlands. The hills of
> Winston. It was no long journey to a man who knew the way, who had
> lost every other way. There he would go. There, in the secret coves, far
> away from the world and vengeance, a deserter might hide forever . . .
> (303).

The solution is the proper one for the novel. Where else could Pleasant
go except to the hills of Winston? But in working it out, the novelist
involves himself, it must be put on the record, in certain technical difficulties. In the sequence leading up to the Battle of Shiloh, we lose Pleasant, the focus of interest shifts, becomes generalized and diffuse, and
when we rediscover him in the battle, something has been lost and is
never, perhaps, completely recovered. No, that is not true. It is recovered,
but only at the last minute, in the splendid conclusion.

This technical defect does not, in one sense, matter—nor do certain
more minor ones. The conception of the story is firm, but the real reason
such a defect does not matter is the spirit of the work. We are not reading
a realistic novel. The work is full of realistic effects, the details of a real
world and real people, but the whole is more like a ballad than a novel—

a quintessential poetry of action, pathos, humor, and doom, to be read innocently, in its own terms, in its perspective of distance and a climate of feeling. It is strangely like a dream, springing from a certain society, from a certain historical moment—not a record, but a dream, the paradoxical dream of that society's, that historical moment's, view of itself.

There is no book quite like *The Long Night,* and there will never be another quite like it. It says something about the world of the South not said elsewhere, and something that is true. But more importantly, it offers its own special fascination and its own special pleasure. At least, that is what I always find when I come back to it, the fascination, the pleasure.

Andrew Lytle was born in 1902 in Murfreesboro, Tennessee, and now lives in Monteagle, Tennessee, near Sewanee. Selected publications: *I'll Take My Stand: The South and the Agrarian Tradition,* contributor (1930); *Bedford Forrest and His Critter Company* (1931), Civil War biography; *The Long Night* (1936, University of Alabama Press, 1988); *At the Moon's Inn* (1941); *A Name for Evil* (1947); *The Velvet Horn* (1957); *The Hero with the Private Parts* (1966, essays); *A Wake for the Living* (1975, family history); *Southerners and Europeans: Essays in a Time of Disorder* (1988); *From Eden to Babylon: The Social and Political Essays of Andrew Nelson Lytle* (1989).

On William Faulkner's
Absalom, Absalom!

Lewis P. Simpson

ASKED ABOUT HIS INDEBTEDNESS to Sherwood Anderson, whom he had known personally in New Orleans in the early 1920s, William Faulkner replied, "In my opinion he's the father of all my generation— Hemingway, Erskine Caldwell, Thomas Wolfe, Dos Passos." Strictly speaking, Faulkner's sense of literary genealogy may have derived as much or more from a personal regard for Anderson as from an informed appreciation of his wider literary influence. It was Anderson who had advised the young writer from Mississippi to give up his residence in the French Quarter bohemia of New Orleans, return to his native patch of earth, and write about what life was like there. Heeding this cogent admonition had made all the difference. But neither the advice nor the stories of the well-known midwestern writer account for the compelling creative impulse that led a literary novice from Mississippi to develop into the world famous author of the Yoknapatawpha saga. Faulkner offered a more basic, less arguable assertion about American literary genealogy, and about his own literary descent, when he rounded out his comment on the subject by declaring that the writer who may be considered Anderson's literary father, Mark Twain, "is all our grand-father."

Whatever he owed to Anderson, the author of the Yoknapatawpha stories might have been more accurate in his metaphor if, ignoring generational chronology, he had also described himself as a son of Mark Twain; for Mark Twain was more than a distant forerunner of Faulkner. He created the model of the crucial role Faulkner enacted: that of the southern author as at once a participant in and ironic witness to a drama of memory and history that centered essentially in the never-ending remembrance of the great American civil conflict of 1861–1865. The obligation of the writer to serve as a witness, not to the actual historical event, but to the remembrance of it, was a force in shaping the vocation of the writer in the South from Thomas Nelson Page to Ellen Glasgow to Faulkner, Allen Tate, Katherine Anne Porter, Robert Penn Warren, and Eudora Welty; to, in fact, all of the writers associated with the flowering of southern authorship, especially novelists, in the nineteen twenties and thirties. The prime testimony to the shaping power of remembrance on the identity of the southern writer is offered not in the actual lives of the writers themselves but in certain implicit portrayals of the figure of the writer in their fiction, two of the notable instances being Lacy Buchan in Tate's *The Fathers* and Jack Burden in Warren's *All the King's Men,* but the supreme example being a twenty-year old Mississippian who appears in *The Sound and the Fury* and *Absalom, Absalom!,* Quentin Compson III. On the surface these two Faulkner novels seem to bear no more than a coincidental relation to the war; but in the second of them, Faulkner's most baffling yet possibly finest single work, the portrayal of Quentin brings the drama of southern remembrance to its culminating expression.

Mark Twain's most cogent definition of the postbellum southern sensibility of memory occurs in *Life on the Mississippi.* At one point in this autobiographical work, first published in 1883, Mark Twain remarks that in the North one seldom hears the recent American civil conflict mentioned, but in the South it "is very different." Here, where "every man you meet was in the war" and "every lady you meet saw the war," it is "the great chief topic of conversation." To southerners, Mark Twain declares, the war is in fact "what A.D. is elsewhere; they date from it."

Thus "all day long you hear things 'placed' as having happened since the waw; or du'in the waw; or be'fo the waw; or right aftah the waw; or about two yeahs or five yeahs or ten yeahs befo' the waw or aftah the waw."

Beneath the surface of the humor in *Life on the Mississippi,* the author—who had been brought up as Sam Clemens in the semi-frontier Missouri extension of the southern slave society but had long since assumed the complex pseudonymous identity of "Mark Twain"—registers his realization of the profound effect of the war on his own consciousness of time and history. In his early manhood, before he became Mark Twain, Sam Clemens of Hannibal, Missouri, had permanently separated himself from the South when he withdrew from—or to speak less politely, deserted from—a rag-tag volunteer company of Confederate Missourians and went adventuring on the new frontiers of Nevada and California. While in Nevada as a reporter for the Virginia City *Territorial Enterprise* he adopted as his literary name the familiar cry of the leadsman on the Mississippi River steamboats he had piloted for three years prior to the war. It was as Mark Twain that after the war Sam Clemens went to live in the North, and later, having become a world traveler, at times in Europe. Although always haunted by a complex and troubled sense of his fundamental identity, in *Life on the Mississippi* Mark Twain writes out of a persistent, deeply empathetic relationship with the South. It is of his identity as a postbellum southerner that the author speaks when he says that to grasp the significance of the war the stranger to the South must realize "how intimately every individual" southerner was involved in it. Ostensibly quoting a gentleman he had met at a New Orleans club— who, whether he was a real person or merely a convenient invention of the narrative moment, serves as an effective authorial persona—Mark Twain says that the experience of the calamity of war was so intense and encompassing in the South each southerner, "in his own person," seems to have been "visited . . . by that tremendous episode"—most notably by the "vast and comprehensive calamity" of "invasion." As a result, Mark Twain continues in the guise of the New Orleans gentleman, "each of us, in his own person, seems to have sampled all the different varieties of human experience. . . . " Inseparably connected to the war, the southern comprehension of time and history in Mark Twain's conception is such that "you can't mention an outside matter of any sort but it will certainly remind some listener of something that happened during the war—and out he comes with it." Even "the most random topic" will "load every man up with war reminiscences." As a result "pale inconsequentialities" tend to disappear from Southern conversation; "you can't talk" about business or the weather "when you've got a crimson fact or fancy in your head that you are burning to fetch out."

Mark Twain's description of the effect of the Civil War on the southerner belongs to the account in the second part of *Life on the Mississippi* of his revisitation of the River in 1882. Although he had had his initial experience on the River only twenty-five years earlier, Mark Twain had returned to a world that bore only a superficial resemblance to the one he had known as a fledgling pilot, everything having been changed by the catastrophic internecine struggle that had erupted in the Republic of the United States of America in the seventh decade of its founding. Not to be generally known for a long time yet as the "Civil War—" often in the North still called the "War of the Rebellion" and in the South "The War for Southern Independence"—the unparalleled bloodletting that the grandchildren and great grandchildren of the founders of the Republic were engaged in for four years had changed the meaning of time and history in the most fundamental sense. The civil slaughter and destruction had, to be sure, altered the very structure of American memory. Those Americans who had known the war intimately—and this in some way included all southerners, even those who, like Mark Twain, had removed themselves from the theater of war by going West—now, more self-consciously than the victors in the war, lived in two republics: the "Old Republic"—the remembered republic of the constitutional federation of self-liberated imperial colonies that had freed themselves in a war in that other time "befo *the* waw"; and the actual republic—the integral union of states, the "Second American Republic," the "nation state"— that had come into existence "aftah *the* waw." But for southerners, the defeated citizens of the aborted Confederate States of America, the sense of the displacement of memory was expressed in a more particular, in an essentially more intimate, historical terminology: the "Old South" and the "New South." Implying a displacement of memory different from that suggested by the terms Old Republic and New Republic, the southern effort to differentiate an Old and a New South emerged most simply and clearly, and it may be said most superficially, in the literary endeavor to create "local color" representations of the South. More deeply, the terms "Old South" and "New South" reflected the search by postbellum southern novelists for characters and situations that would transcend the regional concept of the southern literary identity. In their cultural situation southern writers were inclined to see the life of the individual southerner as always in a dramatic tension with history; they seemed almost incapable of imagining the rejection of the historical context of the individual life. As Robert Penn Warren once put it, "History is what you can't \ Resign from . . . ."

Yet after the War for Southern Independence had ended in the massive invasion and complete defeat of the Confederacy, southern writers—in ironic reaction to the feeling of being closed in history—had commonly envisioned what amounted to a southern resignation from history. Ignoring the historical actuality of the Confederacy—a nation that in its brief existence was ever contentious and divided—writers created a rhetorical image of a unified spiritual nation, to quote Warren again, A "City of the Soul." The metaphysical southern nation had, according to the rhetoric of southern nostalgia, evolved out of a stable antebellum civilization centered in the harmonious pastoral plantation and the beneficent institution of chattel slavery. Accepting such a vision of the past—out of the fear, it may be said, of the alienation of memory by history—the southerner was, as Warren observed, truly "trapped in history." The metaphysics of remembrance being equated with historical reality, one questioned the ideal image of the past at the risk of being suspected of treason.

But the literary imagination in the South did not yield altogether to delusionary remembrance. Reality at times intruded itself even into the rhetoric of an apologist like Thomas Nelson Page, creating an implied dramatic tension between memory and history. Removed sufficiently from the motive of apology, this tension promised to become highly fruitful in the case of Mark Twain's younger contemporary, George Washington Cable, but faded as Cable became more and more committed to the politics of promoting equitable treatment for the "freedmen." Among the immediate postwar generation of southern writers the literary promise of the drama of memory and history reached notable fulfillment only in Mark Twain, and this in only one book, *Adventures of Huckleberry Finn.*

This was a novel Mark Twain had begun in the 1870s and put aside. When he had finished *Life on the Mississippi,* he almost immediately went back to the story of Huck and Jim and completed it in a sustained burst of energy. Obviously the experience of returning to the River and completing the book that he had begun earlier as "Old Times on the Mississippi" with an account of the River and its world fifteen years after the end of the Civil War had produced a tension lacking in the initial book about Tom Sawyer and Huck Finn. Although *The Adventures of Tom Sawyer* (1876) has its darker moments, in this book Mark Twain's recollection of life in Hannibal "befo the wah" (in the 1840s) is informed more by nostalgia than irony. But in *Huckleberry Finn* the relationship between past and present—what was "befo the wah" and what was "aftah the wah"—has altered. Always more significant in Mark Twain's imagination, and in the southern mind generally, than what was "du'in' the waw" what was "befo the waw" and what was "aftah the waw" coalesce. In a novel that is basically an exploration of the southern society that fought the Civil War, Mark Twain strongly implies that history is what you can't resign from.

Or, to put it more corrrectly, Huck Finn implies this. Although a boy of no more than twelve or thirteen years of age, Mark Twain's persona in *Adventures of Huckleberry Finn* is not merely the narrator; writing in his own language, the vernacular of the Missouri backwoods, Huck is the highly self-conscious author, the literary artist, the authoritative maker, of his own book. This is evident from the beginning, when Huck says that "you don't know about me without you have read a book . . . by Mr. Mark Twain [i.e. *The Adventures of Tom Sawyer*]," to the final moment, when he says that if he had "knowed what a trouble it was to make a book," he "wouldn't 'a' tackled it." Invested with the authority of the author—in a day when a "writer" was still an "author" and was presumed to have authority—Huck is fundamentally a reliable narrator. He tells it like it was because, in terms of Mark Twain's philosophy of history, he could not do otherwise. Much has been made of what seems to be Mark Twain's trivialization of the logical climax of *Huckleberry Finn* when, after his awesome declaration that he will defy every rule of society and society's God rather than abandon his support of a "nigger" and a slave with whom, in an act of ultimate impiety, he has entered into a bond of brotherhood, Huck becomes a tool of Tom Sawyer's devotion to the rhetoric of the romantic novelists and participates in the resolution of the story in the cruel rigamarole of the "splendid, mixed up rescue." Yet ironically Huck's authoritative honesty is still basically present. He has come close to experiencing the delusion of an elevation to a moral level superior to that of the society in which he lives—a society indubitably marked by its subscription not only to the God-ordained right to own human beings but, according to Huck's witness, to the right to be aggressively ignorant, like Pap Finn; to carry on murderous and meaningless feuds, like the Grangerfords and Shepherdsons; to lynch defenseless bums like Boggs; and to tar and feather con artists like the Duke and the Dauphin. In a society, in short, that wholly betrays the ideal of the rule of reason that had informed the founding of the American Republic, Huck acquiesces in the historicity of his moral condition. Indeed almost immediately after he has spoken the "awful words" affirming his allegiance to Jim, he qualifies his declaration by saying that he will "go to work and steal Jim out of slavery again," for this is the kind of thing he ought to do, "being brung up to wickedness." In his seemingly unsophisticated yet subtle recognition of the immanence of the conscience in society—of the historicism of his own consciousness of good and evil— Huck displays an intuitive awareness of his situation. He cannot breathe at the level of transcendent moral choice. In his way Huck is profoundly aware of the irony of living in the semi-frontier microcosm of a society that had had its origin in a world historical manifesto proclaiming the innate sovereignty of the self—and heralding a "Great Experiment" in governance that amounted to an unprecedented experiment in human nature, this to test whether or not human beings are endowed with a sufficient capacity for rational thought and rational behavior to govern themselves as free "selves." Yet even as it came into being, half of the nation that had invented itself on the assumption of an affirmative answer to this question was already in the process of expanding into the largest slave society in modern times. Having made a book detailing his memory of his own effort to reject this society through an aborted flight to freedom with Jim, Huck asserts that he will now exercise the prerogative of the transcendent sovereign self and "light out for the territory" to escape being "civilized." He has "been there before." But even as he announces the second flight to freedom, Huck knows the desperate futility of his gesture. He cannot escape the burden of the historical actuality of his experience with Jim by referring it to the realm of nostalgic memory.

Yet if in his effort to penetrate the inner reality of southern society, Mark Twain resolved the tension between memory and history in favor of history, the influence of his exemplary effort did not appreciably undercut the subservience of the southern literary mind to the metaphysics of remembrance. This reason is no doubt to be found in the fact that Mark Twain wore the comic mask but not altogether so. The multivolume compilation of southern literary piety called *The Library of Southern Literature* (prepared, the title page pointedly announces under the "direct supervision of Southern men of letters") was published in the first decade of the twentieth century. While such an undertaking would not have been as feasible ten years later in the aftermath of World War I, the drama of the tension between memory and history created in the southern literary imagination by a war that had ended over fifty years ago was not only still present, but—in spite of the preoccupation with the before and after of the "Great War"—found its fulfillment as the definitive force in the writers of the "Southern Renascence": in (to speak only of a few novelists) Allen Tate, Caroline Gordon, Andrew Lytle, Robert Penn Warren, and, most profoundly, Faulkner.

The question of how the memory of the first world war enhanced the memory of the Civil War in the twentieth-century southern literary imagination is illuminated by a comparison of the difference between the attitude toward the memory of war assumed on the one hand by Faulkner and on the other by his precise contemporary Ernest Hemingway. Like Faulkner, Hemingway acknowledged the primary significance of Mark Twain, even to the point of saying in *The Green Hills of Africa* that "all modern American literature comes from one book . . . *Huckleberry Finn* . . . . There was nothing before. There has been nothing since." But in his hyperbolic theory of American writing, the midwesterner Hemingway ignored entirely the question of Huck's historical context and made him into a "Hemingway hero," who, however incongruously, may be compared to Jake Barnes in *The Sun Also Rises*. A figure of the writer (or the "author") and the chief actor in his own story, Jake, like all Hemingway heroes, finds the major motive of his life in the self-creation of a strangely stripped down image of a world that, in contrast to the memory obsessed world of Quentin Compson (in which the "past is not even past") is preoccupied with the presentness of the present, even to the point of rejecting all traditional associations, including that of the family.

To speak of the role of Quentin in *Absalom, Absalom!* is to raise a much discussed problem. As we read the story of the Sutpens in its various reconstructions by the several narrators, do we discover any single character who serves as a focus of the authorial consciousness? On the face of it, is Quentin not simply one among the several characters in the novel, each obsessed by memory, each—including the third-person narrator—a self-conscious narrator (and actor), each the contributor of a highly subjective interpretative version of the fall of the House of Sutpen? The voluminous library of Faulkner criticism offers such different, and at times contradictory, responses to the narrators' interpretations of the story of the Sutpens that we may well reach the conclusion that the underlying motive of *Absalom, Absalom!* is contradictory: a strenuous effort to recover the past, the novel is yet a demonstration of the ambivalence of the effort. Yet in spite of the narrative maze we encounter in *Absalom, Absalom!*—which is further complicated, it should be added, by the presence of the unidentified third person voice amid the identifiable voices—there is reason to interpret it as finding its ultimate focus in Quentin. "Ishmael is the witness in *Moby Dick*," Faulkner once commented, "as I am Quentin in *The Sound and the Fury*." It may be argued with some plausibility that Quentin is not only the chief participant-witness in *Absalom, Absalom!*, but in his imaginative struggle to grasp the meaning of the lives of Henry Sutpen and his family, white and black, is—as a persona of Faulkner, the author, the maker, the ordering artist—the same enclosing presence in the story of the Sutpens that Faulkner had conceived him to be in his earlier story about the Compsons.

Powerfully established at the beginning of the novel—when Quentin sits with Miss Rosa in the September heat of the "dim airless room" of Sutpen's mansion—and powerfully reasserted at its end, when Quentin lies in the bed talking with Shreve in the "iron" winter dark of a Harvard dormitory room—the presence of the 20-year-old Mississippian in *Absalom, Absalom!* is more compelling than that of any other character. Hearing Miss Rosa's version of the story about the "demon" Sutpen in the initial scene of *Absalom, Absalom!*—listening to her speak "in that grim haggard amazed voice" as it vanishes "into and then out of the long inter-

159

vals like a stream, a trickle running from patch to patch of dried sand"—
Quentin, a grandchild of the generation of Mississippi warriors who had
fought in the Civil War, discovers after a time that he is no longer listening to the voice of Miss Rosa but is hearing "two separate" voices in himself: one voice is that of the "Quentin preparing for Harvard in the
South, the deep South dead since 1865 and peopled with garrulous
baffled ghosts"; the other voice in this inward dialogue is that of the
Quentin "who was still too young to deserve yet to be a ghost, but nevertheless having to be one for all that, since he was born and bred in the
deep South the same as she [Miss Rosa] was." The two Quentins talk "to
one another in the long silence of notpeople, in notlanguage: *It seems that
this demon—his name was Sutpen—(Colonel Sutpen)—Colonel Sutpen.
Who came out of nowhere and without warning upon the land with a band of
strange niggers and built a plantation*" (4–5).

At this point his dialogic interiorizing of the Sutpen story is interrupted when Quentin becomes aware that Miss Rosa is directly addressing him:

> "Because you are going away to attend the college at Harvard they tell
> me . . . So I dont imagine you will ever come back and settle down here as
> a country lawyer in a little town like Jefferson, since Northern people have
> already seen to it that there is little left in the South for a young man. So
> maybe you will enter the literary profession as so many Southern gentle-
> men and gentlewomen too are doing now and maybe you will remember
> this and write about it. You will be married then I expect and perhaps
> your wife will want a new gown or a new chair for the house and you can
> write this and submit it to the magazines" (5).

Why, Quentin wonders, does Miss Rosa need to suggest that he become a writer so that he can be the teller of her tale? If her need to tell the
story of her relationship with Sutpen is so coercive, why does not she
herself tell it? She is a writer, well-known as Yoknapatawpha County's
"poetess laureate," who "out of some bitter and implacable reserve of un-
defeat" has frequently celebrated the heroes of the Lost Cause in odes,
eulogies, and epitaphs published in the county newspaper. Quentin's
question remains unanswered, at least explicitly. The implicit answer lies
in Miss Rosa's recognition of Quentin as a potential literary witness in the
first scene of *Absalom, Absalom!* Here Faulkner indicates his intention to
repeat, in a more complex way, what he had done in *The Sound and the*

Fury six years earlier, namely, project Quentin as an incarnation of the fundamental, and inescapable, motive of the postbellum southern writer's imagination: the importunate sense, stemming from a compulsive memory of the Civil War, not simply of a personal intimacy with history but, as in the case of Huckleberry Finn, of a connection with history so absolute that it is the very source of his being. When his father tells Quentin that Miss Rosa has a vengeful motive in her idea of involving him in the story of her dastardly treatment by the "demon"—this because she believes, or wants to believe, that her fateful association with Sutpen would never have occurred if the "demon" had not come to Mississippi as the consequence of a friendship with Quentin's grandfather—Quentin counters with an explanation of epic grandeur: "*She wants it told .. so that people whom she will never see and whose names she will never hear and who have never heard her name nor seen her face will read it and know at last why God let us lose the War: that only through the blood of our men and the tears of our women could he stay this demon and efface his name and lineage from the earth*" (6).

In spite of the fact that Quentin himself immediately rejects his bardic explanation of Miss Rosa's solicitation of his pen, he is, as the third-person narrator indicates, not merely playing a game with his father. His conception of Miss Rosa's appeal to the "God who let us lose the War" indirectly reflects the fact that Quentin knows that he and Miss Rosa (and for that matter his father), are as profoundly entangled in the history of Sutpen's struggle to found the House of Sutpen as is Miss Rosa's older sister, Ellen Coldfield, the wife Sutpen takes from a prominent Yoknapatawpha family to be the bearer of his heirs; or Henry and Judith Sutpen, the children Ellen bears; or Charles Bon, the son and heir Sutpen has earlier fathered in Haiti, only to reject him when he discovered that his mother is partly Negro; or Clytie, Sutpen's daughter by one of the "wild" slaves he brings to Yoknapatawpha. And Quentin knows that, in a larger sense, he, and Miss Rosa, and Mr. Compson are also implicated in the anomalies and ironies of a shaping cultural ethos that paradoxically at once commemorates and celebrates the world historical self-defeat of a house that was not only a part of that larger house Lincoln said could not stand divided against itself but was significantly in itself a divided house.

Without insisting at all on a literal correspondence between the House of Sutpen and the House of the South, one can hardly fail to discern implicit symbols of the southern divisiveness in Quentin's knowledge of the Sutpens. He knows, for one thing, that Miss Rosa had a father who as "a conscientious objector on religious grounds had starved to death in the attic of his own house, hidden (some said, walled up) there from Confederate provost marshals' men and fed secretly at night by the same daughter [Miss Rosa] who at the very time was accumulating her first folio in which the lost cause's unregenerate vanquished were by name embalmed" (6). Quentin also knows the more fateful fact that Miss Rosa had a "nephew [Henry Sutpen] who served for four years in the same company with his sister's fiance [Charles Bon] and then shot the fiance to death before the gates to the house where the sister waited in her wedding gown on the eve of the wedding and then fled, vanished, none knew where" (6–7). And Quentin knows much more, too much for any peace of mind. Having "grown up" with all the names associated with the story of Sutpen, Quentin, the third-person narrator tells us, has become a symbolic repository of the memory of the destroyed House of Sutpen and the remembrance of the southern defeat.

> He was a barracks filled with stubborn back-looking ghosts still recovering, even forty-three years afterward, from the fever which had cured the disease, waking from the fever without even knowing that it had been the fever itself which they had fought against and not the sickness, looking with stubborn recalcitrance backward beyond the fever and into the disease with actual regret, weak from the fever yet free of the disease and not even aware that the freedom was that of impotence (7).

Described by the third-person narrator as "not a being, an entity" but, in metaphors of Shakespearean intensity, as a "barracks" filled with ghosts, or more expansively, a ghostly "commonwealth," Quentin emerges more clearly in *Absalom, Absalom!* than in *The Sound and the Fury* as a highly self-conscious, romantic, doomed embodiment of the lost Confederacy. Out of the deepest levels of his imagination of memory and history, he subtly transforms the story of the House of Sutpen into a deeply introverted, and deeply ironic, vision of the drama of the inner history of the southern war for independence. Even as the southern society was engaged in a massive struggle to preserve itself as a slave society, the third-person narrator intimates in his description of Quentin, it had a secret motive, inarticulate, hidden even from itself: a desire to free itself from its enslavement to the "disease" of slavery. Yet, having been forced by military catastrophe to accept the fulfillment of its hidden desire, this society looks back with regret at having been freed by the "fever" of war from the "disease" of slavery. Until the South can openly accept the historical implications of its desire to be free from the social and economic institution of chattel slavery—which, although *Absalom, Absalom!* does not quite make this explicit, had been rationalized by antebellum southerners as their necessary source of freedom—the revolutionary shift from a slave society to a free society is historically "impotent." As the drama of the House of Sutpen unfolds through the witness of Miss Rosa and Mr. Compson, Quentin's struggle to interpret it almost half a century after the end of the War for Southern Independence becomes the focal revelation of this powerful irony. In an earlier age of man Quentin would have been a bardic voice speaking of the glory of "olden times." But in the first decade of the twentieth century—not so much a grandchild as a ghost of the generation of the 1860s—a poet of the American South assumes the role not only of a witness to the unending drama of his own personal struggle to interpret the meaning of the vexed and torturous history of the South, but like Faulkner, the self-conscious role of being an actor in a drama he is both composing and enacting in his own consciousness.

The problem of interpretation that preoccupies Quentin in this drama is the central problem in *Absalom, Absalom!*, why does Henry kill Charles Bon? Three poignant scenes are particularly illuminating. One occurs toward the end of the fifth chapter, when the third-person narrator interrupts Miss Rosa's narrative to present what he imagines to be Quentin's creation for himself of a part of the story that he cannot "pass," this being the moment when Henry, having just shot Charles Bon as the two soldiers arrive back at Sutpen's place after Appomattox, runs up the stairs and bursts into his sister's bedroom. Here he sees Clytie and Ellen, "the white girl in her underthings (made of flour sacking when there had been flour, of window curtains when not)." He sees too Judith's wedding dress,

> the yellowed creamy mass of old intricate satin and lace spread carefully on the bed and then caught swiftly up by the white girl and held before her as the door crashed in and the brother stood there, hatless, with his shaggy bayonet-trimmed hair, his gaunt worn unshaven face, his patched and faded gray tunic, the pistol still hanging from his flank: the two of

them, brother and sister, curiously alike as if the difference in sex had
merely sharpened the common blood to a terrific, an almost unbearable,
similarity, speaking to one another in short brief staccato sentences, as if
they stood breast to breast striking one another in turn, neither making
any attempt to guard against the blows:

Now you cant marry him.
Why cant I marry him?
Because he's dead.
Dead?
Yes. I killed him (139).

Another illuminating scene in *Absalom, Absalom!* occurs when Quentin, listening to his father's account of the relationship between Charles
Bon and Judith, sees the one letter Charles—at Henry's urging—wrote
to Judith Sutpen during his entire four years in the Confederate army.
Taking the letter in hand, Quentin imagines as he reads "the faint spi-
dery script"—written nearly fifty years before on elegant French note-
paper from a gutted southern mansion with a pen dipped in stove polish
captured from the Yankees—that he is listening to Bon's "gentle sardonic whimsical and incurably pessimistic" voice telling Judith in the
final days of the Confederacy he has come to believe they are "*strangely
enough, included among those who are doomed to live.*" Although Bon's
message is enigmatic, Judith takes it to be a proposal of marriage.

While Mr. Compson talks on about Henry and Bon—wondering
whether Henry had warned Bon not to come back to Judith and describing the scene of their encounter outside the gate of the Sutpen place as
they arrive back from the war ("the two of them must have ridden side by
side almost")—Quentin, once again "hearing without having to listen,"
according to the intervening imagination of the narrator, is depicted as
silently imagining the scene for himself.

(It seemed to Quentin that he could actually see them, facing one another
at the gate. Inside the gate what was once a park now spread, unkempt
. . . up to a huge house where a young girl waited in a wedding dress
made from stolen scraps, the house . . . a skeleton giving of itself in slow
driblets of furniture and carpet, linen and silver, to help to die torn and
anguished men who knew, even while dying, that for months now the
sacrifice and the anguish were in vain. They faced one another on the two
gaunt horses, two men, young, not yet in the world, not yet breathed over

long enough, to be old with old eyes, with unkempt hair and faces gaunt
and weathered as if cast by some spartan and even niggard hand from
bronze, in worn and patched gray weathered now to the color of dead
leaves, the one with the tarnished braid of an officer, the other plain of
cuff, the pistol lying yet across the saddle bow unaimed, the two faces
calm, the voices not even raised: *Dont you pass the shadow of this post, this
branch, Charles*; and *I am going to pass it, Henry*) . . . (105 – 106).

The conclusion of the scene is in Mr. Compson's voice: "—— and then
Wash Jones sitting that saddleless mule before Miss Rosa's gate, shouting
her name into the sunny and peaceful quiet of the street, saying 'Air you
Rosie Coldfield? Then you better come on out yon. Henry has done shot
that durn French feller. Kilt him dead as a beef'" (106).

Why does Bon want to marry his sister? Is he in love with her? If so,
his love is clearly subordinated to his passion for revenge on a father who
refuses to acknowledge him. Sutpen had a vivid chance to accept Bon as
his son when the elegant and handsome New Orleanian comes to visit
Sutpen's Hundred as Henry's fellow student and friend at the University
of Mississippi. He had a still more vivid chance to accept Charles as his
son toward the end of the war when the unit Charles and Henry are in is
attached to a regimental unit commanded by their father. If Sutpen had
recognized Bon at either time, presumably things would have been different. But he cannot acknowledge an heir who has a tincture of black
blood. Bon—with no trace of the negroid in his appearance, handsome,
urbane, ten years older than Henry, becomes Henry's idol, and no less a
fatal attraction for Judith. Undergoing the experience of war with Bon,
Henry, who has known since 1861 that he and Judith are half-brother
and half-sister to Bon (and has known as well, though this knowledge
is of lesser import, that Bon is the father of a son by a New Orleans
octoroon) has, it would seem, overcome his revulsion against its incestuous nature and reconciled himself to a union between Bon and Judith.
How has this incredible adjustment taken place? Has the war experience
rendered Henry's feeling of a bond with Bon transcendent over any other
emotion? Or does Henry, unconsciously harboring incestuous feelings
both for his brother and his sister, somehow imagine their marriage as a
consummation of his desire? Does Bon desire the marriage only for revenge on Sutpen? Or is he in love with Judith? For that matter, is Judith
in love with Bon?

In any event it is not until the very end of the war that Henry learns of an impediment to the marriage of Bon and Judith that love, normal or abnormal, can in no wise blink. When he responds to a command to come to Colonel Sutpen's tent (Sutpen has organized a command and gone to the war not long after Henry and Bon), he is told by Sutpen that following Bon's birth he had discovered that his mother, a planter's daughter he had taken as his wife while he was an overseer on a Haitian plantation, had Negro blood. Henry is given an injunction by his father that, since it issues from the same lips as those of his commanding officer, has something of the force of a military order: "*He must not marry her, Henry.*"

We do not know about the meeting of Henry and his father until the culminating, and concluding, three-chapter scene in *Absalom, Absalom!*: the dialogue on the question of why Henry kills Bon that takes place between Quentin and his roommate, the Canadian Shreve McCannon, in their chilled Harvard dormitory room on a snowy night in January 1910. But we learn about Sutpen's injunction to Henry not through a speculative reconstruction of the scene that took place in Sutpen's tent as the two friends talk. The scene comes to us only in Quentin Compson's unspoken recreation. At first, Quentin imagines, Henry refused the order.

> —*You are going to let him marry Judith, Henry.*
> *Still Henry does not answer. It has all been said before, and now he has had four years of bitter struggle following which, whether it be victory or defeat which he has gained, at least he has gained it and has peace now, even if the peace be mostly despair.*
> —*He cannot marry her, Henry.*
> *Now Henry speaks.*
> —*You said that before. I told you then. And now, and now it wont be much longer now and then we wont have anything left: honor nor pride or God since God quit us four years ago only He never thought it necessary to tell us; no shoes nor clothes and no need for them; not only no land to make food but no need for the food and when you dont have God and honor and pride, nothing matters except that there is the old mindless meat that dont even care if it was defeat or victory, that wont even die, that will be out in the woods and fields, grubbing up roots and weeds.—Yes, I have decided. Brother or not, I have decided I will. I will . . . .*

> *—He must not marry her, Henry. His mother's father told me that her mother had been a Spanish woman. I believed him; it was not until after he was born that I found that his mother was part negro* (283).

Quentin's imagination of it is also the only source of the moment that follows immediately after the scene in Colonel Sutpen's tent, the encounter between Bon and Henry at the campfire.

> *—So it's the miscegenation, not the incest which you cant bear. Henry doesn't answer.*
>
> *—And he sent me no word? He did not ask you to send me to him? No word to me, no word at all. That was all he had to do, now, today; four years ago or at any time during the four years. That was all. He would not have needed to ask it, require it, of me. I would have offered it. I would have said, I will never see her again before he could have asked it of me. He did not have to do this, Henry. He didn't need to tell you I am a nigger to stop me* (285).

In Quentin's private recreation of what happened next, Bon extends a pistol and commands Henry to shoot him (Bon is also Henry's superior officer), but Henry refuses, saying "*—You are my brother.*" He continues to refuse even though Bon says, "*No. I'm not. I'm the nigger that's going to sleep with your sister. Unless you stop me, Henry*" (286). Henry does not stop Bon until the two arrive at the very gate to Sutpen's Hundred.

By this juncture in the novel Quentin's telling Shreve about his going out to Sutpen's Hundred with Miss Rosa, discovering the dying Henry there, and then witnessing the burning of Sutpen's mansion can only come as an anticlimax. It is instructive to learn that in the short story out of which Faulkner's novel grew, this is not the case. Unpublished until Joseph Blotner's edition of the *Uncollected Stories of William Faulkner* in 1979, this story, entitled "Evangeline," is, like another Faulkner short story called "Mistral," developed through the use of an "I" narrator and the narrator's friend "Don Giovanni." Don has put the narrator onto a "ghost story" about the mystery surrounding a decaying Mississippi plantation house belonging to a family named Sutpen. Although the details of the plot are somewhat different and not nearly so elaborate, "Evangeline" centers in the narrator's investigation of the story of Judith, Bon, and Henry, and his discovery of Henry's presence in the Sutpen house, where all during the forty years since his fratricidal act, he has lived secretly under the protection of a black woman named Raby, who it turns out, fathered by Sutpen on one of his slaves, is, like Judith, the sister of Bon and Henry. (Raby becomes Clytie in *Absalom, Absalom!*) As though he was unable to assimilate the experience of verifying the secret presence of Henry Sutpen in the Sutpen mansion, the narrator's account of the event is fragmentary and subjectively impressionistic. Yet, it is strangely empathetic, as though the narrator feels a certain identity with Henry:

> It was quite still. There was a faint constant sighing high in the cedars, and I could hear the insects and the mockingbird. Soon there were two of them, answering one another, brief, quiring, risinginflectioned [*sic*]. Soon the sighing cedars, the insects and the birds became one peaceful sound bowled inside the skull in monotonous miniature, as if all the earth were contracted and reduced to the dimensions of a baseball, into and out of which shapes, fading, emerged fading and faded emerging:
> "And you were killed by the last shot fired in the war?"
> "I was so killed. Yes."
> "Who fired the last shot fired in the war?"
> "Was it the last shot you fired in the war, Henry?"
> "I fired a last shot in the war; yes."
> "You depended on the war, and the war betrayed you too; was that it?"
> "Was that it, Henry?" (605–606).

In *Absalom, Absalom!* Quentin's visit to the dark room of the Sutpen mansion where Henry lies dying is more ambiguous in its presentation. In the novel, in contrast to "Evangeline," Henry has fled after he has killed Bon and has returned four years before Miss Rosa and Quentin find him there under the zealous protection of a "tiny gnomelike creature in headrag and voluminous skirts" and "a worn coffee-colored face," his sister Clytie. In the discovery scene in *Absalom, Absalom!* no reference is made to a last shot in the war; Quentin's interrogation of Henry is elliptical. But the scene brings to a subtle climax the increasingly close relationship the doomed Quentin feels with Sutpen's tragic children. The sealing of this relationship is indicated by so small a sign as the colon that marks the transition from the narrator's objective description of how Quentin enters the shuttered "bare stale room" where Henry lies dying to the portrayal of the interior scene in which the identity of Henry is established.

"The bed, the yellow sheets and pillow, the wasted yellow face with
closed, almost transparent eyelids on the pillow, the wasted hands crossed
on the breast was if he were already a corpse; waking or sleeping it was the
same and would be the same forever as long as he lived":

And you are——?
Henry Sutpen.
And you have been here——?
Four Years.
And you came home——?
To die. Yes.
Yes. To die.
And you have been here——?
And you are——?
Henry Sutpen (298).

In the omission of an additional punctuation mark [i.e., "(——*the
winter of '64 now, the army retreated,*") etc.] to denote the shift from the
objective to the subjection mode (i.e., the entry into Quentin's consciousness) the subtle authority of the third-person narrator becomes explicit.
His consciousness has become identical with Quentin's. For those who
know "Evangeline," an anticipation of this moment may be seen in the
"I" narrator's strange rapport with Bon, Henry, and Raby [Clytie] in
"Evangeline." When both *The Saturday Evening Post* and *The Woman's
Home Companion* rejected "Evangeline," Faulkner put the story aside,
but finding that it would not let him alone, he came back to it after a
couple of years and sought to make it work better by replacing the "I"
narrator and Don with two characters he called Chisholm and Burke.
Eventually, the grip of the story on him becoming stronger, he conceived
of transforming Chisholm and Burke into Quentin and Shreve and
making them interpreter-participants in a story that, greatly expanded
and far more sophisticated in technique, would have a suggestive frame
of reference in the Old Testament epic of David and his sons and be a
major part of his symbol of the history of the South, the fictional history
of Yoknapatawpha County, Mississippi. Yet basically, Faulkner conceived, the story expanded into novelistic proportions would have its
center—not in the history, singular yet paradigmatic, represented by
Sutpen: the ravaging exploitation of the southern wilderness that, in not
much more than two short generations, produced the rise and fall of the

Cotton Kingdom—but in a story allusive of the biblical story of King David and Absalom's murder of his brother Ammon. In this story the brothers have just concluded four long years fighting against great odds for a common cause. Ironically, in a civil conflict that has often been called "the brothers" war—and in which brothers, not only in a figurative but in some cases in a literal sense, were engaged on opposing sides—the sons of Sutpen were on the same side. Like most southerners, slaveholders and nonslaveholders, they fought to uphold the more or less official doctrine that the preservation of slavery was necessary for the preservation of a sacred guarantee of constitutional freedom that included their right to own slaves. Forcibly dispossessed of this right, they believed, they would become slaves themselves. The murdered brother and the murdering brother had no quarrel in this respect. But the narrator in "Evangeline," asking Charles Bon if he had been killed by the last shot fired in the war and Henry if he had pulled the trigger, was moved by the knowledge that Bon had not died in the war between the North and South but in a struggle within a society that, even as it fought against the brothers with whom, only three generations earlier, it had made common cause in the American Revolution, was rent by its need for a more coherent, convincing definition of its historical character than the Revolution had provided. The southern struggle for historical self-representation was rendered all the more intense because of the fact that even as the South sought to express its destiny, the effort was repressed by the need to present the image of a society united in support of slavery. In its uncertainty about itself the southern slave society placed an extreme premium on an ideal of order that held above all, as Faulkner said in speaking of Andrew Jackson, that "the principle of honor must be defended whether it was or not because defended it was whether or not." Equating the principle of family honor with the ideal of feminine chastity and the protection of the purity of the bloodline, Henry had finally to slay Charles, even though Mr. Compson says Henry loved Bon, and in "Evangeline" Don says the two were "close as a married couple almost."

In their conversation in the cold dark after they finally go to bed, Shreve keeps on baiting Quentin about the South. Referring to the Canadians, he says, "We dont live among defeated grandfathers and freed slaves (or have I got it backward and was it your folks that are free and the niggers that lost?) and bullets in the dining room table and such, to be always reminding us never to forget." When Shreve, warming to his subject, observes that the southern memory of General Sherman is perpetual, so that "forevermore as long as your children's children produce children you wont be anything but a descendant of a long line of colonels killed in Pickett's charge at Manassas," Quentin at once corrects Shreve's factual error about the battle in which Pickett's charge occurred, adding, in the second most famous statement in the novel, "You cant understand it. You would have to be born there." But when Shreve—in a passage not often noticed in the voluminous critical interpretation of *Absalom, Absalom!*—continues to challenge Quentin about the southern culture of memory, "Would I then? [i.e. "have to be born there"] . . . Do you understand it?", Quentin equivocates:

> "I dont know," Quentin said. "Yes, of course I understand it." They breathed in the darkness. After a moment Quentin said: "I dont know" (289).

When Shreve presents his most drastic challenge to Quentin: "Now I want you to tell me one thing more. Why do you hate the South?", the heir of the Compsons replies "quickly at once, immediately," in the best known words of the novel, "I dont hate it" (303).

> "I dont hate it," he said. *I dont hate it* he thought, panting in the cold air, the iron New England dark: *I dont. I dont! I dont hate it! I dont hate it!* (303).

If, as has been said, Quentin protests Shreve's challenge too much, he has reason to. His very identity, in a way his very existence, is at stake.

"Ishmael is the witness in *Moby-Dick* as I am Quentin in *The Sound and the Fury*": If in his imagination of his authorial role, Faulkner identifies with Quentin in the comparatively simple structure of the story of the doomed Compsons, he does so even more surely, if more subtly, in the intricately structured story involving the relationship between the memorial reconstruction of the doom of the House of Sutpen on the one hand and doom of the House of Compson on the other. Thought of by Faulkner as a symbol of the second—or, it may be said, the first full—literary generation of the postbellum South, Quentin (born 1890) could scarcely have been conceived by a writer of his own generation. Representing a symbolic embodiment of the culmination of the drama of memory and history in Faulkner's generation (Faulkner was born in 1897)—

the generation that became the post-World War I generation—Quentin embodies more powerfully than any other character in southern fiction the drama of the ironic equivocation of the southern literary mind in its quest to discover in the southern memory a postbellum southern identity. The revelation of the inner civil war in the South in the story of Henry, Bon, and Judith reveals how, in his effort to come to terms with the South, Quentin, a romantic southern Puritan, is the doomed reincarnation of an earlier young southern Puritan, Henry Sutpen. In the last moment of a difficult journey back from the war, obeying the southern mode of the murderous defense of family honor—defending an abstract principle that had to be defended lest the order of the world would be lost—Henry had not only killed his brother and made himself into a ghost, he had made Quentin, who would not be born for another fifteen years, into a ghost. "'I am older at twenty than a lot of people who have died, Quentin said'" (301).

Before he called on Quentin Compson to be a witness to, and an actor in, the drama of Henry Sutpen's desperate and despairing defense of the principle of honor in *Absalom, Absalom!,* Faulkner had of course in *The Sound and the Fury* already depicted the ultimate fate of his surrogate. Drowning himself in the Charles River in Cambridge, Massachusetts, on June 2, 1910, Quentin had signaled the despair of those bound by the poetry of memory to a world no longer believed in. In this case it was the world the slaveholders—and, however unwillingly, the enslaved themselves—had made in the American South. Equating freedom with the defense of an illusory principle that they nonetheless conceived to be the vital basis of order, the slave masters had littered battlefield after battlefield with the sacrificial victims of a War for Southern Independence. Like the subtly ironic pathos of Mark Twain's representation of Huckleberry Finn's memory of the antebellum South, the still more refined distillation of pathos in Faulkner's representation of Quentin's memory of the Confederacy, and of the postbellum South, does not simply reflect the drama of the literary representation of the inner history of the Civil War, it is part and parcel of this history. If, moreover—and we must admit the possibility—should either Mark Twain's or Faulkner's representation of the war be deemed at times to be misrepresentation, it is not the less integral to the war's inner history.

Faulkner's *Absalom, Absalom!*

The references to *Absalom, Absalom!* are to the following text:

William Faulkner, *Absalom, Absalom!* (The corrected Text). New York: Random House, 1986. [Prepared under the direction of Noel Polk.]
Uncollected Stories of William Faulkner. Edited by Joseph Blotner. New York: Random House, 1979.

William Faulkner was born in 1897 in New Albany, Mississippi, and died in Oxford, Mississippi in 1962. Selected publications: *The Marble Faun* (1924, poems); *Soldiers' Pay* (1926); *Sartoris* (1929; longer version, Flags in the Dust*, 1973); *The Sound and the Fury* (1929); *As I Lay Dying* (1930); *Sanctuary* (1931); *Light in August* (1932); *Absalom, Absalom!* (1936, revised edition, Random House, 1986); *The Unvanquished* (1938); *Go Down, Moses* (1942); *Intruder in the Dust* (1948); *Collected Stories of William Faulkner* (1950); *Requiem for a Nun* (1951); *A Fable* (1954); *The Reivers* (1961).

On Allen Tate's *The Fathers*

Tom Wicker

SINCE ITS PUBLICATION IN 1938, *The Fathers* has evoked much critical comment and dissection, most of it laudatory. A half-century later, however, Allen Tate's novel is so little known to general readers that I—a voracious consumer of Civil War literature, fiction or nonfiction—confess that I had not heard of it.

No doubt the fault was mine. But I was not able, in preparation for this article, to find a copy in the New York bookshops I consulted, including the admirable Strand, a goldmine of old or obscure works. The New York Society Library, an estimable private institution on East 79th Street, did not have a copy. A mail-order firm that claims to find out-of-print books failed even to respond to my request for *The Fathers*.

The editors of this volume finally provided me with a paperback reprint by the Louisiana State University Press—though several bookstores, upon consulting their catalogues, had insisted to me that no paperback was available. *Sic transit gloria mundi!* Not even critical adulation guarantees a novel's literary survival.

After having finally read *The Fathers*, moreover, I believe the critical attention it once received may owe less to its undeniable merit than to Allen Tate's deserved reputation as a poet, man of letters, and one of the Agrarian essayists. *The Fathers* was his first and only novel; coming from a man who already had achieved literary distinction, it naturally received great attention. Much of it was, and is, deserved—though I am far from agreeing with Thomas Daniel Young who in 1977, in an introduction to the L. S. U. paperback, termed *The Fathers* "surely the most remarkable first novel in American literature."

Contrary to my expectation, Mr. Tate's novel turned out to be only peripherally about the Civil War—though the coming of the war provides the novel's environment, and near its end a brief scene from the edges of the first battle of Manassas is sketched. Allen Tate, in fact, does not appear to have considered *The Fathers* a "war novel." He was writing, instead, of the end of a society, that of the antebellum South; and he does not attribute even that wholly to the war of 1861–65—most of which takes place after the novel's close—but mostly to the internal contradictions of a long-established, nearly ossified southern way of life.

The novel's primary achievement is in a kind of double point of view—that of Lacy Buchan, a youth of fifteen just before the war, who recalls its coming a half-century later, when he is an elderly doctor. Thus, the boy's feelings and words, even his actions, are filtered to the reader through the old man's memory, sometimes his wisdom, more often his continuing search for an understanding of which he is still uncertain.

This approach enables Mr. Tate to overlay the action of 1860 and 1861 with the consciousness of a later time; and it gives Lacy Buchan "a story to tell" about "a score of people whom I knew and loved, people beyond whose lives I could imagine no other life," who were to be "scattered into the new life of the modern age where they cannot even find themselves."

The old man's memory impinging on the youth's sensibility—"my feelings now about that time"—preserves the immediacy of "that time" without allowing that immediacy to dominate. Ultimately, Lacy Buchan's preoccupation is not, anyway, with how war came. Rather, it's as if his memory of that period is the background of a photograph, before which stand people who in the assurances of their lives were unaware, mostly unable to imagine, the cataclysm inevitably being formed by shapes and images shadowy in the distance.

This particularly applies to Lacy's father, Major Lewis Buchan—one of the novel's two symbolic and conflicting forces. Major Buchan not only knew but lived "the moves of an intricate game that he expected everybody else to play . . . everything he was and felt was in the game itself"—that is, in the rituals and customs and understandings by which Virginia society, by 1860, had come to sustain itself, without much question or introspection. Major Buchan "had no life apart" from the intricate game of observing the rules; and the only time Lacy can recall seeing his father blush was when someone incautiously remarked: "If you will allow me to be personal . . ."

"Papa," Lacy observes, "could never allow anyone to be personal." The social *order* had to prevail.

So stratified was the resulting life of the Buchan family that a half-century later Lacy can recall—whether with pleasure or pain it's not clear—the ceremony with which, in his youth, he and his father had started each day:

> [A]s I stood before him he leaned over and kissed me on the forehead. Then he shook hands as he said, "God bless you, my son, in your labors of this day."
> "God bless you, papa," I said (LSU Press edition, 126).

In the immediately following paragraphs, however, the essential flaw of Major Buchan's cherished society emerges—as well as what I consider one of the flaws of Allen Tate's novel. As Lacy leaves for school, an old slave, Coriolanus, always dusts the major's sitting room; then

> [P]apa would glance up from his reading over the rims of his steel spectacles, and say, "Well, Coriolanus, your labors must have fatigued you. You'd better rest a little."
> Coriolanus sat down in a small straight chair near the hearth, but he would not have done it had the "major" not invited him every morning . . . In this way the two old friends enjoyed each other's company.

Chattel slavery itself thus could be camouflaged beneath daily ritual; and master and slave (whose very name obscures if it does not deny his status), both conducting themselves by the rules of the intricate game, could present the appearance of being mere "old friends."

Slavery truly was the worm in the southern apple, as Allen Tate acknowledged in other writings. But it is only one of the internal weaknesses, and not necessarily the most destructive, that destroys Major Buchan's way of life. *The Fathers* suggests that the very styliziation of that life, its dependence upon rules and assumptions to deny its flaws, was the primary factor that caused its precarious balance—in Lacy Buchan's phrase—"upon a pedestal below which lay an abyss I could not name."

In a more conventional novel, it might be supposed that Major Buchan's life would be destroyed by hustling Yankees or the fiery upheavals of war. Mr. Tate more subtly—and I believe shrewdly—brings on George Posey, another but very different southern man, with a good business eye—he will sell slaves, an offense Major Buchan cannot countenance—and a disorderly family background. Impatient with tradition (of the Buchan "connection," he remarks: "They do nothing but die and marry and think about the honor of Virginia"), George Posey is unable to submerge his feelings or his attitudes in the rites that overmatch personal sensibility in Major Buchan's world.

When George wants to marry a Buchan daughter, he does not ask for her hand; he simply announces his intention to the nonplused major. When challenged to a duel by a bullying southern cavalier, George reacts directly: he knocks the man down with his fist. After marrying Susan Buchan, he refuses to attend her mother's burial because the attendant ritual cannot overcome his awareness of the corrupt body; and when on a plantation tour with Major Buchan they see a bull mount a cow, George looks "helpless and betrayed" at the exposed intimacy. In the presence of death and life, George Posey has no capacity to conceal or accept their rawest meanings, as demanded by Major Buchan's code.

The collision between the internal forces represented by the major and George—the settled society challenged by those who will not accept its rules—comes to a climax in a strangely flat scene of double murder. Lacy's brother Semmes, in obedience to the code taught him by the Major, shoots a slave, Yellow Jim, who may or may not have raped the girl Semmes intends to marry. (Note the disparity in the names Mr. Tate gives to the "good slave" Coriolanus, who accepts, and the bad slave, who transgresses.)

George Posey then shoots Semmes—because Yellow Jim is his half-brother, a product of the miscegenation that was inevitably the consequence of human slavery. This appears to be the most explicit statement of Mr. Tate's theme: Semmes shoots Yellow Jim as a necessary act to sustain a society built on the subjugation of a race; but George shoots Semmes as an immediate personal reaction to the murder of his black brother.

I take Mr. Tate's novel to say, therefore, that rule and regulation cannot compensate for the innate flaws of a social order built by men; their natural instincts not only will infuse any such society with flaws but in the end will overpower whatever restraints that society seeks to impose on them. "The abyss" is always there, no matter what games men play to deny its existence.

All this, of course, might have occurred at any time in the antebellum South, or even later. But Mr. Tate set his apocalyptic story in the last months before the Civil War for the reason, I suspect, that if collision with George Posey precipitated the disasters of Major Buchan's family, the war itself was to bring the same upheaval to the South. That war was the certain consequence of the kinds of forces, personal and social, that governed George Posey and the major; and thus the Posey-Buchan drama is symbolic or emblematic of the war to come.

Despite this intelligent scheme and some sensitive writing, *The Fathers* does not seem to me an entirely successful novel. For one thing, its portrayal of southern slavery is romanticized—the previously quoted scene with Coriolanus being not untypical. At his wife's funeral, for another example, Major Buchan takes the hand of her black maid of many years, Lucy, and draws her into the middle of the grieving family gathering. At another point, Coriolanus says he does not wish to outlive the major. And I don't make much distinction between a willingness to own human beings and a willingness to sell them.

This is not an objection to Allen Tate's politics; he makes clear, in other writings, his abhorrence of slavery. It's an objection to the soft-edged portrait in which the peculiar institution usually is seen in *The Fathers*. I don't doubt that some Major Buchans and some Coriolanuses had affectionate relationships; but to present centuries of black bondage in this roseate fashion taints the truth for which Mr. Tate was striving, and which he largely achieved.

At two points, the harsher reality of slavery comes savagely into focus. One is the shooting of Yellow Jim—a lynching, and for a "crime" of which he may not have been guilty. The other is when Winston Broadacre, a youthful friend of Lacy's, crudely offers him sex with a young slave girl.

> "You want some of it?" "Some of what," I said. There was a stir farther back under the pavilion . . . the mulatto wench I had seen earlier . . . was lying on her back . . . "She'll let you have it," Winston said. "I don't want none," I said (73).

Possibly Mr. Tate, in pursuit of his novelistic objective, believed a benign picture of slavery better served his ends; I would rather believe that extensive research since 1938 has left us with a clearer and darker picture of what slavery was like for those who endured it, and those who took advantage of it.

As the war approaches, a whiff of Upton Sinclair also touches Mr. Tate's otherwise unmelodramatic pages. Young Lacy manages to encounter both Generals Longstreet and Beauregard in his brief exposure to battle at Bull Run; President Buchanan appears at another point; and Lacy is present at the death of Colonel Elmer Ellsworth, one of the first Union casualties.

Some unfortunate consequences also arise from the novel's generally successful duality in point of view—the elder Dr. Buchan recounting the experiences of the youthful Lacy that he had been. This provides an effective means of looking at 1860 and 1861, a perspective beyond the immediate experience of those years. In Mr. Tate's handling, however, it tells us little about that "new life of the modern age" into which the characters are later "scattered," or about what happened to them in the years after the war. For example, readers are left to wonder where the narrator himself, Old Dr. Buchan—in the modern phrase—is "coming from," other than his teen-aged experiences of family disaster and the verge of war. We are told nothing of his maturity.

George Posey's postwar life, for another example, is hinted at—no more can be claimed—in one or two sentences in the novel's last paragraph; even these, according to an author's note, were added only in the revised L. S. U. version. Is this a complaint about a novel Mr. Tate never intended to write? Perhaps so; still, these sparse closing comments, for me at least, fail to sustain or explain Lacy Buchan's summation of George Posey in the last sentence of *The Fathers:*

"I venerate his memory more than the memory of any other man."

Finally, the *narrative* lacks drive, as opposed to the novel's careful, subtly constructed intellectual concept. I believe the primary concern of fiction is *the story to be told,* with its consequent effects on the reader's emotions—the evocation of his or her pity or hatred, hope or despair, love, terror, compassion. The most direct appeal of fiction, as of all art, is to the senses.

Allen Tate seems to me to have been less concerned with his story's power to move a reader than with what his characters represented, and with his analysis of the colliding social and personal forces depicted in *The Fathers.* If his novel is no longer widely read or available, despite the critical praise it has received, it may well be because Lacy Buchan's story—and Mr. Tate's—insufficiently compels a reader to wonder what may happen next, to persons—to *lives*—about whom he or she truly cares.

Allen Tate was born in 1899 in Winchester, Kentucky, and died near Sewanee, Tennessee, in 1979. Selected publications: *Mr. Pope and Other Poems* (1928); *Stonewall Jackson, the Good Soldier: A Narrative* (1928); *I'll Take My Stand: The South and the Agrarian Tradition,* contributor (1930); *Who Owns America? A New Declaration of Independence,* with Herbert Agar (1936); *The Fathers* (1938, revised edition, LSU Press, 1977); *Essays of Four Decades,* (1968); *Memoirs and Opinions, 1926–1974* (1975); *Collected Poems, 1919–1976* (1978).

On Joseph Stanley Pennell's
The History of Rome Hanks and Kindred Matters

DAVID MADDEN

JOSEPH STANLEY PENNELL'S *The History of Rome Hanks and Kindred Matters* is the most autobiographical of Civil War novels; the protagonist's drama of consciousness occurs around 1940. Consequently, in *Rome Hanks* more than in any other Civil War novel, a clear understanding of the author's life and of his complex use of the point of view technique is essential if the reader is to respond fully. The novel is the "record of the author's search for the answer to the questions: 'What am I? How did I get to be what I am?'" (*Current Biography, 1944,* 542).

Asked to comment on his life and work for *Twentieth Century Authors* in the early 1950s, Pennell (pronounced as in kennel) responded with details that very closely described Lee Harrington, the protagonist of *The History of Rome Hanks and Kindred Matters* (1944) and of *The History of Nora Beckham, A Museum of Home Life* (1948), second novel in a trilogy, the third volume of which was written but never published: "I was born in Junction City, Kansas [on the 4th of July, 1903], when it was still a 'tough' town. For the place is three miles from Fort Riley; and all famous cavalry regiments—including the Seventh—knew 'Junktown' well. The 'Wild West,' however, had gone. By the time I began to notice things most of the townspeople had forgotten James Butler Hickok. [And Jeb Stuart and Custer and Armisted, and by 1991 most seemed to have forgotten Pennell himself.] And I do not remember the saloons and bawdy houses of my native town. Nevertheless, when I left the town in 1947 there were still respectable women of earlier generations who would not walk down the 'saloon side' of Washington Street.

"My Grandfather Pennell [Judd Harrington in the novel] served with the North Carolina troops in the War-Between-the-States; and my Grandfather Stanley [Tom Beckham] fought in the Ninety-fifth Pennsylvania Volunteers (Goslin's Zouaves) in the Civil War. My great-grandfather [Rome Hanks] on my mother's side, a major in the Fifteenth Iowa Volunteer Infantry, went through the battle of Shiloh and the Atlanta campaign. I am both a Rebel and a Damyankee."

When he was sixteen, Pennell's father, Joseph Jud Pennell, left North Carolina with his father and crossed the plains. He went from making coffins to taking photographs that have earned him a place in the history of American photography. A distant relative was Joseph Pennell the graphic artist.

Photography played an extremely important role in the Civil War and in Pennell's life. Pennell's father is represented in American Heritage's *American Album* by a "curious patriotic scene," the unveiling of a monument in Junction City, Kansas (166). Pennell captures a sense of the life of the small town photographer—Robert Harrington is the son of a southern veteran of the Civil War who moved to the West—in the two novels. Pennell is haunted by his father as photographer and by the photographing process and the photographs themselves. Lee thinks he could have stayed home and become a studio photographer, after his father. He remembers watching his father take photographs. "As Lee lay squinting in the night, this series of pictures of Papa—almost as if he, Lee, were a camera Dry Plate multi-exposed—passed in his mind quickly, not flat as on a screen, but deeper and sharper than life, as are the braces of photographs mounted on a card and looked at parallactically through a stereoscope." "The camera of experiences bats its lens a timertwo" (304–305).

The two novels are Proustian researches of things past, contemplations of selected images, photographic in nature. Mythic metaphors emerge from those memories, accompanied by many storytelling voices. Photographs of men at Shiloh reunion, 1889, "seem now as mysterious" as stereopticon views of Pompeii (11).

His mother, Edith Stanley, to whom he dedicated *Rome Hanks,* but who died before it was published, was a pioneer woman. She "might be said to be the daughter of pioneers, as she did a lot of traveling in covered wagons and saw a lot of Indians." He had a love-hate relationship with his mother, who was the model for Nora Beckham in the two novels.

"I was educated in St. Francis Xavier's School, the Junction City High School, Kansas University [one year], and Pembroke College, Oxford University [three years]. I chose Pembroke College because it was known (and still is) as one of the most 'literary' of English speaking colleges." He left there with a B.A. in 1929. In *Rome Hanks,* Lee's numerous direct and indirect allusions to history, religion, literature, and art reflect Pennell's own classical education in England and contribute to a rich external context for the Civil War events.

Pennell started writing for newspapers during summer vacations while in college. "As a newspaper reporter, I 'broke in' on the Denver *Post,* worked for the St. Louis *Post-Dispatch,* the Kansas City *Star,* the Los Angeles *Examiner* and the Los Angeles *Post-Record.* I was, for a couple of years, managing editor of the Huntington Park *Signal* (California). During hard times, I worked on the radio station KMO of St. Louis (as everything from end man in the minstrel show to continuity writer and announcer for the Farm Hour [heard also twice a week as "Professor of Microphone English'], taught in the John Burroughs School and acted in a St. Louis stock company. (Even now I occasionally see a former fellow player on a movie screen)."

In most fiction and nonfiction (see especially Sam Watkins's "*Co. Aytch*") about the Civil War, writers draw quite frequently upon the theater for key metaphors and similes (influenced in part by their reading of such images in Shakespeare, "all the world's a stage," etc.). As Pennell had been, Lee and Christa, his lost love, are actors in the repertory theater in St. Louis. Pennell adds to his own repertoire of theater metaphors several movie metaphors and devices. He alludes to movie directors (94) and invokes the good name of Eisenstein (155). As Wagnal tells about Shiloh, he links key, summarizing images, as in a movie montage, with such phrases as "I saw . . . I heard . . . I remembered . . ." (109).

In the mid-1930s, Pennell abruptly returned to Junction City. Supporting himself by renting his father's photography store, he wrote in an apartment above. No one except his mother and Thelma Baker, town librarian, knew that he was writing a long novel, that he was not what he appeared to the townspeople to be, an idler taking a seven-year vacation. Before going into the army, he also wrote a draft of *Nora Becham* there.

The image of Pennell as a recluse reading and writing is illuminated if we remember Nathaniel Hawthorne's years as a recluse in his dead father's house in Salem, Massachusetts and recall the several ways he worked his own life into his early tales and novels. But Pennell was more a modern-day writer as man of action—he interrupted his work to go off to war. The jacket photo shows him in his officer's uniform. The fact that the novel appeared in the summer of 1944 and that the author is pictured in uniform would have caused readers quite naturally to think of World War II. Readers today will see many similarities to various wars since, especially Vietnam. The trilogy Pennell planned was another one of those strange artifices writers have used to write autobiography; he used both the fictional mode, as Wolfe, Joyce, and Hemingway did, and the third person device as Adams did in his autobiography *The Education of Henry Adams.*

"As far back as I can remember I have always wanted to be a maker of things. I think it was at Kansas University that I began to think of myself as a writer, a maker of books. It was, however, much later, in time and burned manuscripts, when I began to write *Rome Hanks*. That book took more than five years of my time."

He studied Mathew Brady's famous photographs; Brady is depicted at work in several passages (see especially 74–75). He "read scores of books, looked at many others," about a thousand, including the one hundred twenty-eight volumes of the *Official Records.* Lee also names Civil War diaries, histories, songs, novels, and magazines. He "searched long in diverse obscure corners of obscurity. For my grandfathers had told me little of their part in the Civil War; my grandfather Stanley had recollected a thing or two—but he always exploded into a rage of fine cuss words when he began to tell of how the Rebels let maggots get into his wound when he was a prisoner on Belle Isle. And Grandfather Stanley and Grandfather Pennell called each other 'Mr. Stanley' and 'Mr. Pennell' whenever they met.

"Aside from the newspaper stories I wrote, I published an article on Americans at Oxford in the *North American Review* and some verse in Miss Harriet Monroe's *Poetry, a Magazine of Verse*. These, I believe, were my start." Poems open both of Pennell's novels and appear in them as the work of Lee Harrington. Poems frame *Rome Hanks*. Just as Pennell puts his dedication into a poem, Lee the young poet ends his long meditation with his four sonnets to Christa.

Part of *Rome Hanks,* "The Courtship of Tom Beckham," appeared in *Mademoiselle* in September, 1943. A short story, "On the Way to Somewhere Else," appeared in *Harper's Bazaar* in 1944 and was reprinted in *Best American Short Stories, 1945.*

"After I finished *The History of Rome Hanks,* I joined the army [1942] and served for two years as a private and subsequently a second lieutenant of anti-aircraft artillery." He was public-relations director for the anti-aircraft training center at Fort Bliss. "*Rome* was published while I was still in uniform."

After the war, Pennell returned to Junction City, but left after a dispute over the city's failure to stop the noise of a merry-go-round that disturbed his writing. He had worked on *Nora Beckham,* granddaughter of Rome Hanks, who married Robert Harrington, the photographer. This is a much quieter book, similar, reviews claimed, to Proust, Joyce, and Thomas Wolfe. As in *Rome Hanks,* there are many side stories, but Lee, again the center of consciousness, becomes clearly the focus of the novel.

In *Rome Hanks,* Lee frequently alludes to paintings: "The Night Watch," "The Anatomy Lesson," the work of Sir Joshua Reynolds (15, 17, 89). In the last line, "He watched the spider climbing up the wall over his desk toward an engraving of Friar Bacon's study over Folly Bridge." *Nora Beckham* the second volume in Pennell's projected trilogy, ends with the same image, and thus deepens our understanding of what happened to Lee as a result of his meditations and his service in World War II. "Ah, Lee said, Ah. Nothing's become of me—And my father's dead and Nora's dead and Dee Given's dead and Wagnal's buried in Potter's field. He took another drink and looked at the red and silver artillery shield and the silver bar on his forest green shoulder loop. He buttoned the firegilt buttons and put the cap on his head. The spider—a spider—was again climbing up the wall over the desk toward the engraving of Friar Bacon's study over Folly Bridge" (330).

Some time after 1944, he married Elizabeth Horton, an army nurse, to whom he dedicated *Nora Beckham,* "with all my love." She drew the portrait of him on the cover. Thelma Baker, the librarian who had helped him research *Rome Hanks* and gotten it read at Scribner's while he was in the army, when she was told of Pennell's marriage, exclaimed, "That can't be! He loves me!" She lived in Junction City for many years; apparently, she never married.

After Elizabeth committed suicide, Pennel married her sister. "I now live, with my wife, Virginia Horton Pennell," he wrote for *Twentieth Century Authors* around 1955, "on Tillamook Head, a promontory overlooking the Pacific Ocean" near Seaside in northern Oregon. And that was the last the literary world heard from him.

In Junction City, Pennell had worked on the third volume of *An American Chronicle,* entitled "the History of Thomas Wagnal," a major character in *Rome Hanks* and *Nora Beckham.* About Thomas Wagnal, Ernest Hemingway remarked to Charles Scribner in 1949 that the old soldiers who write to him praising his own war fiction "are like that wicked old man that boy you have in your stable wrote so magnificently about in The History of Rome Hanks. Parts of that were better than anything ever written in America and parts were worse" (*Selected Letters,* 669). But his alcoholism impaired Pennell's creative faculties. Lee is talking to his bottle of ale throughout much of *Nora Beckham.*

Having started a biography of his father, Pennell was working on a straight autobiography when he died of pneumonia in Oregon in 1963. (The year of Evelyn Scott's death and a year after William Faulkner died.)

Thelma Baker submitted *Rome Hanks* to three publishers; it was returned unread.

Rome Hanks arrived at Scribner's late in 1943, when Pennell was 35, just before his induction into the army, says Stephen Berg in *Max Perkins, Editor of Genius* (1978). "Another of those damned works of genius," Perkins overheard his associates say (423). Berg claims that Pennell had been inspired by Wolfe, and that his book bore many similarities to Wolfe's work" (424). Many reviewers made the same observation, but all Thomas Wolfe's fiction, except for a novella, is cast in the omniscient point of view and Pennell's is third person, central intelligence, to use Henry James' term. The Wolfe parallel derives from a misreading of the point of view; it is Lee Harrington who is Wolfian, not Joseph Pennell. "Perkins spoke of the book to everyone," says Berg, "for none in years had excited him so much" (426).

Perkins wrote to Pennell, "I am having a grand time reading it, and I should like to tell you that a colleague here showed me that Pickett's charge piece, and I really do not believe I ever saw a war piece that excelled it, not forgetting Tolstoi" (424). But the novel had two problems, Perkins said. First, Christa, Lee's beloved, was too much like her real-life model, Martha Gellhorn, who was then married to Ernest Hemingway. Second, it was open to the charge of obscenity. Through the mail, they worked on those two problems, and others, over most of the year, until Christa was less based on Martha Gellhorn, and the so-called obscene elements were reduced. To this day, Ms. Gellhorn, who lives and writes in Wales, refuses to allow publication of her letters to Pennell. The book was banned in Boston for 'vulgarity,' thus increasing sales. July 26, 1944, Perkins wrote to Pennell to tell him that sales were about 100,000, that the novel had been picked up by a book club and had gone into an armed services edition (*Editor to Author: The Letters of Maxwell Perkins*, 263).

Orville Prescott correctly predicted that *Rome Hanks* would cause more debate than any other novel of the year. It was certainly the literary event of 1944, when these novels appeared: Lillian Smith's *Strange Fruit*, Ben Ames Williams' *Leave Her to Heaven*, Kathleen Winsor's *Forever Amber*, Niven Busch's *Duel in the Sun*, Charles Jackson's *The Lost Weekend*, Somerset Maugham's *The Razor's Edge*, Saul Bellow's *Dangling Man*, Harry Brown's *A Walk in the Sun*, John Hersey's *A Bell for Adano*, Jean Stafford's *Boston Adventure*, and Caroline Gordon's *The Women on the Porch*. Since 1938, no major Civil War novels had appeared and only two more would show up in the forties: Clifford Dowdy's *Where My Love Sleeps* (1945) and Ross Lockridge, Jr.,'s *Raintree County* (1948). Sinclair Lewis called *Rome Hanks* "one of the richest and most pungent novels of the decade."

The novel was praised and damned (and defended by Perkins in a letter, 255) for its gruesome depiction of the killing and maiming of soldiers and its descriptions of bodily functions. "We saw the rebel officer's face splash the water in a puddle" (18). The woods "smelled like piss and powder . . ." (20). "It was almost dusk then—and I kicked something. I picked it up before I saw that it was a young golden-haired head with its blue eyes open" (25). "Once I fell down and put my hand in the mouth of a corpse" (26). "Nights in bivouac sounded like the turn-on of a thousand hoses" (4). There are many instances of sex, including masturbation, buggery, whores. Wagnal even imagines that Katherine fanticizes General Stuart in bed with them (214).

In chapter 10 (80) Lee dotes on his own body and its infirmities, augmenting the effect of Wagnal's descriptions of the effect of war and disease thus far and anticipating Lee's memory of Pinkney's various descriptions of the body. This is the only chapter that is completely italicized, suggesting that Lee's meditation on his body comes some time after the meditation that ends the novel. This chapter suggests two metaphors for the novel, the body politic and war as an anatomy lesson. Wagnal's early references to the body-snatchers (7) and to the resurrectionists (139) of Edinburgh suggest a parallel to the way old men snatch the bodies of the young and hurl them into war. At the end, imagining his birth, Lee returns to the infirmity of his own body since birth, weak lungs (359).

Even before Norman Mailer's *The Naked and the Dead* (1948) and James Jones' *From Here to Eternity* (1951) Pennell had gone beyond Hemingway and other war novelists in rendering the speech of soldiers realistically, although all four still used "f___." *Rome Hanks* was banned in Boston and in a few other places at a time when *Strange Fruit* was banned for the single use of the word. Many copies of both novels were sold to readers searching out such words, and left unread once the thrill wore off.

The obscenity charge and certain references to explicit language in reviews may have stimulated sales, but the confusion noted in reviews suggests that many who bought it were unable to read it with enough comprehension to get through it. By 1957, when Robert Lively put *Rome Hanks* on his list of the 15 greatest Civil War novels in *Fiction Fights the Civil War,* very few people remembered it.

Professor of History Paul Rossman of Quinsigamond Community

College in Worcester, Massachusetts, impressed most by the description of Pickett's charge that had impressed Max Perkins, wanted to use *Rome Hanks* in his class, but it was out of print. The trouble he had getting *Rome Hanks* reprinted was far greater than Thelma Baker's difficulty getting it published. Rossman sent it to one hundred publishers for re-issue before Second Chance Press took it on in 1981. To the publishers of that small press, it was one of the greatest books ever written. But it sold only 6,000 in hard cover and paper. However, it was the first fiction ever offered by the History Book Club, which bought 1,500 copies. Historical Times Book Club also offered it. And David Donald, a major Civil War historian, assigned it in a core curriculum at Harvard. There was some film interest, too.

Both *Current Biography 1944* and, ten years later, *Twentieth Century Authors* summarized reviewer response to *Rome Hanks* as being "sharply divided"—from "self-indulgent, confused, torrential style and undisci-plined, sprawling construction" to "a permanent acquisition to world literature." However, having taken a close look at the reviews them-selves, one must conclude that they were mostly positive, though many critics had serious reservations, generally having to do with structure and style. Even the negative reviewers made some strong positive statements: "obscure" but "powerful and promising"; "not a true historical novel" but "it will appeal to adults who enjoy adventure and spice"; "the method of the book is pretentious and clumsy," but "you can piece together a bot-tomside view of the Civil War that is worth putting beside Brady's photo-graphs, Grant's 'Memoirs,' 'The Red Badge of Courage,' and J. W. De-Forest's 'Miss Ravenel's Conversion' . . ."; "surface absurdities and wild overwriting," but its "repetitious style . . . develops considerable force"; "perplexing, irritating. . . . masses of formless, purposeless experimental writing," but it is a "brilliant, powerful" novel. The *Newsweek* reviewer called it "haphazardly put together," but had high praise for Pennell's descriptions of Civil War battles as being better than the descriptions that journalists on the scene were offering of World War II battles (Pennell himself was then in the service).

Novelist Hamilton Basso expresses the double attitude generated by the book's effects: "Mr. Pennell, like Wolfe, commits just about every sin known to literary man, and, again like Wolfe, thinks up a few all his own. His book is chaotic, undisciplined, and formless, it is extravagant and sentimental, its prose is so emotionally supercharged that it often sputters all over the place, and by and large, it will give those who appreciate novels like Mr. Brown's 'A Walk in the Sun' [a short World War II novel, written in simple, economical style] a very bad attack of chills and fever indeed. Despite this, however, and I readily admit that it is a lot to despite, Mr. Pennell's book strikes me as being a work of unusual talent, and, among other things, the best novel about the Civil War I have read, with the natural exception of 'The Red Badge of Courage' . . . Mr. Pennell, with any luck at all, ought to have a long career as a novelist and, I hope, a happy one. He should be leery, though of anybody who urges him to walk in Thomas Wolfe's shoes. He can get places in his own." Like all the other reviewers, Basso failed to see that Pennell's command of point of view already placed him less in the company of Thomas Wolfe than in that of Henry James, James Joyce, and William Faulkner.

Neither generally negative nor positive reviewers revealed an understanding of how point of view works in fiction. Diana Trilling rejected the novel, partly because "Mr. Pennell tells us simple and obvious things so elaborately as to make us believe he is being profound." On the contrary, Pennell as author says very little because the novel is set in the emotions, imagination, and intellect of the protagonist, Lee Harrington, on whom the author sustains focus. Ms. Trilling makes the amateuerish mistake of attributing to the author the thoughts of his character, a mistake in no way mitigated by the fact that Lee *is* one of the most autobiographical characters in fiction.

The style derives directly from the third person, central intelligence point of view. Reviewers noted, often disdainfully, a certain experimentation in style, apparently unaware that it is Lee and/or Wagnal, not Pennell who indulges in Joycean wordcrafting, such as "wishing for the lipsalved lady with the viciousdashing look on her" (56) and "they were clothed in roughandready plainasanoldshoe garments" (173). Midwesterners Lee and Wagnal share Pinkney's southern love of the sheer sound of words, such as *"plowhannels!"* (157). Kansan Pennel is more convincing in his use of Southern dialect than most pure-bred Southern writers. (See the long paragraph on page 116.) Lee, as young poet, would be quick to use literary and lyrical phrases (see 169–170) and indulge in word play as a way of making the past his own through inventive expressions.

The absence of quotation marks in dialog and the grouping of speeches by several different characters in paragraphs, extremely unusual in 1944, was cited on reviewers' lists of confusing experimental features of Pennell's novel. Given the fact that there is so much storytelling within storytelling, readers should consider how confusing the use of quotation marks would prove to be. Apparently, reviewers and readers blithely ignore the author's own explanation for omitting quotation marks in "Note to the Reader": "to make the narrative flow from one alembic without entailing either too much cloudiness or clarity."

In his intelligent and overwhelmingly positive review on the front page of the *New York Times Book Review,* Nash K. Burger called the novel "a landmark among novels of its type," and claimed that "there is considerable experimentation of style and structure in the work, and it is all very well done indeed," but he too fails to illuminate for his readers the author's point of view technique. One may safely assume that the reaction of reviewers is likely to be that of readers as well.

Pro or con, *no* reviewer describes within a context of clear understanding how all the elements and techniques work together to produce a work of art. Many of those techniques Pennell's readers might have encountered in Melville's *Moby-Dick,* in Proust, Joyce, Dos Passos, Faulkner, and Conrad. *Rome Hanks* may have seemed (and may seem even today), next to Faulkner's *Absalom, Absalom!* and Evelyn Scott's *The Wave,* the Civil War novel most original in conception. In these three, more than in other Civil War novels, point of view is the crucial technique and Pennell's use of it posed problems of orientation for reviewers and other readers.

Readers may make the mistake of taking Lee as merely a point of view device the author is using to present battles and other Civil War experiences. On the contrary, Lee is a direct result of the author's autobiographical impulse; more importantly, *Rome Hanks* is a work of art, produced in large part by Pennell's use of point of view, not, as reviewers suggested, in spite of it. Pennell's Lee Harrington is like Faulkner's Quentin Compson, especially in *Absalom, Absalom!.* Quentin is Faulkner's most autobiographical character, in spirit more than in fact. Pennell's Lee, on the other hand, is much more literally an autobiographical character than Quentin is. Quentin is an ostensibly marginal character whose marginality in several stories and novels is developed artistically and thematically in such a way that he becomes the major character. A major difference between Lee and Quentin is that Lee, unlike Quentin who tells stories to his Canadian roommate Shreve, has not yet surrendered to a compulsion to tell stories of the War (he has told Christa only what little he knew at the time and only to impress her romantically).

For the reader who keeps Pennell's point of view technique clearly in mind, what seems experimental to the untutored reader may follow quite naturally after the first three chapters.

Pennell opens with a device he will use often: italicization to set passages off for various purposes, another feature of experimental writing before 1944. Except for "Note to the Reader" and the dedicatory poem, Pennell uses italics for the same practical reason most people do: to signal that the passage functions in some way different from the main body of the text and for that reason its importance is stressed. On page 302, near the end of the process, Lee will remember this opening passage verbatim. The reader who grasps the function of this technique at the start may experience the passages more intensely. This first instance provides Lee and the reader with a compressed impression of most of the major narrative elements, character relationships, and themes, while employing one of the major techniques that will create artistic unity—italicized passages that anticipate key moments to come.

Lee remembers three stories simultaneously: his recent relationship with Christa (around 1940) and the Civil War stories Wagnal and Uncle Pinkney told him soon after.

The compulsion to remember makes the more general, distilled images come to Lee out of chronological sequence. Here are the major instances: prelude (see 302); 5 (see 111); 55 (see 62); 136 (see 147 and 214); 157 (see 225); 338 (see 352).

In the two italicized paragraphs that open the novel, Pennell suggests how the reader is to read *Rome Hanks*. "*You awake, Lee thought. . . .*" indicates that the point of view will be third person, central intelligence: every element of the novel will be filtered through the perceptions, sensations, emotions, the consciousness of a single character, Lee Harrington.

When Lee awakes "*in the vast night of all the years,*" he cries out: "*How could I have known?* [about the war]. . . . *All right!. . . . I go back and look again and heed and look again and heed. . . . forgetting why (Christa's face and hair and bored voice). . . ."* Here, we are told why he went North to seek out Wagnal to implore him to tell him about his Yankee great-grandfather, Rome Hanks, and why he went South to seek out his Uncle Pinkney to implore him to tell him about his grandfather Judson Wade Harrington—it was because of Christa's disdainful response to his feeble attempt to impress her with his glib recital of only the few facts and notions about his Grandfather Harrington he then possessed.

This passage opens the first chapter: "Yes, Christa said. Yes; I'm sure your Grandfather must have been a fine old Southern gentleman." It is in that chapter that Pennell more securely sets up the third person, central intelligence point of view. The first line of the second paragraph, "She is bored, Lee thought. . . ." and the opening of the third paragraph, "And now here he was, Lee Harrington, sitting across the table from the most beautiful and proudest girl he had ever seen," paraphrases Lee's conscious thoughts at that time and place. Then Lee repeats in his own thoughts the statement she had made in Pennell's third person narration.

The space break indicates a leap in time from that scene in the department store lunchroom with Christa to his own room years later, after her statement has stung him into seeking out Wagnal and Uncle Pinkney and after he has read a great many books about the Civil War. "Lee looked at the photograph and the four sonnets he had pulled out from under the desk drawer." The implication is that the photograph is of Christa who has rejected him and that the sonnets are love poems to her. As he launches into the remembering process, he creates a parallel between himself and Christa and Dante and his ideal love Beatrice. Christa is his muse, as Beatrice was Dante's, even though Christa is, ironically, a negative inspiration. Another implication of the parallel is that Lee as Dante has a Virgil (Wagnal and Uncle Pinkney combined) who will guide him through the Divine Comedy of the American Civil War.

Pennell frames the novel with that scene in Lee's room (4–5). Having referred to them at the start and several times during the course of his meditations, "Lee picked up the four sonnets and began to read them to the photograph" (361). "Thus, Lee said sententiously to the photograph" of Christa, "love ends . . ." (362).

Lee has failed as a lover, as a poet, and, as the last line of Chapter 1 intimates, as a citizen in his hometown: " . . . I *am* an exile—an exile, Goddamn them all to hell!" Lee's compulsion to recall and, with slow deliberation, to fix in memory the stories he has listened to about his ancestors in the Civil War prompts him again, in the italicized opening of chapter 2, to reach forward to remember Wagnal's distillation of his entire story: "*God help me, boy, I'm old and Katherine is dead and Dick's dead at Savage's Station. . . .*" Then Lee tries to put his memories into some chronological order by recalling his mother and her attitude about himself and about Wagnal. Because his mother used to ask, "Whatever is to become of you, my poor boy?" we may suppose she is among those from whom Lee feels exiled as he remembers his own and his ancestors' pasts.

In the opening of chapter 3, Pennell continues to orient the reader to the pervasive third person, central intelligence point of view technique with such phrases as "Lee remembered," "Lee thought," and "Lee said." In passages only a few lines longer, now and then, the author's presence is more clearly sensed. "Yes, Lee said aloud, it is strange—damn' strange. He looked at the sonnets with warm, hypnotized eyes. Strange, he said, strangely" (114).

For two hundred pages after that passage, Pennell seldom offers such passages of author narration because he has established the third person, central intelligence process and because Lee begins to imagine the lives and thoughts of others. With so few passages in which the author narrates—always from Lee's point of view, however—the reader, to remain securely oriented throughout the novel, must avoid the misapprehension that Lee is writing, because Lee has never even attempted to write about his own life or his ancestors; nor is he speaking to a person in the room. He is either remembering or thinking or speaking aloud to himself or to some creature (the spider) or object (the photograph) in the room. The reader overhears, so to speak, his memories and meditations. Again, the primary narrator is Pennell, though always through Lee's consciousness.

It is Wagnal and Uncle Pinkney who have a compulsion to tell stories, responding to Lee, the listener. "The eagerness of a listener," says Jane Eyre, the narrator of Bronte's novel, "quickens the tongue of a narrator." As Lee remembers the various stories, Pennell re-orients the reader frequently with such phrases as "Wagnal said," "Pinkney said," and "Lee remembered." To keep the focus on the storyteller-listener process, Pennell also has Wagnal and Pinkney address Lee directly. "I saw your grandfather beneath the bluff," Wagnal tells Lee. He calls him "boy" or "sir." Uncle Pinkney calls him Lee—"Now Lee. . . . mark what I tell you, boy!" (194)—because Lee's father was named Robert Lee after General Lee and because Lee and Pinkney are bound together in kinship: "You and I can sit here under the honeysuckle vine and talk about war; and I can tell you . . . how we. . . ." (182).

With the opening of chapter 4, the alert reader will have become fully oriented to Pennell's complex use of point of view.

As stated earlier, most of the negative comments made about the novel on its appearance derive from the inability of those reviewers to perceive the workings of Pennel's use of the primary technique of point of view, which affects style and every other technique and device and the narrative, character, and thematic elements in any work of fiction. But technique not only enables a fiction writer to organize and control all the elements of a work, technique in itself expresses a major aspect of the work, and that is especially true of Pennell's novel.

For instance, Pennell uses the technique of juxtaposition to create an expressive pattern. Lee is fighting the war, in memory and imagination, simultaneously on both sides, and that process is dramatized several times when Wagnal telling stories is juxtaposed to Pinkney telling stories. Pinkney's world is contrasted, by juxtaposition, to Wagnal's (167) and then Wagnal's is juxtaposed to Pinkney's (177); their personalities and styles of speaking are contrasted. They are juxtaposed again at pages 204 and 236.

And at one point Pennell juxtaposes Lee's imagining his grandmother Myra's frontier experiences to Uncle Pinkney's storytelling (225); next, Wagnal. Pennell clusters three kinds of narratives, all remembered by Lee. Lee's final memory of Wagnal's story-telling, mostly about Rome Hanks, "That's it, Wagnal said. It was an old song," is juxtaposed to a contrasting chapter in which Lee imagines his greatgrandfather Rome's meditations: "Rome would awaken again . . . Again and again now he would remember . . ." (297)

One effect of juxtaposition is the profound sense of simultaneity for both Lee and the reader. Two or three things when experienced simultaneously are felt more intensely. For instance, as Wagnal tells about the fall of Vicksburg on July 4 (100), Pinkney will tell about the high tide of the Confederacy on the same day, same year, 1863 at Gettysburg (183); readers who know even a little Civil War history will experience both events simultaneously at both points in the novel.

At Lee's birth on the 4th of July 1904, fireworks suggest Vicksburg and Gettysburg. With the firing of cannon (even though it is one from the Spanish American war), Lee's entire life within the context of the Civil War is dramatized (353). In Lee's omniscience-reaching imagination, all three events occur simultaneously. The effect of simultaneity is one of the major achievements of the process Lee has been going through.

Pennell's controlled repetition of word, phrases, lines, passages, and his use of the device of parallel help reinforce simultaneity and enable Lee to see and feel a rich and complex historical context for his meditations on the Civil War. For instance, Pinkney invokes the Revolutionary War by declaring that his father fought at King's Mountain.

Another major effect of the process Lee is going through is his sense of parallels between characters: Rome is to Wagnal what Reeve is to Jud Harrington; Doc Gaines, who delivers Lee, is ironically a comic version of Lee as he comes to be obsessed with the War; Clint Belton parallels Bull Pettibone in Pinkney's story. Wagnal's cabin parallels the room where Lee will remember the stories Wagnal told in the cabin. Above all, Wagnal and Katherine parallel Lee and Christa.

Listening to Wagnal and Pinkney side by side, Lee discovers that grandparents on both sides were guided by or obsessed by the pursuit of the ideal and of a woman as the embodiment of that ideal. "Maybe if women were not watching," Lee imagines Rome thinking at the end of Rome's meditation, just before he hears Clint's footstep on his porch, come to kill him for being witness to his disgrace—cringing in fear under the bluff (293). Lee, who has held Christa up as the ideal woman for himself, names, in the last chapter, ideal women throughout history (360).

Some reviewers were appalled by what they called Pennell's cynicism. Again, it is characters who pose both the concept of the ideal and the attitude of cynicism produced by the corruption of the ideal. Wagnal refers to "the uses of man as a firstrate absurdity" and says of Katherine's sister, Una: "And it was Una who was already planning the evolution of an imperial purpose to satisfy the cold perfect pattern of her geometric vanity" (98). In the mansion's garden, he observes that "the little temple was built as a ruin," suggesting the South's "Lost Cause," to which Uncle Pinkney also scornfully refers. In the midst of battle, Pinkney the Southerner asks, "Where am I? And What, in god's name, am I?" (183) For Wagnal, "The Great West" beckons, but its promises remain unfulfilled.

Before he began to write, Pennell himself experienced the process that his autobiographical protagonist, Lee, experienced. The novel's primary purpose then is to enable the reader, also, to go through that complex process, that experience. It is *not* simply to tell the story, interesting as it is, of Rome Hanks or of Lee's other kin, as the title may lead readers to expect.

Pennell stresses the importance in that process of the oral storytelling tradition. Lee tried to tell stories to Christa, a cynically reluctant listener. Both Wagnal, the Yankee, and Pinkney, the mountain southerner, tell stories to Lee. "Boy, Wagnal said, everything is strange: You sitting there on that kitchenchair . . . ," the eager listener (112).

In serious fiction, first person narratives are almost always about the narrator, and it is as much to the narrators, as revealed in storytelling, that Lee responds as to the various stories they tell about his kin and their friends and enemies.

In addition to Wagnal and Pinkney, Lee recalls several other, minor storytellers, making his own consciousness all the more complex. Long ago, Grandpa Tom Beckham told Lee a little about his war experience. Even as Lee remembers Wagnal telling him about Grandpa Beckham, he recalls things his Grandpa said: "I can hear my grandfather now, Lee thought" (281). Katherine told Wagnal the bizarre and violent story of Jabez (126–35); Wagnal retells it to Lee; Lee then remembers the tale.

The author and the reader experience what Christa's attitude denies her: the process of "looking and heeding," a process that transcends storytelling alone. Lee experiences that, too, as he listens to Wagnal. But stories are only the inciting events: they are elements in a process. Because she clung to stereotypes and clichés, Christa did not even experience the storytelling. Many confused readers of *Rome Hanks* were probably like Christa, reluctant to respond, bored, even hostile, and confused. The ideal reader will *want* to experience the kind of process Lee is experiencing.

Remember, thinking, and speaking aloud, Lee does not always reveal how he feels about what he has heard and read. It is the reader who may imagine the effect on him, which is profound, considering the fact that he recalls everything in such extraordinary detail, even allowing for the natural enhancement his emotions and imagination and intellect bring to the details he has heard and read about.

The effect of this complex process on Lee is suggested by the effect on Wagnal of his own storytelling, especially as contrasted with the effect one may imagine Uncle Pinkney's storytelling has on *him*. Wagnal's stories are less *about* Rome Hanks and others than they are expressions of Wagnal's own character. Wagnal is somehow changed, as his listener, Lee, is. Pinkney, on the other hand, seems relatively unaffected; primarily, he is a deliberate, self-conscious Southern Appalachian Mountain storyteller in the way he uses words and pours on the southern accent.

As Lee searches among his kin and kindred matters for his place in the life-death pattern, he traces, like the spider, a web—of blood kin relationships, following Southern kin who fought in the North at Gettysburg, and northern kin who fought in the southwest at Shiloh. The "kindred matters" referred to in the title includes Wagnal who, as non-kin storyteller, affects Lee as much as the actual kin he tells about—more than Uncle Pinkney affects him.

Chapter 1 is mirrored and climaxed in the final chapter, lending a certain symmetry to the novel, but some readers may feel that the novel ends most effectively as Wagnal ends his last story on page 296. Near the end, after about page 315, the storytelling style and tone of the novel seem to change. Lee begins to use some of the phrases of the omniscient, sometimes satirical narrator: "On the day when we see the covered wagon of the Beckham family nearing the Town . . ." (328); "It is to be noted that Nora said nothing . . ." (342); and the satirical style of the two chapters describing his own birth (347). The question arises, Were the last 50 pages written first, or is the change to a more prevalent omniscient imagining a natural development in the process Lee is going through?

As part of that process, Lee speaks aloud, but not necessarily to himself; rather he is speaking as a way of remembering the stories more clearly and forcefully. "Wagnal was all at sea now, Lee said aloud" (7). As we experience Lee's stream of consciousness, it is dramatized when he suddenly speaks aloud, as if the oral tradition has taken hold of him, even though he isn't ready to make another attempt, after the deeply abortive one with Christa, at telling other people.

But like most recluses, Lee does talk to himself. "Now, Lee said, his voice falling to a soft chant, I am afraid of cities when I am walking along alone at night. . . ." (52). Sometimes Lee speaks to himself about Uncle Pinkney even as he remembers his uncle remembering (199). Sometimes he speaks to Wagnal, contributing to Wagnal's own memory and meditation (110). Lee talks to the spider, weaving a web as *he* is: "Lee posed the question to the spider" above his desk (36). Talking aloud, he animates the inanimate. "Look, Lee said fiercely to the blank wall. Look!" (50). "He was my grandfather, Lee said tenderly," to the four sonnets he has written for Christa (58).

Reviewers put Pennell's scrambled chronology on their lists of experimental devices. Again, an understanding of point of view would have cleared up any confusion. Events for the storytellers are not, finally, structured in chronological time but in memory-time, and so are Lee's memories of the memories others have told him. Remembering, Wagnal and Pinkney *tell* Lee, mostly about *other* people, then as *Lee* remembers, what they told him becomes part of his own life.

Lee's meditations on his body (chapters 10, 80) suggest that while memory, imagination, and intellect can move at will from past to present, the body is always dying in the immediate present. Phrases such as "Now I know" remind the reader of the present (98). Pennell is delineating a young man's meditations on the past, within a framework of the present, and quite naturally Lee would mesh present and past, returning to his relationship, for instance, with Christa at those points where he remembers Wagnal's stories about himself and Katherine. "Wagnal sobbed a little—like distant thunder, Lee thought . And I sobbed with him. For I loved Katherine too—as I loved Christa and Anne and love—" (135). The past is still alive in Lee's total response to the way it is alive in Wagnal's remembering voice. About a hundred pages later (257), after Wagnal has told of Katherine's death, he (or Lee) recalls an event before her death; and for Wagnal and Lee and the reader, she, one of the most vital characters in the novel, is alive again.

Pennell suggests in his note to the reader that memory is more important than accuracy and facts. "All anachronisms are conscious, as the narrative is filtered through the memories and desires of several narrators who may be either ignorant or untruthful—or both." Wagnal himself tells Lee that his memories of battle (34), and of Katherine (121), may be inaccurate.

Many lines attest to or suggest the importance of memory. For instance, "And each memory is a shock that racks this big, clumsy arthritic frame. . . . No. . . . I cannot stand the light over these things, for when I see it over them, I know again that I was young and I am old now . . ." (169–70). And Lee remembers his affair with Christa up to the point where she rejected *his* stories about his Civil War great-grandfathers (148–157).

Forgetting is a torment, "Well, I'll be Goddamned! they had forgotten everything . . ." (36), says Wagnal, who, about 100 pages later exclaims," I forget. . . . I forget how it was then exactly . . ." (146). Uncle Pinkney feels the pathos of being forgotten. "Who remembers gen'l Dick Garnett now?"(198). Lee has set for himself the painful but exhilarating task of *not* forgetting.

Many major American novels from *The Scarlet Letter* to the present are novels of meditation on events that illuminate American history, the American Dream, the American character. The character relationship that embodies that meditative process is the hero-witness relationship. Rome Hanks and Lee's other kin, and Wagnal as well, are heroes who stimulate the meditations of Lee, the witness.

As the characters remember and meditate, their imaginations come into play. Pinkney's less then Wagnal's, Lee's especially. Wagnal imagines General Grant's thoughts (see last paragraph, 254). Wagnal is obviously imagining the event in Clint Belton's life with Katherine's sister, Una, and their thoughts. (See especially chapter 28, at 236). Later, he imagines Clint seeking out Rome to kill him. Having heard Wagnal tell what he has had to imagine, Lee himself is able to imagine Rome's thoughts up to Clint's arrival; Lee then remembers Wagnal's telling him about the Clint-Rome confrontation as Wagnal had imagined it.

Having heard all the stories, Lee, as early as page 55, feels a compulsion to imagine his grandfather Tom Beckham's life, until he merges his own consciousness with Tom's: Tom "lay there for what seemed a long time, for the flies were not only at his thigh but at his face and hands. Jesus, they bit, Lee thought reverently. And he could hear them droning . . ." (71 and 311).

From about page 271 on, through the power of his imagination as it thrives on fragments he has picked up during his life, especially from listening to people talk, Lee becomes, in a sense, his grandmother, Myra, too, and his father, Robert. And his mother, Nora: Lee goes from "Why, I can see my mother, drying her eyes. . . ." to "She saw herself as she leant against the screen door at dusk" (338–39). And then he even imagines his mother giving birth to himself.

Even before the novel begins, Lee has gone through a long awakening process: "*You awake, Lee thought, in the vast night of all the years*" opens the novel. "*How could I have known? I tell you, I didn't know!*" (2) The process of *waking* to *knowing* becomes part of who he becomes, a creature of his own meditation.

The dynamics of storytelling and listening, remembering and meditating, and imagining, in a sustained process such as Lee undergoes, produces, as one achievement of human consciousness, a kind of omniscience, the sense of which is profoundly exhilarating. Lee and Wagnal, who are in many ways so much alike, acquire this power most obviously. In all his stories, Wagnal aspires to know and do everything: "Everything was going on in the world; nothing was stopping until I could finish what I was doing and go see it happen, go take part in it, go everywhere and be everything" (137). For him, strangeness and fascination become pervading experiences of consciousness (112–13).

The lives of Wagnal's friends are so important to the formation of Wagnal as a person that he not only tells what they did that he actually witnessed but imagines and then tells Lee their very thoughts. Lee must have sensed that Wagnal has achieved a kind of omniscience, because one of the effects on Lee of Wagnal's omniscient-like storytelling is that Lee himself begins to imagine the lives of others.

Lee even imagines Rome, also, aspiring to a kind of omniscience. Rome once told Wagnal that curiosity "should be directed . . . toward a history of the world in general terms" (54). Lee imagines Rome meditating on this larger view: "Rome saw all the world as lying simultaneously in dark and quiet . . . places which he had never seen except on the lantern slides of his brain. . . ." (285). Later: "Now Rome had begun more and more to see the wide continent of North America spread out before his mind's eye in one great nocturnal panorama" (299).

Why does Pinkney seem not to aspire to omniscience? Perhaps because in his Southern culture many people already tended to think of themselves within a larger context as a habit of mind?

When he met Christa, Lee "had not even vicariously lain under the bluff at Shiloh . . ." (48). But he finally achieves a degree of omniscience, as this passage suggests: "I have lain under the banks at Shiloh . . . ," Lee thinks, "and talked to the pale major from Springfield, Illinois and heard the boy from Fairfield, Iowa blubber. I worked Webster's guns on the landing and lay wounded all night on the banks of Owl Creek. . . . I am the soldier who never fired a shot. . . . I buried no dead. . . . Yet because of something that happened before my grandfathers came to Kansas, I know these things. I know . . ." (see long passage, 43–44).

The compulsion to remember stimulates Lee's own imagination and that phase of the process is the most crucial. Point of view generates that process; style and several other techniques and devices control that process to create a work of art. Confusion of style, chronology, and other "problems" are the product of reader inattentiveness not of a lack of artistic power in the author. In the imagination humankind transcends captivity in "self," in the limited sense of that word. We do not often re-imagine the facts of our own past, as Lee does not *his*, but in making the humanistic leap to imagine the lives of *others*, he most truly creates himself. Lee fails as lover and poet but succeeds as a human being by becoming, at the end of the process, the man who remembered, imagined, and meditated on his and his ancestors' pasts.

Such a man is capable then of passing that experience, in artistic form, on to others; Lee does not yet do that. That is what Pennell himself does, in a great novel that puts the reader through the stages of the same process. The Civil War and its impact are freed from the inertness of mere facts and stereotypes to become real and vital for each person within his or her imagination. It is first there that it has either emotional impact or meaning; without that process, the Civil War as a public experience that all Americans can share in a wide variety of ways remains inaccessible.

Joseph Stanley Pennell was born in 1908 in Junction City, Kansas, and died in 1963 near Seaside, Oregon. *The History of Rome Hanks and Kindred Matters* (page citations are to the 1944 first edition and the 1983 Second Chance Press reprint) and *The History of Nora Beckham, A Museum of Home Life* (1948), first two volumes in an unfinished trilogy, are his only books.

On Ross Lockridge, Jr.'s,
Raintree County

DANIEL AARON

ROSS LOCKRIDGE, JR.'S, NOVEL, a mix of history and myth, encloses a single day, July 4, 1892, in legendary Raintree County, Indiana. As the hours tick on from dawn to midnight, flashbacks (some fifty in all) to distant decades gradually fill in the lives of the principal characters who have converged at Waycross Station near the town of Freehaven for the ceremonies. Thus the past is recaptured in the present and the future anticipated in the past. By the end of the day, and 1,060 pages later, all the pieces of what amounts to a giant jigsaw puzzle have fallen into place and the pageant-history of America from the presidency of James K. Polk to Grover Cleveland's brought to a close.

Scrambled chapters don't always mesh smoothy, but the timing of the cutbacks, the abruptness of the scene shifts, and the withholding of essential information until late in the narrative add a degree of suspense to the novel. Its elastic structure seems especially suitable for a writer trying to pour into his single book the history and culture of a people, his own spiritual autobiography, and everything he had ever read, heard, thought, and dreamed.[1]

Raintree County, published in 1948, has no plot to speak of unless it be the unfolding story of John ("Johnny") Wickliff Shawnessey, himself a surrogate of the author, who sets forth like the questing child in Whitman's poem and gathers to himself every object "he looked upon and received with wonder or pity or love or dread." Through the twenty-four hours of the Grand Patriotic Program, Johnny relives more than a half-century of his lifetime. Once again he is initiated into the mysteries of nature and sex, immersed in the affairs of friends and rivals, in the social activities of his time and place, and—his most sustained experience of all—in the Civil War, an event that reverberates through the whole of *Raintree County.*

The war doesn't seem to have been uppermost in Lockridge's mind when he began to think about writing the Great American Novel. Only later did it become the grand and terrible stage-setting for the hero's and the nation's maturation. In fact, *Raintree County* didn't spring apparently from any single historical episode but rather from a Whitmanesque vision the young Lockridge felt obliged to vouchsafe long before he discovered a way to dramatize effectively the "legend called American History, bloody, irrational, and exciting like the Bible."

His first attempt to objectify this vision was "A Pageant of New Harmony" dashed off in 1937 to commemorate the rise and fall of Robert Owen's Utopian community. It ended with an affirmation of beneficent tendency: "the great past still pours its giant strength into the present and our very life is fashioned from the dreams of other days." Two years later he began "The Dream of the Flesh of Iron," a pessimistic and turbid allegorical work, vast in conception but sophomoric and inchoate.[2] "The Dreamer," in pursuit of "The Beautiful One" (signifying elusive Truth and Beauty) is balked by "The Rival" or "The Enemy" (namely lust and gross materialism). The rotten old civilization collapses at the end; a new one is in the making.

Readers of *Raintree County* should have no difficulty detecting the thematic ghosts of these apprentice pieces in the ideas and characters of the finished novel, the shape of which was already taking form in Lockridge's imagination. Some time in 1941—he was then in his late twenties—he set out to write a work about his Indiana homeland at the turn of the century. What he appears to have had in mind was a prose "Song of Myself" written in the manner of Thomas Wolfe's self-absorbed autobiographical fiction that would out-Joyce Joyce by confining the action of the projected novel not to just twenty-four hours but to a series of days.

He labored several years on this plan until the design he had been groping for suddenly materialized before him in a flash of illumination. He would crowd his novel into one synoptic day but push back the time period to the Civil War era (including the years that immediately preceded and followed it) and base the hero on his maternal grandfather, John Wesley Shockley, who had lived through this period and whose life was both real and shadowy enough to provoke his grandson's fancy. Now he had license to range freely across the nineteenth century cultural landscape, blend the national and local, fact and legend. In the guise of John Wickliff Shawnessey—Hoosier shaman, poet, pedagogue, and soldier and author of a remarkable unpublished masterpiece—he could, as he put it, "express the American myth—give shape to the lasting 'heroic' greatness of the American people."

Of all the writers represented in *Classics of Civil War Fiction,* Lockridge probably comes closest to seeing the war from the perspective of a mystical midwesterner, although to be sure from a marked nothern bias. For him the Old Northwest was the heartland of the nation, Lincoln country (as it was for his midwestern kindred spirits Francis Grierson, Vachel Lindsay, Sherwood Anderson, Carl Sandburg, and Edgar Lee Masters) and the attempt to pull down the Union an impious act. The gallantry and sufferings of the Confederates may stir his admiration and pity, but the defeat of a recreant South confirms his hero's belief in a providential design.

The war in *Raintree County* is registered, interpreted, and justified by Johnny Shawnessey as he drifts back to the times of "blood and iron." His direct involvement begins in 1863, a low point in his life, when he is estranged from his mad southern wife and mourning his young son, dead through her negligence. Heretofore, the portents and first years of the war have been reported second hand and serve as a kind of mood music. But now it is reenacted in Johnny's meditations. It comes to life in the conversations carried on during the long July 4th day and most graphically in the cutbacks to the war episodes from Johnny's enlistment to the Grand Review in Washington, May 23–24, 1865.

A sizeable chunk of the novel is given over to battle scenes and descriptions of Johnny's soldiering in the Army of the West. Lockridge competently re-tells the familiar and much written about accounts of army experience: how raw recruits were bloodied into veterans and grew accustomed to the "song of the bullets," what it was like to cope with real and fancied terrors, the impulse to panic, the arduous marches through devastated countrysides, the dismal bivouacs, the camaraderie and fierce elations, the fear of dying in "a foreign place." Occasionally his inventions of hand-to-hand conflict and exploits of derring-do ring hollow, as if he had Hollywood already in mind when he composed them, but at his best, he dispenses with heroics and writes with agreeable flatness and directness.

Not surprisingly, given the tone of the writing that followed the recently ended second world war, Lockridge's Civil War is studiedly deprettified, saturated in blood and booze. His novel is occasionally ribald, to the dismay of some of his reviewers, and strains against the proprieties, but it contains none of the expletives thinly disguised in *The Naked and the Dead* (published in the same year) and breaks no taboos. It was enough for Lockridge to explain the "immense profanity" of the soldier as an expression of his "enormous disgust with the inhumanity of his life. What the soldier endured was fit to be described only by verbal excretions. The Civil War soldier cursed fighting, eating, marching. He cursed awake, and he cursed asleep. He was cursing the great insanity of War with the bitter curse of experience." Johnny reads the Gettysburg Address in a Chattanooga whorehouse. He learns to drink, looks benignly on his lustful drunken companions, and grows inured to smashed bodies and sundered arms and legs, to dysentery and suppurating wounds. Certainly *Raintree County* can't be faulted for want of realism or inadequate research. Ross Lockridge read lots of books.

All the same his Civil War is scenic, discussed rather than deeply probed. The progress of the armies from Chickamauga and Missionary Ridge to the investment of Atlanta and the March to the Sea unrolls panoramically, the authorial voice intermittently soliloquizing on America, democracy, history; the action is interpolated with dreams and visions and rhetorical set-pieces. Clearly Lockridge's model wasn't the Melville of *Battle-Pieces* or any of the war obsessed writers like John W. De Forest or Ambrose Bierce or Stephen Crane but Walt Whitman for whom the war was at once a personal and a national crisis and a ratification of *Leaves of Grass*. Johnny, chronicler and seer, ponders the meaning of the "War" without palliating its horrors or plumbing its tragedy. In *Raintree County* it is the *mise en scéne* that antedates Fort Sumter and continues after Appomattox; it is also the hinge that links the ante bellum republic of the Golden Day with the emerging industrial nation.

Why did it hapapen? How to interpret its consequences? Did it spell triumph or degradation? These questions, insinuated into the narrative from the beginning, are intimately related to Johnny's speculation about his own destiny, his own success and failure. They are aired in the debates between him and three of his boyhood friends which function as a chorus on the issues that split the Union and which symbolize philosophical positions and social attitudes.

Big florid Garwood P. Jones, Johnny's slightly older classmate at Pedee Academy, is the fictional incarnation of The Rival or The Enemy in Lockridge's already mentioned abortive poetic work. He stands between Johnny and Nell Gaither, Johnny's first and only love (a later verson of The Beautiful One) and dooms their union. Doughface, fraud, demagogue, corruptionist, racist, despiser of Lincoln and quintessential cynic, Garwood sits in the United States Senate in 1892 and is angling to become the Republican nominee for the presidency. The Civil War for him is simply an episode in a vast power struggle between two economic systems and a prime opportunity for his own advancement.

Financier Cassius P. Carney, like Senator Jones, has also found Raintree County too small an area to contain his large ambitions. Calculating and prudent and since adolescence impatient of inefficiency, disorder, and waste, he sees no meaning in the war, morally or ideologically; it has only honed his genius for consolidation. He sees it as a training for business. By 1892 he has become a "bloodless abstraction," the cool young clerk of ante bellum Freehaven all but obliterated in the unloved money-worshipping older man.

Professor Jerusalem Webster Stiles, the improbable principal of Pedee Academy and the third and most important member of the trio, not without reason shares the initials of Lockridge's hero and grandfather. Although ostensibly Johnny's opposite (for the "perfessor" is a Menckenian type, a pagan, Puritan-basher, scoffer, and iconoclast), he is in reality his alter ego, the only one in Raintree County who discerns and savors his former pupil's wisdom and innocence. Johnny easily counters the sophistries of Garwood and Carney but finds Stiles's dark pronouncements on the War much harder to dispose of.

"How in your theory of history, John," Stiles asks him, "do you encompass this bloody name [Sumter] on which the Republic foundered? Take away the flagwaving and the patriot shrieks, and what do you have?—a few hundred iron balls bounding on brick walls from which a dyed rag fluttered! For this, the Republic resorted to four years of mass murder" (first edition, 475). The issues seem pretty simple to him. He dismisses the cant of Liberty and Union. The South fought to keep the Negro "a slave and productive, the North to keep him from becoming too productive, which meant making him free." War is "neither moral nor immoral." It's just something that happens to vainglorious men, "the clash of forces ruthless and natural." The Civil War gets lost "in a swirl of proper nouns," in the names of battles and battle leaders, but what it comes down to is "the death of a million men in a series of bloody explosions and stinking camps." And what did the dead die for? "Liberty, Justice? Union? Emancipation? The Flag? Hell, no. They died so that a lot of slick bastards" could exploit the natural and human resources of America and make it possible for "several million poor serfs" to exchange their European slums and ghettos for American ones (767).

Johnny can't shrug off this sardonic declaration and is half-inclined to concede its accuracy. He hadn't foreseen the debacle of Reconstruction, the KKK, the magic growth of the industrial nation, the "tidal glut" of immigrants, the scandals of the Gilded Age, the bitter railroad strikes in 1877, and the "mining and stripping and gutting and draining, and whoring and ravaging and rending the beautiful earth of America" (772). Yet the child of Emerson and Whitman must reject the summation of his teacher and friend as a partial one. The Civil War, he asserts, was fought to preserve the "Republic" or "Union," illusory and unanalyzable concepts but connoting "the denial of tribal boundaries and tribal prejudices." The South fought for freedom to enslave others, the North to keep alive "the last, best hope of earth." The South produced Robert E. Lee, the North Abraham Lincoln. "As a series of physical facts, we know how terrible the War was. As a series of Moral Events, it was necessary and even sublime" (495).

From his transcendental perch, Johnny watches the impious doers of

God's work. He is even ready to admit a certain grandeur in the flatulent and crowd-pleasing orations of Senator Garwood and a degree of validity in the cheerful fourflusher's reply to the Professor's diatribes against the crooks and politicians: "you read too much. Go out sometimes, jerk off your specs, and take a look at this nation. This nation is big enough for everyone in it" (767). Of course Garwood, the unregenerate American, mouths words which are merely sounds to him, whereas for Johnny they resonate with historical undertones.

And so do the reminiscences of General Jake Jackson, Johnny's old corps commander and, as it happens, the keynote speaker at the July 4th activities. In 1892 the General is preoccupied with pension bills and the plans for the erection of a huge soldiers' and sailors' monument in Indianapolis. It will consist, he announces, of a peace group ("a great big gal about a hundred sizes bigger than real in the middle holding up a flag" and grouped around her "a farmer, a blacksmith, a veteran, and a dinge at her feet holding up a busted chain") and a war group, the latter a melange of raised sabres, guns, horses' heads, and broken drums. The monument is a cliché in stone and not to be taken seriously, but the General's volumes of military memoirs, sonorously titled and written in the "grand style" of the period, still breathe. His "customed pompous language is steeped in the sadness of the greatest of all wars" (598).

For all its genial and not so genial satire, its somewhat mannered obstreperousness and calculated impiety (echoes of Sinclair Lewis and John Dos Passos here), *Raintree County* is at bottom a reverent and celebratory book. Lockridge-qua-Whitman beheld These States as a Poem and exalted the Poet as one whose educated eye detected patterns in the welter of historical phenomena. To stimulate "the feeling of historic preoccupation," he drew upon any fact or artifact, lofty or low, that would allow his readers to partake of "the sacred communion:" Myths, folklore, and legend, popular songs and poems and novels, Johnny Appleseed, Uncle Tom, John Brown, strikes and prize fights, military and political crises, and especially the words of Abraham Lincoln that illuminated as nothing else the "few hard facts of history."

Passages from Lincoln's speeches resound through the novel. They put the War, and indeed all American history, into the "right context" and, like the words of Jesus, have a "moral gravity" that gives "the feeling of a human life lived in relation to Humanity." Lockridge's Lincoln is a homely made-in-America product, but he is even more a mythic hero ordained for mighty tragedies—America's link with the ages. Shakespeare, Johnny observes, presaged Lincoln's fate in *The Tragedy of Julius Caesar,* "the prelude to another red drama of assassination in a Republic as little known to him as Caesar's Rome" (946). His play steered the hand of John Wilkes Booth.

Sparingly employed, such fancies can be provocative, but Lockridge also celebrated the martyr-President in windy exclamatory prose. ("Where are the days of Abraham Lincoln? They are yours, Republic! They are yours, American earth dense with the roots of prairie grass! They are yours, mythjetting Time . . . He was a memory and a hundred thousand memories, mostly of the earth . . . He was a memory of big trees felled for clearings . . . Lincoln, the seamy, memoryhaunted face, the fabulous flesh of Sangamon County . . ." (477). And not only Lincoln. Lockridge had a fondness for apostrophizing things American, for bardic chants, expostulations and catalogues, for rhetorical questions and rhetorical answers, and for long dream sequences in which he solicitously recorded "the sleeping soul"of a hero. He thought these effusions were artistic and profound and that readers, fed up with the usual pap would think so too. Hence it came as no surprise to him when *Life* magazine, soon to clamor for yea-saying statements commensurate with Henry Luce's "American Century," featured a homespun excerpt from *Raintree County* on the eve of its publication, and when it was made the Book-Of-the-Month Club's January 1948 selection.

Success proved to be his poison. The promotional hoopla and booming sales left him deflated and despondent. Doubts about his accomplishment, enhanced by the barbs of his fault-finders and more so by the reservations of his admirers, soured his triumph. Already beyond the reach of his concerned family and friends, he felt physically and mentally burned out. (His memorialist called it "a case of literary shell shock.") A month after the news that *Raintree County* had topped the *Herald-Tribune*'s national best-seller list, and at a moment when he appeared to be emerging from the swamp of depression, Lockridge went into his garage, shut the doors, and turned on the engine of his new car. He was thirty-four years old.

Raintree County languished after his suicide. Now long out of print, although still plentiful in second-hand bookshops, it is rarely mentioned in surveys of modern American literature. There are plausible reasons to account for its swift eclipse. As many of Lockridge's reviewers complained, his book was awash in talk, self-indulgent, undiscriminating, repetitive, over-ambitious, too complex and intricate for the general audience, too boyishly confessional and intellectually naive for the sophisticated.

One has only to compare it with Margaret Mitchell's *Gone With the Wind,* the well-researched romance by a natural and accomplished storyteller and defiant partisan of the southern view of the War Between the States, to understand why her book became and remained a popular classic and Lockridge's did not. She instinctively divined the taste of her public (especially readers enchanted with Scarlet O'Hara's nineteen inch waist and Rhett Butler's electric kisses) and resorted to time-tested literary formulas and stereotypes without embarrassment: a strong-willed beauty, a dark and insolent lover, a complement of "darkies," "bucks," and "niggers" straight out of Thomas Nelson Page and Thomas Dixon, her friend and corrrespondent. In Mitchell's Georgia, Yankees are aflame with greed and lust and eyes smolder, glow, gleam, and glitter. Nothing in this tumultuous tale is likely to distract or perplex the reader.

Raintree County, on the other hand, is a man/boy book. Because of its chronological shifts and authorial divagations, what there is of plot line is hard to trace. It is less focused than *Gone With the Wind,* less breathlessly dramatic, more subjective, bookish, meditative, metaphysical. Not that Lockridge can't match Mitchell's sensationalism; if anything he is less squeamish in depicting violence, death, and sex, only his bodice-rippers have white southern hands, not black. But novels that feature idyllic plantation scenes, the lazy grace of booted cavaliers, gallant ragged Confederates, and the Lost Cause, ordinarily catch on better with the public than those that envisage the South as a swamp of prejudice and sensuality, poke fun at John C. Calhoun, and condone the destruction of Atlanta as necessary and just.

Raintree County is hardly the classic Ross Lockridge felt sure he had written but one of those good/bad books difficult to categorize in which the gold and the brummagem are fairly evenly mixed. (Melville's *Mardi* is another example, if on a considerably higher level). It is best in its unpretentious segments—mostly vignettes, asides, impressions—often arresting and shrewd. For instance, he will remark on the War's "epic rhythms, epithets, heroes . . . a newspaper Iliad of seasons, maps, and proper nouns," on the battles whose names "had swum slowly into the columns of the papers, had lain there wallowing bloodily for days, and had swum slowly out again." Or he will passingly reflect on cigar smoke, "incense of the Republic," that pervades his novel from beginning to end and "hovers in the smell of all the pullman cars and diners, and all the lobbies, court rooms, courthouse toilets, all the Senate chambers, hotel rooms, and statehouse corridors. The Republic is rolled up in thin brown leaves and smoked all over the Republic" (293).

Unhappily for Lockridge, the vogue of lusty, folksy, autochthonous American Stuff had already peaked, except in Hollywood, by 1948. To the new crop of literary satirists, all talk of Americans as a "mythic race," all the hymns to "hob-nailed rail-splitters," all the ceremonial clichés of American history were so much "corn," a term that came into popular usage about this time. Even the Civil War was now fair game. In Flannery O'Connor's story, "A Late Encounter with the Enemy," a dotty 92-year-old "general" is loaned out annually on Confederate Memorial Day to the city museum "where he was displayed from one to four in a musty room full of old photographs, old uniforms, old artillery, and historical documents." His fondest memory is the Atlanta premier of a Civil War film when usherettes wearing Confederate caps and short skirts escorted him to the stage where the Hollywood master of ceremonies introduced him to the cheering audience as one "who had fought and bled in the battles they would soon see daringly re-acted to the screen."

Raintree County never got from impatient reviewers the thoughtful reading it needed and deserved. Some of them praised its lyricism, energy, ebullience, its patches of skillful narrative, but came down hard on its egregious flaws. Four decades after its "short echo-walk between the ballyhoo and the hoot" (to quote Vladimir Nabokov out of context), it is now more evident than it once was that Lockridge did manage to recover something valuable from his risky dive into American history. His vulnerable novel, old-fashioned and ingenuous for all its gimmickry, has become in its own right a piece of Americana.

1. John Leggett's *Ross and Tom. Two American Tragedies* (New York: Simon and Schuster, 1974) is my only source for Ross Lockridge, Jr.'s, life and career, unpub-

lished compositions, and correspondence. As will be seen, I have made extensive use of Leggett's sensitive and even-handed biographical study, but he is not responsible for my hunches and speculations on the material he has provided.

2. Described in a reader's report as "an immensely long narrative poem, divided into short lyrics, interspersed with frequent prose passages of exposition. This is all about War and the Machine, human depravity and human aspiration, pretty well tangled up and expressed through symbols that aren't very fresh" (Quoted in Leggett, 67–68).

Ross Lockridge, Jr., was born in 1914 in Bloomington, Indiana, and died there in 1948. *Raintree County* (1948) is his only book, and is out of print.

BIBLIOGRAPHY

SELECTED NOVELS, STORIES, POEMS, AND PLAYS

Including works discussed in this collection and works by the authors of the essays. This chronological list suggests the number of notable Civil War works in any given period and which periods were the most fertile (the 1930s, for instance), for southern and northern writers.

1852 Harriet Beecher Stowe *Uncle Tom's Cabin*
1863 Henry Morford *The Days Of Shoddy: A Novel of the Great Rebellion in 1861*
1864 Epes Sargent *Peculiar: A Tale of the Great Transition*
       John Townsend Trowbridge *Cudjo's Cave*
       Augusta Evans Wilson *Macaria; Or Altars of Sacrifice*
       John Greenleaf Whittier *In War Time* (poems)
1865 Walt Whitman *Drum Taps* (poems)
1866 John Esten Cooke *Surry of Eagle's Nest: Or, the Memoirs of a Staff-Officer Serving in Virginia*
       Herman Melville *Battle-pieces and Aspects of the War* (poems)
1867 John William De Forest *Miss Ravenel's Conversion from Secession to Loyalty*
       Sidney Lanier *Tiger-Lilies; A Novel*
1874 Albion Winegar Tourgée *Toinette: A Novel*
1881 Colonel William C. Falkner *The White Rose of Memphis*
1883 E.P. Roe *His Sombre Rivals*
1884 Charles Egbert Craddock (Mary Noailles Murfree) *Where the Battle Was Fought*

Bibliography

1885 Mark Twain *Adventures of Huckleberry Finn*
George Washington Cable, *Doctor Sevier*
Silas Weir Mitchell *In War Time*

1886 Virginius Dabney *The Story of Don Miff, as Told by his Friend John Bouche Whacker: A Symphony of Life*

1887 Frances Courtenay Baylor *Behind the Blue Ridge*

1891 Ambrose Bierce *Tales of Soldiers and Civilians*

1892 Joel Chandler Harris *On the Plantation: A Story of a Georgia Boy's Adventures during the War*

1893 Thomas Cooper De Leon *John Holden, Unionist: A Romance of the Days of Destruction and Reconstruction*
Harold Frederic *The Copperhead*
Thomas Nelson Page *Meh Lady: A Story of the War*

1894 Thomas Nelson Page *The Burial of the Guns*

1895 Stephen Crane *The Red Badge of Courage*
Bret Harte *Clarence*

1896 William Gillette *The Secret Service* (play)

1897 William E. Barton *A Hero in Homespun, A Tale of the Loyal South*

1898 W. H. H. Murray "A Ride with a Mad Horse in a Freight-car"

1901 Winston Churchill *The Crisis*
John Uri Lloyd *Warwick of the Knobs: A Story of Stringtown County, Kentucky*

1902 Ellen Glasgow *The Battle-Ground*
Mark Twain "The Private History of a Campaign that Failed"

1903 John Fox *The Little Shepherd of Kingdom Come*

1904 Upton Sinclair *Manassas*

1905 Charles Egbert Craddock (Mary Noailles Murfree) *The Storm Centre*

1906 Molly Elliott Seawell *The Victory*

1907 Lydia Collins Wood *The Haydock's Testimony: A Tale of the American Civil War*

1909 Francis Grierson *The Valley of Shadows*

1911 Mary Johnston *The Long Roll*
Edward Peple *The Littlest Rebel*

1912 Mary Johnston *Cease Firing*

1915 James Lane Allen *The Sword of Youth*

1921 Thomas Dixon *The Man in Gray: A Romance of North and South*

1927 Allen Tate "Ode to the Confederate Dead," *Mr. Pope and Other Poems* (1928). Revised 1937
James Boyd *Marching On*

Bibliography

1928 Stephen Vincent Benét *John Brown's Body*
1929 Evelyn Scott *The Wave*
1931 John Peale Bishop *Many Thousands Gone*
     Joseph Hergesheimer *The Limestone Tree*
     T. S. Stribling *The Forge*
     Eugene O'Neill *Mourning Becomes Electra* (play)
1932 DuBose Heyward *Peter Ashley*
     Leonard Ehrlich *God's Angry Man*
1933 Roark Bradford *Kingdom Coming*
     Josephine Herbst *Pity Is Not Enough*
1934 MacKinlay Kantor *Long Remember*
     Stark Young *So Red the Rose*
1935 F. Scott Fitzgerald "The Night Before Chancellorsville," *Taps at Reveille*
1936 Andrew Lytle *The Long Night*
     Margaret Mitchell *Gone With the Wind*
     William Faulkner *Absalom, Absalom!*
     MacKinlay Kantor *Arouse and Beware*
1937 Clifford Dowdey *Bugles Blow No More*
     Caroline Gordon *None Shall Look Back*
     Edgar Lee Masters *The Tide of Time*
1938 Allen Tate *The Fathers*
     Donald Davidson *Lee in the Mountains* (poems)
     William Faulkner *The Unvanquished*
     John W. Thomason, Jr. *Lone Star Preacher*
     Hervey Allen *Action at Aquila*
     Thomas Wolfe "Chickamauga," *The Hills Beyond*
     Gwen Bristow *The Handsome Road*
1940 Willa Cather *Sapphira and the Slave Girl*
     Harry Harrison Kroll *Keepers of the House*
1941 Louis Bromfield *Wild Is the River*
1942 James Street *Tap Roots*
1944 Joseph Stanley Pennell *The History of Rome Hanks and Kindred Matters*
     Howard Fast *Freedom Road*
1945 Clifford Dowdey *Where My Love Sleeps*
1946 Robert Penn Warren *All the King's Men* (chapter four)
     James M. Cain *Past All Dishonor*
     Frank Yerby *The Foxes of Harrow*
1947 Ben Ames Williams *House Divided*

Bibliography

1948 Ross Lockridge, Jr. *Raintree County*

1952 Shelby Foote *Shiloh*
Ward More *Bring the Jubilee*

1955 MacKinlay Kantor *Andersonville*
Robert Penn Warren *Band of Angels*
Flannery O'Connor "A Late Encounter with the Enemy," *A Good Man Is Hard to Find*
Richard O'Connor *The Guns of Chickamauga*
Davis Grubb *A Dream of Kings*

1959 Hamilton Basso *The Light Infantry Ball*

1960 Mary Lee Settle *Know Nothing*
Ovid Williams Pierce *On a Lonesome Porch*

1961 Robert Penn Warren *Wilderness*

1964 Robert Lowell *For the Union Dead* (poems)
John William Corrington *And Wait for the Night*
James Gould Cozzens "Men Running" and "One Hundred Ladies" in *Children and Others*

1967 William Styron *The Confessions of Nat Turner*

1969 Stephen Becker *When the War Is Over*
Richard Marius *The Coming of Rain*
Eugenia Price *New Moon Rising*

1972 R. H. W. Dillard "Gettysburg," *After Borges*

1974 Michael Shaara *The Killer Angels*

1977 Robert H. Fowler *Jim Mundy*

1979 Thomas Keneally *Confederates*

1980 Douglas C. Jones *Elkhorn Tavern*
Richard Slotkin *The Crater*

1981 Berry Fleming *The Affair at Honey Hill*

1984 Gore Vidal *Lincoln*
Tom Wicker *Unto This Hour*

1985 John Calvin Batchelor *American Falls*
David Madden "Willis Carr at Bleak House," in *The Bread Loaf Anthology of Contemporary Short Stories*

1986 Lawrence Wells *Rommel and the Rebel*
Rita Mae Brown *High Hearts*

1988 Andrew Hudgins *After the Lost War, A Narrative* (poetry)
Terry Bisson *Fire on the Mountain*

1989 Allan Gurganus *Oldest Living Confederate Widow Tells All*
Richard Adams *Traveler*

Notes on Contributors

Daniel Aaron was born in Chicago, Illinois, in 1912 and now lives in Cambridge and teaches at Harvard. His writings focus on American political history: *Men of Good Hope: A Story of American Progressives* (1951); *America in Crisis, Fourteen Crucial Episodes* (1952); co-author, *The United States: A History of the Republic* (1957): *Writers on the Left* (1961); co-editor, *The Strenuous Decade: A Social and Intellectual Record of the 1930's* (1970); *The Unwritten War: American Writers and the Civil War* (1973). He has edited several volumes, including *Studies in Biography,* 1978 and *The Inman Diary: A Public and Private Confession* (1985). He is one of the founding editors of Library of America.

Peggy Bach was born in 1929 in Ohio and grew up in Indiana and Kentucky. She has published essays on Mary Lee Settle and Djuana Barnes and essay reviews on the works of Anaïs Nin, Simone de Beauvoir, Margaret Atwood, Nadine Gordimer, David Madden, and Wright Morris, among others. Her essays on Evelyn Scott have appeared in *The New Orleans Review, The Southern Review, The Southern Literary Journal, Louisiana Literature, The Southern Quarterly,* and *Modern Fiction Studies.* For her work on Scott, she has received a grant from the Louisiana Endowment for the Humanities, the Kentucky Foundation for Women, and in 1990–91 an NEH Independent Scholar Fellowship to work on the authorized biography of Evelyn Scott. Her poems have appeared in *Ken-*

tucky Poetry Review and *The Chattahoochie Review*. She is coeditor with David Madden of *Rediscoveries, II* and *Rediscoveries, Nonfiction*.

Stephen Becker was born in Mount Vernon, New York, in 1927. He is the author of an unusual Civil War novel, *When the War Is Over* (1970), that has many admirers. *Dog Tags* (1973) was reissued in 1987, and five of his other works are still in print in Europe. The following novels are either still in print or being actively discussed: *The Chinese Bandit* (1975), *The Last Mandarin* (1979), *The Blue-eyed Shan* (1982), and *A Rendezvous in Haiti* (1987). He has translated many novels and published widely in several other genres. He has received both a Guggenheim Fellowship and an NEA grant. He is currently Distinguished Lecturer in English, University of Central Florida.

Rosellen Brown was born in 1939 in Philadelphia, Pennsylvania, and teaches at the University of Houston. She taught American literature for several years at Tougaloo College in Mississippi, and creative writing at Boston University, Goddard College, and Bread Loaf Writers' Conference. She has published *Some Deaths in the Delta* (1970), poems; *The Whole Word Catalog* (1972, 1978); *Street Games* (1974), stories; *Cora Fry* (1977), poems; *Tender Mercies* (1978), a novel; *The Autobiography of My Mother* (1981); and *Civil Wars* (1984), a novel. Three of her stories were reprinted in *Prize Stories: The O. Henry Awards* and another in *Best American Short Stories*. She has received several Guggenheim and other awards.

James Cox was born in 1925 in Independence, Virginia, where he now lives. For many years, he taught at Dartmouth College. *Mark Twain: The Fate of Humor* was published in 1966. He edited *Robert Frost: Twentieth Century Views* (1962). Recipient of many academic grants, awards, and teaching honors, he has published numerous essays in the field of English Renaissance drama and poetry (Shakespeare, Milton, Peele), along with essays on C. S. Lewis, Poe, Darwin, Hume, humor, and autobiography.

R. H. W. Dillard was born in Virginia in 1937. He is a professor of English and chairs the Creative Writing Program at Hollins College in Virginia. Novelist, poet and critic, he published the first of several books of poems, *The Day I Stopped Dreaming About Barbara Steele,* in 1966. *The Book of Changes* (1974) was his first novel. His most recent books are *The Greeting: New and Selected Poems* (1981), which includes his poem "Gettysburg," *The*

First Man on the Sun (a novel, 1983), and a critical monograph, *Understanding George Garrett* (1988). His essay on *The Battle-Ground* is his first work on the fiction of his fellow native Virginian, Ellen Glasgow, since he finished his doctoral dissertation on her novels in 1964.

George Garrett was born in 1929 in Orlando, Florida. He has published many novels and books of stories, including *The Finished Man* (1959), *Which Ones Are the Enemy?* (1961), *Cold Ground Was My Bed Last Night* (1964), *Death of the Fox* (1985), and *Entered From the Sun* (1990). Among his many books of poems are *The Reverend Ghost* (1957) and *For a Bitter Season: New and Selected Poems* (1967). He is also the author of a biography of James Jones (1984) and a critical monograph, *Understanding Mary Lee Settle* (1988). He has taught English and creative writing at Hollins College, Princeton, among other places, and is now at the University of Virginia.

Robie Macauley was born in Grand Rapids, Michigan, in 1919 and lives in Boston. He is the author of two novels, *The Disguises of Love* (1952) and *A Secret History of Time to Come* (1979), and a collection of short stories, *The End of Pity* (1957). With George Lanning, he wrote *Technique in Fiction* (1987, revised edition). He is a former editor of *The Kenyon Review*, fiction editor of *Playboy,* and is now retired from Houghton Mifflin where he was executive editor. He teaches a class at Harvard and is codirector of the Ploughshares International Seminar at Castle Well in the Netherlands.

David Madden was born in Knoxville, Tennessee, in 1933. He has worked for the past ten years on *Sharpshooter,* an unusual Civil War novel; ten chapters have appeared in literary magazines and fiction anthologies. The best-known of his seven novels and two books of stories are *Bijou* (1974), *The Suicide's Wife* (1978), and *The New Orleans of Possibilities* (1982). He has published twenty books of nonfiction, including *Rediscoveries II,* with Peggy Bach, and works on Wright Morris, James Agee, James M. Cain, and Nathanael West. Writer-in-Residence at Louisiana State University, he is helping to establish the Civil War Center at LSU.

Ishmael Reed was born in 1938 in Chattanooga, Tennessee, and now lives in Oakland, California. Novelist, poet and critic, he published his first novel, *The Free-Lance Pallbearers,* in 1967. *Yellow Back Radio Broke-Down* came out two years later, followed by *Mumbo-Jumbo, Conjure: Selected Poems, The Last Days of Louisiana Red.* In 1986, *Reckless Eyeballing* and *Cab Calloway*

Stands in for the Moon appeared. His latest books are *Writin' is Fightin',
Thirty-Seven Years of Boxing on Paper* (1988) and *The Terrible Threes* (1989).

Mary Lee Settle was born in Charleston, West Virginia, in 1918. She has
published many novels, including *The Love Eaters* (1954), *Celebration* (1986),
Charley Bland (1989), and a quintet: *O Beulah Land* (1956), *Know Nothing*
(1960), about the Civil War, *Fight Night on a Sweet Saturday* (1964, rewritten,
retitled, republished in 1982 as *The Killing Ground*), *Prisons* (1973), *The
Scapegoat* (1980); the quintet was published as a boxed set in 1988. *Blood Tie*
won The National Book Award in 1978. Her memoir of World War II, *All
the Brave Promises, Memoirs of Aircraft Woman 2nd Class 2146391*, appeared in
1966. She has also published two books for young adults *The Scopes Trial*
(1972) and the *Story of Flight* (1967). She lives in Charlottesville, Virginia.

Lewis P. Simpson, Boyd Professor-Emeritus of English at Louisiana
State University where he has taught southern literature for several decades,
was born in 1916 in Texas. Most of his books deal with aspects of southern
culture: *The Man of Letters in New England and the South* (1973); *The Dispossessed Garden: Pastoral and History in Southern Literature* (1975); *The Bra-
zen Face of History, Studies in the Literary Consciousness in America* (1980);
Mind and the American Civil War: A Meditation on Lost Causes (1989). He was
cofounder and coeditor of *The Southern Review,* Second Series, editor of
LSU Press's Library of Southern Civilization, and has edited four books on
The Southern Review and Cleanth Brooks, among other subjects.

Robert Penn Warren was born in Guthrie, Kentucky, in 1905. He was
America's first Poet Laureate, the year before he died in 1989. Two of his
novels deal with the Civil War, *Band of Angels* and *Wilderness, A Tale of the
Civil War*; a major section, chapter 4, of *All the King's Men* also deals with the
war. He won the Pulitzer Prize for *All the King's Men* (1947) and for a book
of poems *Promises* (1958). His first book was *John Brown: The Making of a
Martyr* (1929). With Cleanth Brooks, he started *The Southern Review,* and in
their poetry and fiction textbooks, they contributed to the New Criticism
movement. His *Selected Poems: 1923–1975* appeared in 1976. Among his
many novels are *Night Rider* (1939), *Flood: Romance of Our Time* (1964),
Meet Me in the Green Glen (1971), and *A Place to Come To* (1977). Both Warren and Lytle, along with Tate, were contributors to *I'll Take My Stand, The
South and the Agrarian Tradition* (1930). He wrote several books dealing with

the Civil War and with racial problems in the South: *Segregation: The Inner Conflict in the South* (1956); *The Legacy of the Civil War: Meditations on the Centennial* (1961), *Who Speaks for the Negro?* (1966), and *Jefferson Davis Gets His Citizenship Back*.

Tom Wicker, born in North Carolina in 1929, is a political columnist for The New York *Times*. He is the author of one of the major Civil War novels of the 1980s, *Unto This Hour* (1984), and of five books of nonfiction, including *A Time to Die* (1975), about the Attica prison riot, and seven other novels, including *Facing the Lions* (1973). His most recent work is *One of Us: Richard Nixon and the American Dream* (1991). He lives in New York and Vermont.